THE HOME LANDSCAPER

55 PROFESSIONAL LANDSCAPES YOU CAN DO

Landscape Designs by
Ireland-Gannon Associates, Inc.

Project Manager: **Michael J. Opisso**

Landscape Illustrations by
Ray Skibinski

Written by
Ann Reilly & Susan A. Roth

Created by
Susan A. Roth & Company

HOME PLANNERS, INC.
3275 WEST INA ROAD, SUITE 110, TUCSON, ARIZONA 85741

Designed and Produced by:
SUSAN A. ROTH & COMPANY
3 Lamont Lane
Stony Brook, NY 11790

Publisher: Susan A. Roth
Art Director: Remo Cosentino
Associate Editor: Pam Peirce
Copy Editor: Lisa McGaw

Landscape designs by:
Ireland-Gannon Associates, Inc.
Rt. 25A, Northern Blvd.
East Norwich, NY 11732

James Morgan
Michael J. Opisso
David Poplawski
Damon Scott

Regional consultants:
Northeast: Carol Howe
Mid-Atlantic: Michael J. Opisso
Deep South: Nancy Jacobs Roney
Midwest: Harrison L. Flint
Florida & Gulf Coast: Robert Haehle
Rocky Mountains: Allen M. Wilson
Northern California & Pacific Northwest: Jo Wilson Greenstreet
Southern California & Desert Southwest: Margaret West
Regional map consultant: Pam Elum

Artwork by:
Landscape renderings: Ray Skibinski
Landscape plot plans: Michael Iragorri
How-to artwork: Ron Hildebrand
Maps: Jack Crane

Photographs by:
Susan A. Roth: 8, 9, 10, 12, 13, 14, 16, 18, 19, 20, 21, 22, 23, 24
   top, 25, 27, 28, 29, 31, 35, 37, 159, 160, 161, 162, 164, 173
Carl Saporiti: cover, title, 6, 15, 24 bottom, 25, 26, 39, 152
David Goldberg: 155
David Poplawski: 172

Published by Home Planners, Inc.

Editorial and Corporate Office:
   3275 West Ina Road, Suite 110
   Tucson, Arizona 85741

Distribution Center
   29333 Lorie Lane
   Wixom, MI 48393

President & Publisher: Rickard D. Bailey
Publications Manager: Karin Lotarski

10   9   8   7   6

Library of Congress Catalogue Card Number: 89-85209
ISBN softcover 0-918894-73-5
ISBN hardcover 0-918894-80-8

CONTENTS

INTRODUCTION

This book is unique among gardening and landscaping books. It is one of a kind. The *Home Landscaper* is the only book available that provides plot plans and illustrations of professionally designed landscapes for which the reader can order actual customized blueprints. Though you will read in the first chapter about what makes a successful landscape design, you don't have to attempt to design one for your own home, unless you want to. All the design work is done for you in the second and third chapters, where you will find actual plans that you can follow yourself. The understanding gained by reading the first chapter will help you to appreciate the professional quality of the designs in the next two chapters.

This unique idea results from the collaboration of two talented companies: Home Planners, Inc., architects and publishers of blueprints for do-it-yourself home builders and contractors; and Ireland-Gannon Associates, Inc., a nationally recognized award-winning landscape design-build firm. Both companies are tops in their fields. Home Planners, Inc., was founded in 1946 and has published over 135 books of home plans, and sold more than one and a half million blueprints for their designs. Their home plans are featured regularly in special issues of *House Beautiful, Better Homes and Gardens, Colonial Homes,* and other leading shelter magazines. Ireland-Gannon Associates, Inc., has been serving the prestigious North Shore of Long Island since 1943. In 1978, the company formed an association with the acclaimed Martin Viette Nursery, a major horticultural center in the Northeast. Ireland-Gannon has been honored with over forty awards in the last twenty years, including several Grand Awards from the Associated Landscape Contractors of America and Superior Awards from the National Landscape Association.

ABOUT THE DESIGNS IN THIS BOOK

In this book, architect and landscaper have combined their talents to create professional-quality landscape designs for the do-it-yourselfer and landscape contractor. The book offers fifty-five landscape designs to choose and learn from. Because most people have a bit of difficulty imagining what a one-dimensional planting scheme would actually look like in the flesh, a full-color illustration accompanies each plot plan in chapters 2 and 3. These show the landscape after it has matured and filled in a bit, creating the mood and feeling of the landscape design and demonstrating how a professionally designed landscape can enhance a home.

The forty landscapes presented in the second chapter are designs for front yards and entryways. These landscapes are designed to complement a selection of Home Planners' house designs — designs that represent popular homes from twenty-three styles of architecture, ranging from contemporary to traditional, Colonial to Tudor. (If any of the houses shown here strike your fancy, turn to p. 178 to see floor plans and to p. 200 to find out how to order complete architectural blueprints.) A front yard is on continual public view; its design works well if the landscape complements and enhances a home's architecture in the way furniture enhances the interior. The professionally designed landscapes included here offer a range of designs, from neat, formal landscapes to enhance elegant homes to informal cottage-garden landscapes to match country farmhouses. Whatever the style of your home, you'll be sure to find a similar-looking house — and a ready-made landscape design to go with it.

The third chapter offers fifteen backyard designs. Because a backyard is the family's private outdoor living space, it should be landscaped to meet the family's individual needs rather than to match a particular style of architecture. These backyard landscapes are designed with particular themes in mind, themes that match most families' needs, such as a children's play yard, a yard for the suburban food gardener, or a yard for formal outdoor entertaining. Any of these thematic backyard designs will work well with almost any style architecture.

The landscape plot plans included in the book show the placement of the plant materials within beds, foundation plantings, and shrub borders, and they indicate the outlines of the walkways, driveways, and other features of the landscape. Because plants vary in their adaptability to different climates and regions of the country, the plans included in the book include a list of general types of plants coded to the plot plan. The shape of the planting beds, position and spacing of the plants, and scale and contours of the paved areas are the essence of the designs.

You can order a large-sized blueprint package of each of these landscape designs customized for your region. These easy-to-read blueprints include a list of professionally selected plants that will perform well in your region. Most landscapes are available for eight different regions of the United States and Canada, but because not all home styles are built throughout the country, some plans may be customized only for selected regions. (See p. 178 for more details on the blueprint package and for ordering information.)

Most of the landscape illustrations are rendered with plants selected for the Mid-Atlantic region of the United States. Customized plant lists for other regions substitute plants when necessary, using ones with a similar landscape effect, such as the same season of bloom, flower color, and foliage texture.

HOW TO USE THIS BOOK

The first chapter of the book provides a mini-lesson on home landscaping. You will read about the design principles that professional landscapers put into practice. Then browse through the second and third chapters, which contain the plot plans and illustrations of the landscapes. You can study these and see how the principles discussed in chapter 1 are put to work in each of these designs to create truly professional-looking landscapes. Use what you learn and see here as an inspiration for creating your own landscape plan (see chap. 4), or copy any design presented here that would work with your home and family's needs.

If you would like to plant and install any of these landscapes on your own property, use the plot plan provided in the book to guide you, modifying it, if needed, to fit the exact contours of your house and property. (Chap. 4 offers suggestions on modifying the plans to suit your particular piece of property.) It isn't absolutely necessary to order the blueprint package offered with each design. However, the larger size of the blueprint with its accompanying regionalized plant list, and the other useful information in the six-page blueprint package, will be invaluable.

INSTALLING THE LANDSCAPE

Most do-it-yourselfers can install any of these landscapes themselves. If you use the designs in this book, there is no need for you to hire an expensive landscape architect or designer to create a landscape design. And you are getting a bargain in the deal. Most top-notch firms, such as Ireland-Gannon Associates, Inc., charge between $500 and $1,000 just to design the planting scheme for a half-acre property. For a fraction of that cost, you can order a large professional-quality blueprint package featuring the planting scheme coded with plants selected especially to thrive in your area of the country.

If you don't want to do the installation yourself, you can hire a landscape contracter—a professional installer—to do the job. Keep in mind that many landscape contractors are not skilled designers, even though they may advertise themselves as landscape designers. Their skills lie in maintaining a lawn, planting or removing trees, or regrading the land, but when it comes to actual landscape design, their talents may be limited. (See chap. 4 for more information about hiring a contractor.) By hiring a contractor to plant and install one of the landscape plans from this book, you can be assured that you are getting a beautiful, top-quality design—a design created by an award-winning landscape design firm.

Whether you do it yourself or hire a contractor, a landscape need not be installed all at once. Don't worry about taking several years to complete the planting. You can begin landscaping the front yard by first planting the large shade trees and installing the walks, driveway, and lawn. Next put in the foundation planting and follow that with the shrub borders along the edge of the property. In the back, begin by planting trees and privacy screens and follow up with patio and garden beds. Installed and planted over several years, larger and more elaborate landscapes are more easily handled by a weekend do-it-yourselfer. Spreading the work over several years may also make hiring a landscape contractor more affordable to average homeowners.

Whether you follow the plot plans exactly or modify them to suit the terrain, these professionally designed landscape plans can transform your home from ordinary to outstanding. Landscaping is an investment in the enjoyment and value of your home, so why not begin with the best?

Chapter 1

Landscaping the Professional Way

Learn the Principles and Techniques Professionals Use to Create Effective Landscape Designs

Let's pretend a minute. Let's pretend that somehow you come into possession of your dream house. Maybe you won the lottery, Publishers Clearing House sweepstakes, the jackpot at Thursday night bingo, or whatever. No matter how you managed it, your dream house is brand new, empty, has never been lived in, and is begging to be furnished and decorated. Would you know how to go about it? Do you have a clear picture in your mind of the fabrics and furniture you'd choose? Would you select period pieces of dark polished wood or go for chrome and white leather? Would the walls be painted, papered, or paneled? Are you the wood-floor-and-Oriental-carpet type or the wall-to-wall type?

Chances are you already know the answers to many of these questions. You know what your dream house would look like—indoors. But do you know what it would look like outdoors? What would the landscape be like? Does your imagination conjure up a parklike setting of rolling lawn and stately trees? Or a pleasing jumble of flowers and a split-rail fence draped with roses? Now, here's a question: Have you thought about where your dinner guests will park their cars? (Assume you didn't win so much that James will park the cars for them.) Will you be able to park in the driveway and easily carry groceries to the kitchen? Will the guests arrive at the front door or will they become confused and enter the kitchen instead?

A home's landscape design contributes dramatically to its appearance. When well done, the landscape creates a setting for the home that complements and enhances the architecture. An ordinary-looking home can be made eye-catching. A grand, imposing structure will be anchored to its surroundings with an equally impressive landscape. A well-designed landscape is a permanent capital improvement in your home—it contributes not only to the aesthetics of your home, as does the interior decor, but also to its value, which its furnishings do not. In addition to its other benefits, a well-designed, well-executed, and well-maintained landscape can add anywhere from 10 percent to 40 percent to a property's value, according to real estate appraisers and nurserymen.

Masses of bright yellow 'Goldsturm' black-eyed Susan complement the warm color of the home's wooden siding and deck.

A home's landscape can be thought of as outdoor decoration, and just as there are unlimited ways you could decorate your living room, there are many ways you could landscape a house. To be successful, however, the landscape style should complement the home's architecture as well as create the outdoor feeling you would like to achieve. For instance, a country house might be landscaped with fieldstone walls, picket fences, and numerous flower beds to create the feeling of a country farmhouse, like the house on page 54. For a more formal appearance, like the country house on page 58, a row of symmetrical trees and a straight brick walk do the job nicely.

Given the importance of a landscape to the beauty and value of a home, it is a pity that most homeowners haven't a clue about how to design an attractive and functional landscape. More often than not, whatever paltry shrubs, narrow driveway, and front walk the builder installed suffice for years.

If the homeowner adds more plantings, these are often lined up along walkways and driveway, and instead of inviting visitors into the yard and to the home's entrance they, in effect, wall it off. The shrubs chosen are usually common, boring plantings installed with little sense of proportion, scale, or seasonal interest. Frequently, shrubs are planted too close together and too close to structures, so that in a few years' time the shrubbery is overgrown and in the way.

Skilled professional landscape architects and designers understand how to select and position plants and paved areas to create a beautiful and functional landscape that enhances a home. If you had unlimited funds, you might hire one to create a setting for your dream home (or to help transform the house you already have into a closer approximation of your dream house). Short of that, you can learn about landscape-design principles by reading this chapter and then studying the professional landscape designs in the following chapters to see these principles in action.

Many of these designs can be adapted for use in landscaping your home. You will probably want to copy the landscape that was designed for a house of similar architecture, although there's nothing wrong with mixing and matching, if the result promises to please you. You can even order complete blueprints (see p. 174) with a customized list of plants chosen to do well in your region of the country. (If you haven't already done so, please read the Introduction to this book. It explains how to use this book and what is unique about it.)

HOW A PROFESSIONAL LANDSCAPE DESIGN CAN ENHANCE YOUR HOME

Builders often skimp on landscaping, putting in a straight, narrow walk to the front door and lining the front of the house with an unexciting row of yews. A professional landscape designer is more creative, enhancing the appearance of the house with the layout of the landscape and choosing plants that are beautiful in their own right. The house illustrated on this page is a good example of how a professional landscape can transform an attractive house into a knockout.

Landscape design: Howard Purcell

A circular drive leading beneath the extended boughs of a shade tree, eye-catching statues, and an elegant espalier give this beautiful home a distinctive finishing touch.

Professional landscapers understand how to arrange and integrate the softscape (plant materials) and the hardscape (paved areas, fences, and other structures) into a pleasing and functional whole. A good landscape design makes access to the various parts of the house and the outdoor living spaces easy. The design considers where people will walk and locates walkways for routes most commonly traveled. Walks lead to all entrances, but the design makes it evident which is the main entrance. The landscape plan will provide adequate parking for your family and guests, and allow for easy maneuvering of cars. You don't want your property to look like a parking lot, so skillful design of these areas becomes an important consideration.

A professional design can increase your outdoor living space by creating private places for relaxing and entertaining, providing you and your family with a place to enjoy the outdoors. Landscaping also improves both the indoor and the outdoor climates by moderating sun and wind. A screen of tall evergreens, such as hemlocks or pines, can be located to block street noises, to trap dirt, and to provide privacy. Deciduous trees, such as oaks and maples, can be positioned to shade and cool the house in summer but let in warming sun in winter. Evergreen hedges positioned on the north and west sides of a house will slow winter winds, lowering heating costs.

In just the way a person's clothing can flatter the figure, so can landscaping be used to "trick the eye" and flatter a house. A well-designed landscape can make a house or the property seem larger or smaller, as desired. For instance, a house landscaped with towering trees will look smaller than it actually is, but the same house flanked by trees only slightly taller than the roof gains in stature. A diminutive house can be turned into a quaint cottage with the addition of a picket fence, tumultuous flower beds, and a towering shade tree. To make a small house appear more substantial, anchor the house with medium-height trees, a formal hedge, and a symmetrical planting of foundation shrubs.

TRANSFORM YOUR YARD INTO OUTDOOR LIVING ROOMS

If you want to enjoy your property to the fullest, landscaping can create outdoor spaces that fulfill many of the same basic needs as the rooms in your house. The landscape design can create sep-arate areas for relaxation, recreation, entertaining, cooking, dining, and even storage in as pleasant and comfortable an environment as possible.

As you study the plans in this book, try to think of the landscape as consisting of a floor, walls, and a ceiling, just like a house. The creation of a total landscape design is not that much different from decorating the interior of the house. These three principal segments—floor, walls, and ceiling—can be created and decorated with plants and construction materials, or with a combination of both, to form outdoor rooms or living areas where you can enjoy many outdoor activities.

Floors

The lawn, other low-growing plants used as a ground cover, and construction materials such as wood, concrete, brick, flagstone, gravel, and other paving materials create the outdoor floor. Before making any decision about which types of flooring to use, consider how much use the area will receive and how the plants or pavement fits with the rest of the landscape design. Budget and maintenance considerations should also enter into the decision.

A grass lawn is the most common landscape

The charming fence, painted white to echo the house trim, enhances the quaint character of this cozy home.

floor and fits into almost any design except perhaps a woodland garden. You will probably want a lawn for recreation areas and children's play yards where you might be playing games or sports because they are softer and more resilient than paving or wood.

Hard-surfaced floors are called for in recreational areas that will receive heavy use, such as tennis courts or barbecue and dining areas. Large paved areas, such as patios and decks, are frequently designed to occupy a major portion of the backyard, if this fits into the overall design and scale of the property. Walkways, like hallways, should be wide enough to permit easy access and surfaced with a material that is easy to walk upon without slipping.

Ground covers such as ivy or pachysandra work wonders in covering large areas not subjected to heavy foot traffic. A low ground cover, such as juniper or wintercreeper, provides a bolder texture than lawn and can be used to sculpt beautiful curves and cover shady ground where grass won't grow well. Because they are low, ground covers won't block a view. Though they are part of the garden's floor, ground covers do act somewhat like walls because they tend to direct where people walk. Most people—at least those over about age fifteen—will walk around a

bed of ground cover rather than through it. For this reason, you might want to locate a border of ground cover along the street to direct people to the walk. Ground covers also make a perfect low-maintenance covering on slopes where mowing grass is difficult.

As you will note when studying the designs in this book, a floor of ground covers is the best way to unite a shrub border and to connect two separate areas of the design. A ground cover of vinca (myrtle), for instance, creates a tapestry of foliage and flowers beneath masses of shrubbery, rather like the way a fine Oriental carpet sets off the furniture in a study. Once such a ground cover fills in, it keeps out weeds, and shades and cools the soil, improving the health of the shrubs and reducing maintenance requirements.

Where possible, designers use construction materials for walks, decks, and patios that match the construction of the house. This creates unity. For instance, the brick walls used in the landscape on page 68 are built of the same brick used on the facade of the house. Where houses are built entirely of clapboard or shingles, the hardscape should complement the house in texture and color and blend with the style of the architecture. For instance, the walkways in the country farmhouse on page 54 are made of fieldstones,

This pretty poolside garden is a perfect example of how skillful landscape design creates outdoor living rooms. Brick paving and mulch form the garden floor, a lattice fence, shrubs, and tall perennials act as walls, and an arbor and a canopy of trees serve as the ceiling.

Landscape design: Conni Cross

which further enhance the country feeling of the landscape and echo the fieldstone walls.

Walls

Hedges, shrubbery, and constructed walls and fences act as outdoor walls, serving many landscape functions. They can define boundaries, separate one garden area from another, provide privacy from neighbors, or block unsightly views. Used to border a small garden or courtyard such as for the house on page 73, a wall creates a sense of intimacy and enclosure. They are also useful as backgrounds for flower gardens or low shrub borders. Tall walls also provide shade and can help to slow a wind.

All shrubbery should be considered as part of the walls of the landscape, whether planted as formal straight-sided wall-like hedges or arranged into free-flowing informal masses. Where you wish the landscape walls to provide year-round privacy, evergreen shrubs, both broadleaf and conifers, are the answer. These can provide barriers from neighboring properties or from a street at the back or side of the yard. Deciduous shrubs are also popular walls, especially in the backyard, where they provide privacy during the months your family uses the yard.

Many deciduous shrubs, such as spirea, weigela, and viburnum, will provide welcome floral color during the spring and summer months. Some living walls also provide fragrance, berries, and a home for birds. Plants with thorns or sharp leaves, like barberry, holly, and pyracantha, make useful walls where you want to discourage animals and other intruders, especially if the plants are used without a fence.

Constructed walls can be wooden or metal fences or sturdy brick, stone, or masonry walls. As with flooring materials, walls look best when they reflect the building materials or style of the house. A white picket fence looks charming with an Early American home or a Cape Cod cottage (see p. 44), but would be laughable around a contemporary house. Cost and longevity are also considerations; brick is usually more expensive than wood, but requires less maintenance and replacement over the years.

When planning a wall, a designer considers its height in relationship to the property's needs for privacy and security. Local zoning regulations may also limit the heights of fences. In some cases, the type of boundary fences used within a neighborhood should be considered so the garden wall blends with surrounding properties.

When cost is a consideration, chainlink fence is often the most economical security fencing, although it isn't a particularly attractive choice. Using one coated with black vinyl (as in the children's play yard on p. 130) helps the fence to blend innocuously into the landscape. Such fences can also be masked with shrubbery.

Low walls separate different garden areas and direct traffic without restricting views. They often are more decorative than useful, but they can double as garden seats or be topped with planters. The wall in the landscape on page 118 creates a sense of entry and provides some privacy from a busy road without blocking light or views. Sometimes low walls are more decorative than functional, such as the wall in the landscape on page 72, which adds weight to the landscape and balances the mass of the three-story brick house, but would not keep out an intruder.

Ceilings

While the sky is actually the ceiling of the garden, trees and overhead structures also form part of the landscape's ceiling. By partially blocking the expanse of sky, trees and structures frame and enhance the view of the sky. Ceilings provide relief from the sun or the rain, as well as creating beauty overhead and interesting shadow patterns on the ground.

Trees are the primary garden ceilings, contributing shade, overhead structure, and strength to the landscape. When choosing trees for this use, select ones with interesting silhouettes, colorful fall foliage, or attractive spring flowers. Many trees also have characteristic shapes that lend themselves to certain styles of landscaping. Linden trees and Callery pears have formal oval shapes that go well with stately homes, while red oaks and crab apples are more irregular and chunky, befitting more informal homes.

When working with existing trees, you may wish to prune away some of the lower branches to provide clearance under the trees for sitting or dining. Mature trees also may need selective branches thinned out to allow more light to penetrate to plants below.

Vines can create ceilings when grown on overhead structures. When allowed to twine through overhead trellises and arbors, vines provide beauty and shade. Hanging baskets of flowers suspended overhead add color and visually tie the floor and the ceiling together.

The perfect curve of the lawn is reinforced by a brick border and mounds of low shrubs.

Overhead structures can be made of wood, fiberglass, plastic, or canvas. An umbrella is the simplest of all ceilings, albeit the smallest and most restricted in use. Ceilings made of solid material provide the best protection from the elements, while those that are partially open allow more air to circulate and some sunlight to come through, creating pleasing shadows.

Trellises and arbors can link the patio to the house, providing a visual transition that brings the outdoors in. Choose overhead structures that complement the construction material of the garden floor and walls and harmonize with the architectural style of the house. A white lattice trellis decorated with wisteria has an old-fashioned elegance that would complement a Colonial or formal brick home. A more massive stained wood structure would go better with a contemporary home.

APPROACH YOUR LANDSCAPE DESIGN WITH AN ARTISTIC TOUCH

As you look over the designs in this book, you will notice that each landscape enhances the home it was designed for and has a visual appeal of its own. Each is unique, but certain qualities become apparent as you study one design after another. The landscapes work successfully because their designers weighed certain basic artistic principles when choosing and laying out the plants and pavement used in the designs. Each property may be unique, but the methods the landscape designer uses to solve the problems and create the landscape are the same. The designer creates a pleasing landscape by skillfully respecting the space, line, form, pattern, texture, and color used in the landscape.

Space

The frame of reference in which the landscape designer works is the space occupied by each part of the landscape. A design is planned and executed in relation to the available space on the property, whether it be a courtyard garden or a half-acre woodland. The space in which the designer is working influences the use of the other elements of design.

Line

The contours of the hardscape and softscape create the lines of a landscape. These may be curved or straight, horizontal or vertical. Curved lines have a freer, more natural feeling than straight lines, which are crisp and formal. Vertical lines give strength, and horizontal lines imply permanence and flow. Squares and rectangles are formal, whereas circles and curves are more informal. Oblique angles suggest power and boldness, although too many different angles appear weak and distracting.

Line leads the eye from one area of the landscape to another, unifying the design within its space. Lines may be continuous or broken but, when broken, there must be no visual stop; rather, your eye should be able to pick up a continuity of movement for a harmonious design. For instance, the curved line of the lawn in the design on page 112 is broken by the driveway, but the eye picks up the continuation of the curve on the other side.

All good designs have a balance between horizontal and vertical lines. Line can be generated by repetition of shapes, sizes, textures, and colors. The choice of line depends on the space and the style of the house and the landscape—and promotes harmony, unity, and contrast.

The skillful designer can manipulate the lines of a garden to create an illusion. Lines—perhaps from the contour of a flower bed or the placement of a walk—running across the narrow part of a garden make it seem wider, while lines running the length of the same narrow space emphasize and exaggerate the narrowness.

Form

The three-dimensional shapes of a landscape are its forms. Plants may have upright, spreading, arching, weeping, rounded, columnar, pyramidal, or irregular forms. The overall form of a well-designed landscape results from combining and repeating plant forms that balance and complement each other. Too many forms alternating with each other become visually disturbing. It is more pleasing to group similarly shaped plants, using a contrasting shape as an accent. For impact, the professional designer often masses groups of the same type of shrub to create a strong statement.

The selection and placement of plant materials within the lines of a landscape creates depth of form. Depth of form results not from the individual shapes of the plants, but from how the shapes are grouped together within the lines of the landscape.

There are basically two types of depth of form: closed, which is a compact, massed form, with few spaces in between; and open, with spaces or

A curved walkway made of randomly cut stone creates the perfect informal air to complement this flowery setting.

The strength of the walkway design lies in the bold straight lines created by closely spacing square-cut pavers, which echo the long lines of the patio's stone edge.

voids being an important feature. While the cottage garden of a Cape Cod home might be best landscaped using a closed form, a sleek, modern home would be more pleasingly landscaped using an open form. In the design on page 40, the pyramidal shape of the river birches repeats throughout the landscape within the curving line of the ground cover, creating an open depth of form.

Texture

Referring to the surface finish of plants and other materials, texture appeals to the senses of sight and touch. The character of the foliage, bark, branches, and flowers of plants creates their textural impact. Plants are usually categorized as having a fine, medium, or coarse texture. Shrubs such as boxwood or azalea have tiny fine-textured leaves. Large-leaved plants, such as most rhododendrons, aucuba, or Oregon grape, appear coarse-textured.

Knowing how to combine and contrast textures is one of the most important design skills a landscape designer can have. Too many contrasting textures is unpleasant and busy. Overusing plants of the same texture is monotonous. An interesting design is achieved by grouping plants of similar textures and contrasting these with plants of a different texture. Textures of plants must combine well with the textures of the hardscape, too.

For textural harmony, landscape designers consider all elements included in a plan: house, pavement patterns, fencing, and other background material. As a general rule, use smooth-textured construction materials together and rough textures together, unless you intentionally want to create a broad contrast. For instance, smooth bluestone pavers are in keeping alongside a smooth wooden fence or leading to a fine-textured wooden deck, while rough-textured wooden benches would look attractive in front of a fieldstone wall.

Texture also influences weight. Plants with stiff branches or rough, coarse, large, or dull foliage appear heavier than plants with loose branches and smooth, fine, or glossy foliage. A combination of both results in a better balance within the design. Landscape designers also manipulate texture and weight to their advantage by creating visual illusions. Fine-textured plants appear further away and are calming, while bolder-textured plants appear closer and are more exciting. Small spaces can be made to feel more roomy with fine-textured plants and large areas more intimate by

14

Above: Construction materials, such as the gray and brown wood tones and the turquoise pool, contribute landscape color. The appeal of this scene lies in its repeated straight and curving lines—notice how the rounded pool shape is echoed in the steps within the pool and how the horizontal lines of the deck are balanced by the vertical lines of the cabana.

Top Left: Many ornamental trees, such as birch, feature brilliant fall foliage color and decorative bark for year-round appeal. Center left: Flowers, such as hydrangea, contribute outstanding color to a landscape. Bottom left: Gleaming berries, as from pyracantha, offer landscape color in fall and winter.

planting coarse-textured plants in the distance, since they will appear closer.

Color

In the landscape, color comes from foliage, flowers, berries, bark, and construction materials. Though we think primarily of flowers as providing the most vivid landscape colors, foliage may be many shades of green, purplish, or variegated during the growing season and yellow, red, or bronze in autumn. Color has a strong emotional appeal and influences the impact of a design.

Repetition of color in a landscape creates a pleasing patterning and visual unity within the design. Masses of the same flowering plant make a bold color statement and will be found in professional designs; mixtures of many different colors lose unity and pattern and look too busy. Skillful use of color can also be used to create accents and lead the eye to the focal point of a design.

Colors are described as warm or cool; red, orange, and yellow are warm colors, and blue, green, and violet are cool colors. Warm colors tend to advance, becoming more stimulating and aggressive than cool colors. They therefore make good accents and look best in a relatively small area. When warm colors are used in a large area, they make it seem smaller. Cool colors recede and are more relaxing. They look best used in large areas, although cool colors used in small areas will make the area appear larger. It is best to decide upon one dominant color and combine it with smaller amounts of one or two complementary colors.

When combining colors, different harmonies can be relied on. Complementary harmony uses colors that are opposite each other on the color wheel, such as red with blue and yellow with violet. Analogous color harmony uses colors that are adjacent on the color wheel, such as yellow with orange, or blue with violet. Monochromatic harmony uses different tints and shades of the same color, such as that used in an all-pink or all-blue garden.

Pattern

The arrangement and use of solids and open spaces within the depth of form creates pattern. The silhouette of a design against its background is an important aspect of pattern. Pattern is also achieved by repetition of form, texture, and color by massing plants. It may be naturalistic or stylized, and it is essential to the movement and rhythm within the design.

Each part of your landscape should be related to the others with a recognizable pattern not only of plants, but also of construction materials. For instance, each landscape in this book employs the same brick pattern throughout. The same paving material used in the front entry is used for the walkway to the backyard, and the same type of wood is used in decks, steps, and possibly the trim on the house.

Balance

Visual stability in a design creates balance. It is attained by placing plant materials and garden structures with their size, color, and texture taken into consideration. Balance may be actual or perceived, which is why a landscape does not need to be symmetrical to be in balance. One side of a design may be heavy in weight due to large forms, strong colors, or rough textures as long as it is balanced by a larger section where plants are smaller, lighter colored, or of a more delicate texture.

The strong, horizontal lines of this Southwestern-style home are dramatically balanced by the equally strong vertical lines of the huge cactus.

A large tree on one side of a landscape can be balanced by a grouping of shrubs on the other side. A garden structure on one side of the garden can be balanced on the other side with a tree. To help you achieve balance, draw imaginary lines through the center of the landscape. The placement of balancing features does not need to be measured exactly, but the visual impact of the weight of the design elements on each side should be equal.

Dominance

When one size, form, pattern, texture, or color of a landscape feature commands attention, it dominates the other features. Dominance is closely related to balance, and even though the other features are subordinate to the dominant feature, all features must be unified. Dominance is used to accent a plant or a garden feature and make it a focal point. The two trees placed on each side of the brick wall before the brick Federal house on page 72 dominate the design while still directing the eye beyond them to the house. They also frame the view and are balanced by the repeating pattern of the trees to the side of the house.

Contrast

When elements of a design are placed so they emphasize their differences, contrast is created. To be interesting, a design must have some variety and thus contrasting areas. This is accomplished by juxtaposing a strong vertical line with a horizontal line, combining different plant shapes, foliage textures, or colors, or alternating closed and open spaces. One or more elements can be used for contrast. For example, in the design of the Colonial house on page 46, the open, rounded shape and red foliage of the Japanese maple contrasts with the dense, pyramidal shape and dark green color of the Hicks yews planted around it.

Rhythm

The flow of plants and their colors, which carries the eye easily from one part of the design to the other, creates the design's rhythm. Rhythm can be attained by repetition and contrast of size, form, line, and color. A rhythm evolves from repeating a color, shape, plant, or group of plants throughout a design. Exact repetition is monotonous, and can be modified, for example, by repeating pink instead of red, or by repeating a smaller group of the same plants instead of repeating a mass of the same size.

When a planting gradually changes from large to small plants, or from coarse-textured to fine-textured, this creates a visual rhythm. Line and form will carry the eye in a definite direction or rhythm, too.

Scale and Proportion

Scale and proportion derive from the size relationship between the components of the landscape design with each other and with the size of the space the design occupies. A professional landscaper would not normally use large plants in a small area, because their size will be overwhelming—out of scale—and make the space seem claustrophobic. Likewise, small plants are out of scale and seem lost in a large area.

The mature size of plants should be in proportion to the house, patio, deck, or lawn area around which they are planted. Tall, towering trees are demanded by the scale of a three-story house, such as that on page 72, but would be too overpowering for a one-story ranch. Likewise, the form and mass of plant material must be in scale with the landscape design. A tiny island of ground cover planted beneath a tree makes the tree look top-heavy; a large tree demands a proportionally large bed beneath it to anchor the tree visually to the ground. When the correct scale and proportion between the landscape elements is achieved, the design becomes visually unified.

SELECT THE PERFECT LANDSCAPE PLANTS

Plants perform a variety of uses in a home's landscape. They form the basis for the garden's floor, walls, and ceiling. They provide privacy, color, shade, noise abatement, wind screening, erosion control, cooling, food for your family or wildlife, and most of all, they add value and beauty to your property.

A professional landscaper selects the plants to be used in a design for their ability to perform the foregoing functions as well as for their ability to satisfy the aesthetic needs of a landscape. Different plants perform well in various regions of the country, but no matter where you live there are attractive landscape plants to choose from. Each landscape plan pictured in this book is available with plant lists tailored for most regions of the country (see p. 174).

Trees

Trees are the tallest elements in a landscape, providing a framework for the setting and giving the design visual strength. Tall shade trees, such as oak, maple, and sweet gum, provide line, pattern, and form from their height and structure and cast cooling shade. Ornamental flowering trees, such as pear, magnolia, and dogwood, are smaller and contribute color, line, pattern, and form from their flowers, foliage, and fruits.

Shade trees may be planted singly as specimens, or grouped for a woodsy look. They provide strong vertical lines in the garden while creating an overhead canopy of horizontal or curving lines. Their forms are primarily rounded, pyramidal, or weeping. When used alone, smaller, ornamental trees draw the eye, creating a colorful focal point; when repeated, small trees create pattern and rhythm in the design. Tree foliage reflects light and is studded with shadows, contributing pattern and texture, and the movement of the foliage with the breeze brings the garden to life.

Shrubs

Shrubs offer the most versatility among landscape plants. They are invaluable as foundation plantings, as screens and hedges, in shrub borders, or as accents. When choosing shrubs, consider how their form and the texture of their foliage and branches work with the landscape design. Choose shrubs whose mature size won't be out of scale with the landscape. Although shrubs can be kept small with proper pruning, this adds greatly to gardening chores—and all too often shrubs are improperly pruned into unnatural shapes, ruining the designer's picture. Skilled landscape designers choose and space shrubs so that their mature sizes will not block windows, crowd driveways or walks, or obscure a desirable view.

Shrubs should also be chosen with their seasonal interest in mind. Evergreens are generally used in entry gardens because they provide year-round background color. Flowering shrubs offer floral color in spring and summer, and many contribute fall color from foliage or berries.

Using Shrubs in Foundation Plantings and Entryways

Shrubs form the mainstay of foundation planting and entry landscaping. When planted around the perimeter of the house, shrubs hide the foundation from view and dress it up, although their function does not stop there. Shrubs in the foundation planting are critical to the first impression of the house and reflect the creativity of the owner. They frame the house, outline windows, and soften corners. With few exceptions, plants in

Shrubs have many landscape uses. Top-left: Inkberry anchors a raised deck to its surroundings and camouflages its base. Top-right: A shrub border of azaleas provides privacy and spring flowers. Bottom-left: Low junipers hide a house foundation. Bottom-right: Boxwood provides an evergreen background for a flower border.

these areas should be evergreen and be varieties that will not soon become too large for the area or require frequent pruning.

A foundation planting is not a place for a collection. Professional designers limit the planting to three to five different types of shrubs, choosing ones that harmonize and complement each other. These are usually planted in masses for better impact, with a single taller, pyramidal or columnar shrub used adjacent to the front door or at a corner, although this is not a design necessity. Place lower growing and horizontally shaped shrubs under windows, where they will not turn into a problem. Avoid a single row of shrubs, but create a bed with a background, foreground, and midground, if space allows. Arrange the shrubs in groups where their different heights and forms can contrast with each other.

Shrub Borders

Shrub borders often create walls along a property border or a background of a flower garden. They can be used to separate different areas of the landscape or to hide security fences. Shrub borders can be of mixed plants or of a single variety, but look most attractive when several plants of the same shrub are massed together, whether the bor-

der contains evergreens, deciduous shrubs, or both. When the border repeats masses of the same texture, form, line, or color, the display becomes unified and visually pleasing (see pp. 12-15). When shrubs are used as a background for a flower garden, it looks best if the border consists of only one kind of plant, so the border doesn't detract from the flower garden.

Hedges and Screens

When planted close together, usually in a uniform row, trees and shrubs can be used to create hedges and screens. When sheared into a straight-sided shape, hedges take on a uniform, serious character, which best fits formally designed landscapes with other straight lines. Sheared hedges are a bit out of vogue these days because they require pruning several times a year. A row of shrubs can be left unpruned, or can be pruned by thinning with hand clippers, so that they grow into their natural graceful shapes. Such informal hedges look more graceful and require little maintenance. Hedges, whether informal or formal, make a bold statement and are useful for marking lines of the garden or a section within the garden. Tall hedges act as screens to ensure privacy or hide eyesores.

Tall hedges can conserve energy by moderating wind and sun. Hedges of plants such as Austrian pine, arborvitae, spruce, or fir can reduce wind velocity by 15 to 75 percent, depending on the plant and the density of the planting. These ever-green barriers can cut heating costs by up to 30 percent in the winter when placed within 40 feet of the house and blocking the prevailing wind, which usually comes from the north or west.

When using a hedge as a windbreak, the hedge works best if the plants are staggered rather than standing in a single row; otherwise the air currents are simply deflected over the tops of the trees. Maximum wind reduction occurs at a distance of four to six times the height of the hedge, so plantings should be established this distance from the house. For example, a hedge 8 feet tall should be planted 32 to 48 feet from the house.

Lawns

Grassed areas give a feeling of spaciousness to the landscape, unify it, and add a finishing touch to the garden. Lawns are visually pleasing but also serve the practical purposes of providing a place for lounging or playing.

There are many different varieties of lawn grass, each having its good and bad points. Choose a lawn grass or mixture suited to your climate and one that requires only the amount of maintenance you are inclined to give it. If this is done, the lawn will thrive; otherwise it is sure to languish. If the lawn will be heavily used, choose a grass that will withstand the traffic. Tall fescue and perennial ryegrass are the types that best withstand wear and tear. Your local nursery or county agricultural extension agent should be able to advise you.

All too often, the lawn shape is an after-thought. The lawn occupies whatever space is left over after the other plantings are put in. But the size and shape of lawn areas make a statement also. Lawns unify different areas of the landscape. Their fine texture sets off the other plants in the design and creates the finishing touch—a carpet—to the house, trees, and shrubs. Notice how the lawn areas in the landscape on page 48 create graceful curves throughout the landscape, repeating the curve of the brick entry landing. These areas of fine-textured emerald green give a sense of calm and unity to the landscape that would be lacking if the areas were squared off or filled with masses of flowers or shrubbery.

Notice how the strong curved shape of this lawn holds the eye and adds excitement to the landscape.

Ground Covers

Low-growing plants that blanket the soil are called ground covers. These plants work well in low-traffic areas and in parts of the garden where a high-maintenance lawn is not desired or would be difficult to mow. Ground covers used on slopes assist in preventing soil erosion as well as making the area easier to maintain. Beds of ground covers beneath shrubs unify the planting design and set off the shrubbery while improving the soil. In general, ground covers require little maintenance once they have filled in.

The choice of ground covers is extensive, offering foliage of different shapes, textures, and colors; and some, such as vinca, pachysandra, and ajuga, contribute flowers as well. Use flowering ground covers or masses of shade-loving perennials under trees and shrubs that bloom at the same time to create pleasing color harmonies.

Professional landscapers normally use only one type of ground cover in a given area, as you can see in the designs in this book. This technique makes the area seem larger and eliminates the choppy appearance that would result from a mixture of ground covers. Also, when ground covers are combined, one frequently outperforms the other, crowding it out.

Vines

Because they are climbing woody plants, vines make excellent landscape plants for screening small areas, covering fences, arbors, and trellises, and softening corners and rough walls. They are especially useful where space is at a premium. Vines can also be allowed to climb up the side of the house, although sometimes tendrils can damage mortar and loosen clapboards. It is often advisable to grow a vine on a trellis placed in front of the house rather than allow it to grow directly on the house.

Vines growing on a house wall, or on a trellis placed next to the wall, will block the sun's heat in summer and insulate against the cold in winter. Deciduous vines should be placed on south and west walls to block summer heat and allow winter warmth to come through. Evergreen vines should be used on a north wall, where their foliage deflects winter wind and their stems and leaves act as insulation.

Flowers—Annuals, Bulbs, Perennials

Garden flowers—bulbs, annuals, and perennials —die back to the ground at the end of the growing season. In following years, most bulbs and perennials sprout again and rebloom, year after year; annuals perform once and then die. Because they lack the year-round structure provided by woody plants—trees and shrubs, and most vines and ground covers—garden flowers have special uses. They were once massed together into showy flower beds in the backyard. Only recently have innovative landscapers been including quantities of perennials in landscape designs for front yards. When long-blooming, low-maintenance perennial varieties are selected, such as daylily, 'Goldsturm' coneflower, and astilbe, their flowers and foliage provide welcome bursts of color and texture.

Whether you are choosing spring-flowering bulbs for their show of early color, perennials for their dependable seasonal performance, or annuals for their months of bright flowers, garden flowers make the most impact in a landscape design when they are planted in large drifts of a single variety. Their floral color will then make a dramatic statement during seasons when few trees and shrubs are blooming.

Note that the designs in this book include masses of bulbs or perennials within beds of ground cover such as vinca or pachysandra. When combined this way, the perennials' lack of structure during the cold months will not leave a noticeable hole or patch of bare ground in the landscape design. When planted at the same time, both ground covers and perennials can each get established and will not compete with one another. Establishing perennials within an existing expanse of ground cover may be more difficult.

Annuals must be replanted every year as transplants or seedlings and they will not do well in an established bed of ground cover. Neither will the ground cover appreciate being disturbed by the digging necessary to plant the annuals each summer. If you wish to grow annuals, try combining them in a bed with early-spring bulbs; the annuals can be planted around the withering bulb foliage for a successful companion planting. Annuals add bright welcoming color when included in planters located on the walk or landing leading to the front door.

POSITION THE PLANTS FOR BEST EFFECT

Where you position landscape plants within a landscape design is just as important as which plants you select. A plant's position determines how successfully it contributes to the overall design of the plan as well as how successfully it serves any intended practical function.

Using Plants as Accents

Garden accents are incidental features used to highlight a particular area of the landscape and draw the eye to it. This may be done with an unusual plant shape, foliage texture, or hue, or with a splash of color from flowers. Accent plants are usually single specimens that contrast with and stand out from nearby plants. Including a strongly upright plant, such as San José holly, among a group of lower-growing, horizontal plants such as spreading yew creates an accent due to the sharp change in line and form. A large clump of tall, feathery ornamental grass makes a novel accent. Fountain grass, for instance, adds a graceful accent of weeping line and fine texture that contrasts well with dark green foliage and bolder textures.

Locating Shade and Ornamental Trees

Shade trees around a house do more than create a structure and give strength to the landscape. They can also be effective energy conservers. For this reason, their positions should be chosen carefully.

Shade trees are best planted far enough from the house that their limbs will not eventually grow onto the roof or cause damage if they break off in a storm. A good rule of thumb is to plant a shade tree at least 20 feet from the house. Before planting, the proposed location of shade and flowering trees should be considered both from inside the house or the garden and from several angles outside the property as well.

Deciduous shade trees planted 20 feet from the house on the south or west sides will shade the house during summer, lowering the indoor temperature anywhere between 8° and 20°F. In the winter, when the trees' leaves have fallen, sunlight strikes the house and helps to reduce heating bills.

Trees should be planted far enough apart to allow summer breezes to blow through them. Space the trunks so that the branches will not quite touch when the trees are mature. When trees are planted too close together, winter wind funnels through the spaces between the trunks. To lessen this problem, if close-growing trees already exist on the property, they can be underplanted with shrubs.

Shade trees are usually best located to the sides of a house, where they will frame the house rather than block it. When the vertical lines of a tree's trunk cut through the view of the house, this makes the house appear less significant and stops your eye from traveling toward the front door, which should be the focal point of the design. Framing a house with trees makes it appear larger or longer than it is and leads your eye to the front door.

Usually smaller than most shade trees, ornamental flowering trees demand a location that draws attention to the best of their attributes.

Landscape design: Howard Purcell

The purple foliage of the Bloodgood Japanese maple, which contrasts with surrounding greenery, draws the eye, creating a dramatic focal point.

The decorative white fence echoes the white house in color and style, unifying the house and landscape into a harmonious scene.

They can be planted singly as an accent, in a group to create a weighty mass, or repeated in a row to create a straight or a curving line. A flowering tree shows itself off well in almost any area of the garden, but looks truly effective with a simple background that plays up the flowers and silhouettes the outlines of the branches. Place small trees as specimens on the lawn, along a fence, or at the front of the house without too much distracting material behind them. They can be used to frame or partially block views (see p. 29) and to create a line and pattern. Used in the distance, flowering trees become a focal point and provide depth to the design.

Spacing Shrubs

An important consideration in positioning plants in the landscape is spacing shrubs. All too often homeowners plant shrubs too close together so that in a few years they crowd each other, the house, and walkways. Landscape designers face a dilemma: if they position young shrubs correctly, so that when mature their branches just touch, the new planting looks skimpy for many years. When planted close enough to give the bed or border a full and lush appearance soon after planting, the shrubs quickly get too large for their spaces and crowd each other. Usually a compromise is reached so that a new planting will fill in within a few years and have a useful life of fifteen to twenty years before the shrubbery is overgrown. Or course, correct pruning over the years can control growth and prevent the shrubs from

ever becoming too large. And when a skilled professional chooses plants whose mature heights are not too large for their locations, the landscape plants perform practically forever.

Locating Beds and Borders

Sometimes called an island bed, a bed is a planting area accessible from all sides. It is located in either a lawn or a paved area. Whether filled with flowers or shrubs, beds work most effectively on large properties where they can be used as a device to break up large areas and thus make the garden feel more intimate while still not completely blocking the view beyond. Island beds can separate garden areas, especially active- and passive-use areas. Since, by definition, they are freestanding, they must be designed to look attractive from all sides.

Beds should be in proportion to the rest of the property. Any bed occupying more than one-third of the lawn area will most likely appear out of proportion. Beds in formal gardens call for straight edges and a symmetrical design, but in an informal planting, they can be free-form. Designers plan curves to be gentle because those that are too sharp look contrived and busy. Soil within a bed can be mounded to create a berm and give a flat garden needed dimension.

Bedding plants should be chosen with care so the area looks distinctive and not merely like a functional hedge. A bed makes an ideal location for a magnificent specimen plant, perhaps with a mass of lower-growing plants surrounding it. Also, a berm can be planted with interesting dwarf conifers or turned into a rock garden. Annuals, perennials, and bulbs work well set out in beds, but leave the bed empty after the growing season. It is best to have a year-round structure anchoring the bed, such as a tree or mass of shrubs, so it is not an empty space when bulbs, annuals, or perennials are not growing and flowering. Beds can be designed with an existing tree in the center or located about one-third of the way from the bed's end. But the size of the bed must be large enough to anchor the height of the tree visually.

A peninsular bed can hide the backyard and the entrance to the backyard from the street if the property is on a corner. There will still be access to the backyard, but it will be hidden from view.

Borders differ from beds because they are three-sided, backing up to the house, a fence, a wall, or other garden structures. Borders may be planted with garden flowers, shrubs, or both.

The generous shape and proportions of this island bed anchor the tall maple to its surroundings, while providing an informal setting for displaying low azaleas, rhododendrons, and a clump birch.

They are called mixed borders when shrubs are combined with garden flowers.

Borders work best when the tallest plants grow in the back and the smallest in front, but they look more interesting if the plant heights mingle, with taller plants edging forward of shorter ones in places. Effective mixed borders result from combining groups of deciduous and evergreen shrubs in the background and midground, and mingling perennials and bulbs with them in the foreground and midground for an ever-changing display of flowers and foliage.

SELECT THE PERFECT LANDSCAPE STRUCTURES

The paving, fences, walls, and any garden ornaments used in a landscape design are often called the hardscape, while the plant materials are called the softscape. The hardscape plays an important role in any landscape design, contributing line, pattern, form, color, and texture.

Materials

Well-designed landscapes use paving materials for driveways and walkways whose color, texture, and pattern complement the construction material of the house. While some materials, such as concrete, brick, or stone, can be used in both driveways and walkways, this is not always possible, as the driveway needs to support more pressure than a walkway. Wood, for example, is rarely used on a driveway, but works well on pathways if the house is by the seashore or has a

naturalistic, weather-beaten look. In a case like this, the driveway can be edged in the same wood as the walkway to unify the two.

Bricks are available in different textures and colors and can be used on driveways, walkways, patios, and steps. Used bricks are rougher in texture and therefore more suitable for walkways. A common brick measures 3¾ by 8 by 2¼ inches. Other types of brick are Roman brick, which measures 4 by 12 by 1½ inches, and paving brick, which is 4 by 8 by 3½ inches. Bricks do not need to be embedded in mortar or concrete, although this gives them more permanence and keeps out weeds, but can be laid in a 2-inch base of sand, as long as a car will not be driven over them. If the soil does not drain well or is in an area with severely cold winters, lay 3 to 5 inches of crushed rock under the sand. After the bricks are laid in their pattern, brush more sand on top until the cracks are filled.

Common patterns for brick are running bond, basket weave, herringbone, diagonal herringbone, pinwheel, and circular. Each pattern has a different texture and mood, some being more formal and others more busy looking. When laying a brick walk that turns sharply or meets a brick patio or terrace, the direction of the pattern can change to indicate a turn or transition (see the design on p. 76).

Concrete is one of the most inexpensive paving materials, although not always the most attractive. It can be laid in any shape, and may be the easiest way to deal with a circle. Smooth concrete

Mortared brick laid in a herringbone pattern has a busy texture that complements a romantic style of architecture.

Mortarless brick laid in a running-bond pattern looks clean and crisp—perfect for contemporary homes.

is slippery when wet; a textured finish is safer and can be made more attractive with a sweeping circular design. Adding heavy aggregate to concrete strengthens it and makes it more attractive, as does dividing it into sections broken up with pieces of treated wood. Concrete can also be beautified by coloring it, stamping it, or topping it with colored stones.

Pre-cast interlocking concrete pavers are strong and easy to install. They come in a variety of shapes, textures, and colors and, while more expensive than concrete, are more economical than brick, flagstone, slate, or other stones. Quarried stones such as granite, marble, bluestone, and slate are often used as paving materials. Dimensioned stone, since it is cut, is easy to work with because it is usually flat. Fieldstone can also be used, but it is necessary to find stones as flat as possible and to bury part of the stone so that the surface is flat and easy to walk on.

Pressure-treated lumber has preservative forced deep into the wood and lasts longer than wood that has simply been dipped or painted with preservative. Pressure-treated wood is not toxic to plants and the preservatives will not leach into the soil; however, extreme caution should be used when sawing the wood to prevent inhaling or ingesting the dust particles. Do not burn pressure-treated wood.

Authentic railroad ties measure 8 to 10 feet long and have variable heights and widths; they are usually treated with creosote, a preservative toxic to people and plants. Landscape timbers are usually made of pressure-treated pine and are 8 feet long and either 6 by 6 or 6 by 8 inches, or 8 by 8 inches. They are preferable owing to their non-toxicity, longevity, and uniformity.

Installing Driveways and Walkways

In many cases, the driveway is the first section of the house to be seen and so is an integral part of the landscape. Driveways are often paved with concrete, blacktop, or gravel, depending upon the climate and the style of the home. Special cement blocks that allow grass to grow through the holes in them add an informal look to a country setting. Concrete, while the least expensive, stains easily; blacktop softens in the heat and requires sealing every year or two.

Brick, flagstones, or cobble can be inlaid in the driveway's pavement to create a decorative pattern that matches the walkway to the door or the landing in front of the door. Brick can also be patterned to mark parking spaces or to create a courtyard feeling in a circular driveway (see the design on p. 110). In smaller or hilly properties where level outdoor recreational space is at a premium, an attractive pavement material or pattern allows the driveway to double as a patio (see the designs on pp. 103 and 106).

Walkways provide ease of movement from one area of the garden to another and also provide a feeling of continuity, especially if the same paving material used at the entry leads to the side and the backyard. Landscape designers are careful that the lines of the walk do not cut the design up so much that the property seems choppy or smaller than it is.

The landscape designs presented here demonstrate that a straight line may be the shortest distance between two points but is not necessarily the best landscaping principle. Only in formal gardens are walkways straight. Turns are attrac-

Inlaid brick and an island bed transform this driveway into a dramatic entry courtyard that greets visitors and provides easy access to the home's entrance.

tive, can be used advantageously to block views, can give the feeling that they are leading to something special beyond, and can make the property appear larger than it is.

When a walkway is constructed of a material such as bluestone, the stones can be laid in such a way that the edges of the walkway are irregular. This blends well with a farmhouse or barn-style residence, as shown on page 60. In natural settings, walkways can be paved with wood chips, pine needles, crushed stone, crushed seashells, or gravel. They should be used only on flat or almost flat areas as these materials can wash away on slopes. To keep these materials in bounds, include an edging of wood, brick, metal, or stone.

Garden paths are most often designed to be 24 to 36 inches wide, except for the walkway to the front door, which works best if it is 48 inches wide. Ensure that gates and other potential obstacles are wide enough to allow the lawn mower and other maintenance equipment to pass.

Installing Patios, Decks, and Terraces

Patios and terraces are often constructed with brick, although other materials such as concrete and concrete pavers may be used. A smooth-finished brick is ideal for patios, but be aware that it is slippery when wet. For this reason, it is not recommended around pools.

Decks are almost always built with wood, and materials such as redwood, cedar, and cypress are the most common and durable. Pressure-treated lumber, which is usually pine, is more durable than any of the other woods and should be used when in contact with the ground, if not everywhere on the deck. It is slightly green when new, can be left to weather naturally to a light gray, and does not need painting or staining, although a sealant is recommended for a one-time application immediately after installation.

Decks are usually raised to meet the level of the house to avoid stepping down. This will necessitate steps leading to ground level and railings for safety. Railings should be designed carefully as they are an integral part of the structure. They must be strong enough for people to sit on or lean against, and high enough off the floor of the deck so leaves will blow off or can be swept away.

Building Walls and Fences

Walls and fences play many roles; they mark property lines, camouflage service areas, retain soil in a change of grade, and separate one area of the garden from another. They make excellent backgrounds for shrubs and flowers, while providing privacy and contributing pattern, texture, and line to landscape design. Walls and fences can be functional or purely decorative, made of a variety of materials, and designed in many heights and styles. If the material from which the wall or fence is made matches either the paving or the house, it will tie the landscape together more uniformly.

Walls can be made of brick, concrete, adobe, or stone. Railroad ties and landscape timbers are used for constructing retaining walls, edgings, and the sides of raised planters. Stone is more expensive than brick, but quite durable, and fits well into a country-style or farmhouse landscape. Fieldstone makes excellent dry walls, which can be accented or softened with plants growing between the stones.

Small, low brick or stone walls look striking placed at the entrance to the driveway or the pathway leading from the sidewalk. A low retaining wall can be built into a slope to change the grade when filled in behind with topsoil, adding height and contour to the landscape. Whenever a wall is constructed as a retaining wall, it must be angled back into the fill behind it for stability. The use of this type of wall will make an expanse look larger because there is no visible interruption of the lawn or planting when viewed from above. Such walls work well near an entryway, where they help draw attention to the front door (see the design on p. 78). A low retaining wall can be planted with ground covers or low shrubs that hug the top of the wall and cascade over it, softening the appearance of the stone.

Fences are usually made of wood or metal and have many styles that can contribute to the landscape design. Wooden fences should be constructed of redwood, cedar, or cypress as these are the most resistant to the weather. Chainlink fences work in areas where children or pets need to be confined, and around swimming pools because they allow you to see through them while still providing security. Chainlink is more durable than wood, although not as attractive. The appeal of this kind of fence can be heightened by using chainlink coated with green or black vinyl, or by hiding the fence behind a vine or shrubbery.

Installing Steps

Steps enhance a landscape design and are not just a functional necessity. Steps can be made of wood, bricks, flagstones, or concrete—or a combination of any of these—and can be made more

A feeling of continuity in this attractive landscape comes from matching the weathered wood of the home's deck to its siding. Notice how the graceful lines of the ornamental grass complement the linear pattern of the wood.

attractive if edged with vertical pieces of wood, Belgian blocks, or plants. Landscape timbers, railroad ties, or logs make effective steps in woodland gardens. They may, however, be difficult to place on steep slopes. For safety reasons, construct outdoor steps lower and deeper than indoor steps. The tread on outdoor steps should be at least 12 inches deep and the riser no more than 6 inches high.

Lighting

Outdoor lights illuminate walkways at night, light outdoor activity areas, and provide security. Besides performing these very practical purposes, outdoor lighting beautifies the garden at night, spotlighting a specimen plant, silhouetting an intricately branching tree, and dramatizing the view from indoors. Lighting, when set away from the house, makes even the smallest garden look larger.

Outdoor lights are most easily installed prior to planting so walks and plant roots needn't be disturbed when the underground conduit or wire is laid.

Along walkways, lights are best located at ground level or on posts 24 to 30 inches high with the lights directed downward, away from the eyes, so they emit a soft, pleasant glow. Choose fixtures that make a decorative addition to the landscape. A lamp on a post with the name or street number fits well with almost any style home and can accent a bed of low shrubbery and ground cover.

Landscape design: Conni Cross

A fieldstone retaining wall helps level out sloping ground while creating a lovely spot for a flower garden.

Steps and a landing constructed from brick and landscape timbers attractively link high ground with low ground where timbers are used to hold back a steep grade.

Both functional and beautiful, the bench in the garden acts as a focal point and a comfortable place to sit while enjoying the garden. The symmetrically placed statues frame the entrance and emphasize the formality of the garden design.

Garden Ornaments

Garden sculptures and statuary can add a special focal point or accent to the garden as well as providing year-round interest. The smallest of gardens can use a statue, sundial, or piece of stonework as an eyecatching focal point. Be sure that whatever you use is in proportion to the size of the garden and of a color that does not distract from but, rather, enhances the planting.

Garden accents may be placed amid beds and borders. They may also be placed away from the house and the rest of the garden to carry the eye to a focal point and so create the illusion of distance.

Garden structures, such as gazebos, pergolas, and benches, while serving a function as shelters or relaxation areas, also act as garden ornaments. The architecture, material, and color should blend with the style of the house and the rest of the garden.

Water Features

There is probably no more effective way to create a special place in the landscape than by incorporating a water feature. Still water reflects the surrounding landscape and adds serenity to any setting. The sound of running water soothes the spirit and its movement entertains. If a natural pond or stream does not exist on the property, a small pond or formal pool with a fountain or waterfall can be installed within most homeown-

ers' budgets. Books are available that give detailed do-it-yourself instructions or the work can be handled by a contractor.

Prefabricated pools made of fiberglass come in many different shapes and are long-lasting; pools may also be constructed of flexible PVC sheeting, and then their outline is left to your imagination. Square, rectangular, or circular pools fit well in formal gardens, while free-form pools made to look natural highlight informal landscapes.

In a naturalistic setting, a small footbridge can be used as either a decorative or a functional feature (see the landscape on p. 134). The edge of an informal pool can be planted with bog plants, ornamental grasses, or ferns to impart a naturalistic feeling. To grow waterlilies, a pool must receive at least six hours of full sun a day and be at least 18 inches deep. Local zoning often dictates that yards with an ornamental pool of a certain depth be fenced.

CREATE A BEAUTIFUL GARDEN VIEW

A beautiful garden scene unfolds from a series of changing views as you move through the landscape. There are new views you want to create, existing ones you want to save, and others you may want to hide. Some views remain visible from almost any indoor or outdoor viewpoint; others are surprises to be glimpsed when rounding a bend or entering a gateway.

Studying the Existing View

Before any landscape construction or planting begins on a piece of property, a professional designer studies the area from many vantage points both inside and outside the house. The homeowner may, depending on personal preference, want a patio or a deck, a flower or a vegetable garden, a swimming pool or a tennis court, in sight of the house or hidden from view. The perfect location for any desired landscape features may already exist without removing or adding plant material, but if it does not exist, screening plantings may need to be added, or trees and shrubs may need to be pruned selectively or removed.

When choosing a location for a deck or a patio, there may be one area that affords a better view of the rest of the garden than another; if so, work with it. If its location means loss of privacy from the street, fencing or hedging may need to be incorporated.

Many prominent garden focal points, such as a gazebo, fountain, small patio, or birdbath, serve a dual purpose. They can be the focal point of a distant view, drawing your eye to them, or they can draw the viewer physically to them and then become a viewing point from which to see the rest of the landscape. For example, a gazebo at the far end of a garden looks inviting when viewed from the house; when actually sitting and relaxing within the gazebo, you can enjoy viewing the garden from a different perspective. When choosing a spot for any prominent garden feature, consider both views that you are creating.

Concealment and revealment can turn an ordinary landscape into an exciting one, especially when one is working with a view. It takes a skilled landscape designer to hide a view from sight, using plant materials, construction, or a curving path and then allowing the view to open beautifully all at once. This technique employs the element of surprise or emerging views.

Framing Views

A professional landscape designer will consider the views of the house from many angles—from the street, the walks, and the corners of the property, and then view the property from inside looking out. Focal points and any particularly exciting views become enhanced when framed by landscape plants or other features.

Existing trees or shrubs that block a view may be removed or transplanted, and new trees or the transplanted trees set further to each side of the

Landscape design: Howard Purcell

An inviting garden scene unfolds upon approaching the gate, because the statue beyond acts as an alluring focal point.

line of sight to form a frame around the view. Depending on the size of the property, it is possible that trees or shrubs that frame the view of the landscape from the house will also frame the view of the house from a distance.

The entrance to the driveway can be emphasized by framing it with trees or shrubs, which also serves the purpose of providing privacy and blocking the view of the entry landscape from the street.

When framing a view into a wooded area, two prominent trees set on each side of the line of sight will echo and frame the verticals of the trees in the woods. The result is a feeling of unity that allows the prominent trees to flow into their surroundings.

Color can be used to frame a view. Where a large panorama or distant view exists, frame it with flowering shrubs that bloom in a monochromatic scheme. The flowers will then provide a lovely frame that won't compete with the view for attention and will give depth to the view while leaving it open and spacious.

Screening Views

There are times when it is advantageous to block, fully or partially, a view of the house or the garden. For example, when a magnificent panorama exists from the backyard, blocking that view from the side of the house with a tree or shrub so that the view comes into sight all at once as you enter the back of the property makes for visual drama. This drama relies again on the element of surprise, and intensifies the contrast between small and vast.

When a view overlooks a large area, such as a pond or a large lawn, some blocking of the view may be more effective than framing the entire view. Although the view itself may be breathtaking, by interrupting part of the view with masses of trees or shrubs the view becomes more dramatic because the feeling of depth and distance is enhanced. Blocking part of the view results in framing sections of it. Planting masses separated by open areas has a greater impact than planting the entire perimeter of the view or leaving it entirely open.

There are times when screening a part of a view can enhance the impact of the view that is left unimpaired. Blocking the view to the side enhances the view straight ahead. The blocking can be achieved with plant material or with construction such as a trellis, an arbor, or a fence and garden gate. This technique often works well in landscaping the front of a large home. Groups of trees or tall shrubs, even a wall blocking part of the house, may give depth to the design while revealing an impressive sight as you walk up the walkway or drive into the driveway.

DESIGN A WELCOMING ENTRANCE FOR YOUR HOME

The landscaping surrounding your home's front door creates a welcome, acting as an extension of your home. Whether you are landscaping a new home or replanting around a house that needs a face-lift, the entryway should be of primary importance. Because it is the first part of the house that most people see, it sets the scene for the home as well as the rest of the landscape, acting similarly to a vestibule, where guests are first greeted.

While entry landscaping should be eyecatching, it serves practical purposes too. It should provide easy access to the front door from the driveway, and from the street if desired. This does not mean, however, that the walkway to the door needs to be in a straight line. Straight walks leading from the street dissect the lawn, making it look smaller than it is. A professional landscape designer, to make the entrance more interesting, often positions the walkway across the front of the house or curves it from the street or the driveway, even when the house has a central entrance.

Many homes may have two entrances in front, and the landscaping becomes an important clue as to which is the main one. Usually a less-prominent walk leads to the kitchen, or service, door. Small trees or shrubs may be located partially to block that door, making the front entrance all the more noticeable (see landscape design on p. 46).

While garden paths can be narrower, walkways to the front door look and work best when they are at least 4 feet wide, if this is not out of scale with the rest of the landscape. This width allows two people to walk side by side. The walkway can be landscaped on both sides with an interesting garden floor, but should not be lined with shrubs, as many homeowners mistakenly do, which creates a tunnel effect. Keep in mind that the walk is part of the garden floor and should be left open; by planting shrubs along it you are erecting walls where none are called for. The designs in this book tend to highlight a landing at the foot of a walkway with low plantings on either side, but these do not usually continue along the entire length of the walk. This frames the entrance to the walkway, welcoming your visitors.

Landscape design: Barbara Damrosch

The home has two front entrances; however, skillful landscaping makes it obvious which one is the main door, while providing easy access to the secondary entrance.

The graceful curving walk, which leads up two steps to a courtyard/landing, extends a friendly invitation to all visitors.

Professionals know how to lead a visitor dramatically to the front door by using several levels linked by walks. Study, for example, the entry design for the Elizabethan Tudor home on page 78. The low stone wall encircles the area directly in front of the door, separating it from the lawn and creating a welcome mat at the door. A large, decorative paved area below the front stoop can dramatize a front door and create a permanent welcome mat. (The designs on pp. 82 and 110 use this technique to great effect.)

A low hedge or other plantings can surround an entry garden or courtyard near the door, which creates walls and suggests an outdoor vestibule. A small bench is a welcome sign here, even if rarely used. Planters with seasonal flowers provide cheerful color and a decorative touch.

Where a circular driveway winds in front of a home, inlaying a decorative pattern of brick, cobble, or flagstones into the driveway's pavement creates an outdoor vestibule.

Choosing Landscape Plants

Designers keep the landscaping at the front of the house restrained. The planting should be simple and unified by repeating masses of the same types of plants. As shrubs grow together, there will not be the busyness that would exist if the plants were all different.

Evergreen shrubs work best as foundation plants, because they are on view year round. Low-growing shrubs, such as spreading juniper, Japanese holly, boxwood, dwarf rhododendron, spreading yew, azalea, and euonymus, work best in front of windows, where they will never grow so tall as to hide the windows, create too much shade, or obstruct the view from the inside. Tall shrubs, primarily those with a conical shape, may be used to soften corners or frame the front door. Vines can be used to make corners of doors and windows seem less harsh.

Small flowering trees can be used to advantage against a windowless wall or in front of a window where privacy from the walk or front door might be desirable. In the design on page 78, the magnolia screens the guest room at the front of the house while providing a beautiful, changing view from indoors.

The layout of a landscape and the choice of plants usually reflects the style of the home's architecture. Formal designs make use primarily of straight lines and right angles or simple curves. Plants are often arranged symmetrically, especially around the front door, and may be ones with precise, formal shapes. The trend in landscaping today is more toward the informal, with curving beds, borders, and walks, and with plants left unclipped to reveal their natural grace, although the choice is one of personal preference and style.

A large Georgian, Federal, or French Provincial house would easily conform to a formal style, while a farmhouse or Cape Cod home would adapt well to informal landscaping. When the house is a contemporary design with strong and dramatic architectural features, the landscape plants and construction must be equally clean. Plantings might be sparse and emphasize the dramatic lines of an unusual specimen plant, such as a blue atlas cedar or an espaliered pyracantha.

When selecting plants to incorporate in a front-yard landscape, scale and proportion are primary considerations. The designs in this book keep the plantings in scale with the house. Tall or massive houses demand equally weighty plantings and towering trees to offset and frame them. A ranch home does best with low-growing evergreens across its front, and trees look best when of medium height. Small or average-sized homes can be dwarfed by tall shrubs and trees, while large houses look comical if the trees and shrubs are proportionally small.

Plantings at the front of the house can also visibly affect the scale and balance of the setting. Tall plantings at both corners of the house and astride the door can cause the house to appear smaller than it is, while a lower grouping of shrubs at each corner will result in making the house appear larger and longer. A small, decorative tree at one corner of the house can be used to balance the garage on the other side and will also help the house appear longer.

Using Color

The colors of flowering plants used in the landscape should complement the colors of the house. All too often brightly colored flowering shrubs clash with the house's trim or siding. This problem is sometimes more easily corrected by repainting the trim than by re-landscaping. Many favorite landscape shrubs and trees, such as azalea, rhododendron, lilac, and crab apple, come in many varieties and in an assortment of colors and hues. Picture what they will look like in bloom in front of your house when you are deciding which colors to choose. Usually light-colored flowers look best if planted in front of a dark-colored house and vice versa.

Transition Zones

Landscape designers often plan for a transition between the house and the landscaping in front of the house; this could be a porch, a small front patio, or an entry courtyard. There are design assets to a feeling of enclosure in an entryway. This enclosure might be only as wide as the path or consist of a larger area in front of the house, creating a small garden several feet deep. Enclosure can be achieved with plantings or a low fence and may be accented with container plants. As visitors approach the front door and enter the enclosure, they feel as if they are entering a part of the home, even though they are still outside. This creates the sense of a single space, separated from the rest of the landscape and yet not in conflict with it.

Dealing with Slopes

If the entryway is not at the same level as the driveway or the street, a combination of steps, landings, and turns leading to the front door is more attractive as well as more functional than a straight path and steps (see the plan on p. 44). The turns can be accented with shrubbery or with planters filled with seasonal flowers.

Railings may be necessary on steps where the grade changes significantly, especially if snow, ice, or rain are frequent occurrences. If the risers are not too high—between 4 and 7 inches—and if the treads are at least 24 inches deep, railings may not be needed. Plantings alongside steps should be low-growing and massed, well below eye level, to give a sense of security.

One way to provide privacy from the street without blocking the house with tall plantings and dense shade is with landscape berms, or mounds of soil. These can block the view of the house from the street and add interesting contours to a property. The berm used in the design on page 52 provides privacy to the entry courtyard and gives it a sense of enclosure. A low, decorative wall of brick or stone does the same thing. Contouring at an entryway may also impart the feeling of greater distance from the street. The berms or areas around the wall can be jacketed in low-growing shrubs or ground covers for a natural look.

If the slope extends all the way to the house, topsoil can be used to fill in the area immediately in front of the entrance-way to create a flat area for a landing with steps leading to the walk below.

Containers of colorful annuals placed on the staircase provide a cheerful greeting and a visual transition from garden to home.

Notice the delightful way the pink tulips pick up the pink of the garden gate.

When there is a slope between the house and the entry walkway, the foundation planting can be built into a raised planter with a retaining wall of brick or stone. If the planting area is wide or the slope steep, the raised bed can be two-tiered. Cotoneaster would be a good choice to plant here, as its structured branches will complement the wall without completely hiding it.

Landscaping to Solve Parking Problems

Among the practical needs that good landscaping can solve is to provide a place to park cars. With so many families owning one car for every member of the family over age sixteen, parking can be a serious problem. Professional landscape designers solve parking problems in ways that are an asset to the design, employing several attractive solutions.

Low walls or hedges can curve around and hide parking areas from prominent view, while still keeping them accessible. Where the garage is far from the front entrance, wide, circular driveways that swing in front of the front door can be installed, and plantings placed in the center of the circle to soften the pavement. Separate areas for parking can be indicated by inlaying a pattern of brick or concrete into the driveway, or by using a different paving material.

Where space permits, build a turnaround area into the driveway. This eliminates the need to back out of the driveway and allows space for additional guest parking. Or widen the driveway in one area if space is more limited. Sawtooth or diagonal parking areas can be built to make more efficient use of space for parking.

Professional designs leave enough room for car doors to be opened; they also have access from the driveway to the walks leading to all entrances without requiring anyone to brush against shrubbery. Belgian blocks or other bumper strips edging the driveway help to prevent cars from accidentally running over plantings. Steel edging holds gravel in place.

LANDSCAPE YOUR YARD FOR MAXIMUM OUTDOOR LIVING SPACE

Every home needs an outdoor place for playing, whether it be in the literal sense of the word with young children bouncing about, or in a more figurative sense with adults needing their niche for relaxing, barbecuing, swimming, reading, or napping in the sun. The right landscaping will actually contribute to the enjoyment of the area by making it both more attractive and more functional. A home's backyard usually provides the family's outdoor space for recreation, relaxing, entertaining, and dining. Practicality, privacy, and beauty are the rules when landscaping these areas.

Evaluating Your Family's Needs

Your outdoor living space can and should serve many functions. A professional landscaper will consider the ages, interests, and individual desires of your family members before creating a plan to meet your needs. Here are some questions you might ask yourself:

■ Do you enjoy, and have time to care for, garden plants, or is low maintenance a primary consideration?

■ Do you need space for a children's swing set, jungle gym, or sandbox?

■ Do you want a paved area (which could be part of the driveway) for sports such as basketball, hopscotch, etc.?

■ Do you want a swimming pool, hot tub, built-in barbecue, or tennis court?

■ Do you want to grow edible plants, such as vegetables, herbs, or fruits? How extensive an edible garden do you desire?

■ Do you desire, and have you time to care for, a large flower border? Do you want an area for growing flowers to cut for indoor use?

■ Do you entertain frequently outdoors? How large a group of people do you usually invite?

■ Are you a nature lover? Would you like to attract birds and wildlife to your garden?

■ Is there a beautiful view or vista that should be dramatized, or an unsightly one that should be camouflaged?

■ Do you need privacy from the street or neighboring property?

■ Do you need to have a place for outdoor storage?

■ Does the yard require landscaping to increase sunlight or to provide more shade?

Creating a Place in Which to Relax and Entertain

Landscaping experts feel that the relaxation area should stand alone functionally yet blend with the rest of the landscaping around the home. This can be achieved with proper layout, placement, paving, and planting. Patios, decks, terraces, and barbecuing areas are most convenient if located within easy access of the house, especially the kitchen, and on the same level. But if a better spot exists, such as one with a magnificent view, a sitting area should be located there also. Sliding glass doors leading out to a patio or a deck tie indoors and outdoors together, enhancing the view from both inside and outside the house, as well as making access easier.

Because the primary outdoor relaxation area will get heavy use, the floor should not be of lawn but of a construction material. It should be large enough to hold comfortably a table, lounge chairs, a barbecue, and the number of people you intend to entertain. If you plan large outdoor parties, provide a paved surface large enough so all your guests can stand and mingle comfortably. (The landscape on p. 122 provides ample room for large parties.) All too often, builders include only a tiny patio, one that has barely enough room to hold all family members, much less guests.

When siting a deck or a patio, you can work with what you have in the way of existing trees and topography as long as you don't change the soil level around existing tree roots, for to do so would kill them. Decks and patios can be set in the shade of existing trees, which visually anchors the landscape and makes for a comfortable spot to sit on hot afternoons. If a sitting area is situated in a wooded area away from the house, the pathway and steps leading to it can be made to twist and turn through the trees, creating a walk-in-the-woods feeling. You can place a brick patio under a large specimen tree—a circular pattern looks quite attractive—and add a circular bench around the tree's trunk. Similarly, decks can be built with a well and bench and even a table surrounding the trunk.

Outdoor living areas work well when they connect with the indoors, forming an extension of the house. When a patio or a deck can be reached from sliding doors or French doors that open off the dining room, living room, or kitchen, the out-

A pool for swimming, a patio for lounging, and a table and chairs for dining add to the livability of this backyard.

door space becomes an extension of that room, creating an easily flowing space for entertaining, especially enjoyable in mild climates. Attaching a latticework to the house and extending it over the deck or the patio not only creates shade but makes a visual connection between patio and house. Hanging baskets can be suspended from the latticework to create a living ceiling.

If the land slopes away from the house, an area below can be leveled and connected to the house by a series of wide steps and platforms. Another way to increase usable space in a sloped backyard is to cantilever a deck over the slope, which also creates a spot for enjoying the view below. It is also possible to fill in a sloped area and hold it in place with a retaining wall. The retaining wall should be made of the same material as the paving material to create unity.

Creating Recreation Areas

Though serving an important function, many recreational or intensive gardening areas aren't the most attractive to look at. Vegetable gardens may offer nothing more appealing than an expanse of bare soil for many months of the year; tennis courts offer an expanse of pavement. Landscaping can physically or visually separate these unattractive areas and turn them into a design asset. Situate them as far from the home as possible or out of sight of your primary sitting area. Where space is tight, living or constructed walls can provide separation, and proper landscape design can achieve the effect of distance and separation by creating a foil. A vegetable or cut-flower garden close to the house can be made more attractive by enclosing it within a low, decorative fence or by planting the perimeter with shrubs, as long as the walls aren't so tall as to shade the garden. Creating a decorative shrub border to wall off a tennis court turns function into beauty. Massing plants around the perimeter, while leaving some open areas in between, will create the feeling of enclosure without confinement. Massing and repetition also enhance the design.

If you provide a pathway leading around a wall or shrub border, you will give interest to the garden while playing up the element of surprise, even if the surprise turns out to be only a toolshed. Proper landscaping not only camouflages work or play areas, but can soften any noise they generate. A natural barrier such as a hedge muffles noise more than a fence.

In the case where young children need to be supervised, the play area should be located near the house. Or if it is located further away, a vista can be left open and the space enclosed on the other three sides, leaving ample space yet creating security and privacy.

Landscaping the Property Line and Side Yard

Shrubs or fences typically form walls along property lines, especially in the backyard, where they provide privacy and enclosure, as well as mark boundaries. In formal landscapes these walls might be straight-sided hedges, but such hedges require vigilant pruning several times a year to look their best and are planted less often these days. The landscapes in this book rely on planting masses of shrubs in naturalistic groupings along property lines. On large properties these can be backed up with tall-growing evergreen trees such as hemlocks and pines, which provide privacy from neighbors. Where security is important, fences and walls can enclose the property, but they will look best if they are softened with plantings of trees and shrubs.

The areas between the side of the house and the property line are often overlooked as places to be landscaped, but these areas can be made interesting and attractive. Think of a narrow side yard as you would a hall that leads from one room to another. Use the narrowness to your advantage by creating the feeling that it leads to something special beyond. Install a curving walkway leading into the backyard and, if space allows, place a large shrub at the end of the curve so the backyard cannot be seen. This creates a surprise view as you enter the yard, and it separates the areas.

Pave the walk with the same material used in the walk leading to the front entrance, which helps to create a feeling of unity and continuity. Line both sides of the pathway with colorful ground covers or plant low-growing shrubs along the house to keep the vista open and prevent the area from appearing cramped.

You can use these same techniques even if the area between the property line and the house is not narrow; a large space provides more room in which to be creative, and it may be used for storage or growing vegetables and flowers if it receives all-day sun. Serious gardeners often use side yards that are camouflaged from the street to hold a work area. A greenhouse, cold frame, lath house, or toolshed and potting bench can be located out of view in the narrow space beside the house. If any of these features are located away from the house, it will be easier to use them if water and electrical lines are installed nearby.

The cool lake-like depths of the swimming pool are created by "black" paint, which creates a naturalistic character in keeping with the home.

Swimming Pools

A swimming pool plays an important part in the landscape design, usually acting as the focal point of the landscape. Rectangular, T-, or L-shaped pools are most formal, while kidney or free-form shapes suit naturalistic or informal settings. Pools painted black, actually a dark blue, can resemble real ponds if naturalistically landscaped with native rocks, stones, and plants. Formal pools should be landscaped with pavement that matches the rest of the landscape, while informal ones can have plantings close to their edges.

Most zoning regulations require that swimming pools be fenced and may require that a fence exist between the house's exit and the pool. Select a style of fencing that blends with the rest of the landscape design, or choose vinyl-coated chain-link, which can be landscaped with shrubbery and vines to improve its appearance. Swimming pools can be situated several steps below the

house or the patio with proper excavation, thus allowing the eye to scale the hedge or fence without blocking the view of the pool.

Just as the selection and arrangement of furniture in a room, its color scheme, and the textures and patterns of the fabrics used create a special feeling in your home's interior, landscaping makes a statement about you and your home. A home may be landscaped—or furnished—creatively and successfully in many styles. The design should suit your home's architecture and your personality, while fulfilling your family's needs. Professionally designed landscapes, such as those presented here, enhance a home's beauty while adding to its value. Study the variety of designs for front yards and backyards in the next two chapters to see how you can achieve professional results without hiring a professional.

Chapter 2

Successful Front Yard Landscape Designs

Browse Through These Professional Landscape Designs to Select One Perfectly Suited for the Front of Your Home

Included in this chapter are a variety of professionally designed landscape plans for the fronts of forty houses, representing a variety of typical architectural styles. Study the individual designs, examining the plot plans and the accompanying illustrations to discover which designs will work with your home. The paintings show the landscape a few years after installation, when the new plantings have filled in and matured a bit, so nothing is left to your imagination!

Because few plants adapt to all regions of the country, a plant list is not included along with the plot plan in the book. Rather, a descriptive list of the types of plants used in the design and keyed to the plot plan accompanies each design. Use this key to select your favorite plants to carry out the design, or seek the advice of a nurseryman or landscape designer.

You can also order a complete, full-sized blueprint package for any of these designs, which includes a plant list especially selected to perform well in your area of the country. (See p. 174 for ordering information.) The painting for most landscapes shows the plants recommended for the Mid-Atlantic region. Similar-appearing plants are selected for other regions, where possible. Complete construction blueprints for each of the homes shown in the paintings are available from Home Planners. (See p. 178 for floor plans and p. 200 for ordering information.)

In this award-winning landscape design, a problem slope was transformed into an asset. The ground before the door was leveled and held in place with a picturesque retaining wall to create a broad landing that dramatizes the home's entrance.

Repetition of forms, curves, and paving unifies the landscape design for this traditional New England-style home.

Cape Cod Traditional

The quaint character of this traditional Cape Cod home calls for an intimate, comfortable landscape that reflects the formality of the house without being stiff or unfriendly. Notice how the repetition of curves throughout the landscape works to unite the design into a cohesive whole. The clean, curving line of the large shrub border, which sweeps directly from the foundation planting toward the street, is repeated in the smaller curves of the planting borders along the street and in the shapes of the lawn areas. The stone walk and the driveway feature flowing curves. The front walk attractively leads both to the driveway and to the street, where guests would probably park their cars.

Loose, informally shaped trees soften the lines of the house and complement the curves of the landscape. By positioning these trees at the front edge of the property and in the center of the walkway, the designer buffers the view of the house from the street, creating a sense of privacy while framing the home. Evergreen foundation shrubs used near the house match the traditional style of the architecture. Elsewhere, flowering shrubs provide seasonal color.

This landscape design works successfully because the gentle, repetitive lines and forms, which remain apparent even in the winter, unify the property, making it seem larger than it is.

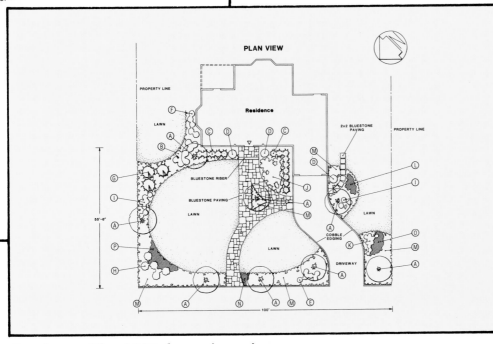

Landscape Plan L200 shown in spring
Designed by James Morgan

Home Plan 2657

Regionalized Plant Lists

Because climate and growing conditions vary greatly throughout North America, it is impossible to list here all the plants for this landscape plan that would do well everywhere on the continent. However, you can order a Blueprint Package with plant lists keyed to this plan and selected by expert horticulturists to thrive in your area.

The six-page Blueprint Package features a large-size version of this Plan View, plus a detailed regional Plant and Materials List. It also includes an illustrated list of hundreds of landscape plants suited to your region, in case you wish to make substitutions, as well as planting instructions and plant adaptation maps to ensure professional results with your new landscape.

See page 174 to order your regionalized Blueprint Package.

Corner properties pose special landscaping
challenges. Here the landscape designer screens
the street with a colorful shrub border.
A formal walkway leads from the main street,
where guests might park, to the front door. A
more informal walk provides access from the
driveway to both entrances.

Williamsburg Cape

This extended Cape poses several challenges to the designer. Situated on a corner lot, the house needs access to both streets, but the noise from cars stopping at the intersection needs to be muffled. The two doors located in the front of the house should be distinguished and the long lines of the house played down. The landscape design provides walks leading to both entries while clearly defining the dominant, main entrance with a formal brick entry court. Partially hidden by an upright shrub, the entrance to the breezeway remains out of view but is still easily accessible by family members. The semicircular planting bed in front of the walkway leading to the breezeway breaks up the long lines of the brick walk and lawn while balancing the large planting beds beside the house.

The landscape on either side of the front door features symmetrically placed trees and shrubs to reflect the formality of the brick entryway. Tall, uniformly oval trees complement the formal design while softening the long lines of the house.

Because the house is located on a corner, access to the street with a front walkway is desirable. For unity and harmony, the same brick used in the walkway across the front of the house is used in the front walk. An extensive shrub border screens the view of the house from the intersection and stifles traffic noise. A variety of shrubs and perennials make up this border, to provide interest throughout the year.

Regionalized Plant Lists

Because climate and growing conditions vary greatly throughout North America, it is impossible to list here all the plants for this landscape plan that would do well everywhere on the continent. However, you can order a Blueprint Package with plant lists keyed to this plan and selected by expert horticulturists to thrive in your area.

The six-page Blueprint Package features a large-size version of this Plan View, plus a detailed regional Plant and Materials List. It also includes an illustrated list of hundreds of landscape plants suited to your region, in case you wish to make substitutions, as well as planting instructions and plant adaptation maps to ensure professional results with your new landscape.

See page 174 to order your regionalized Blueprint Package.

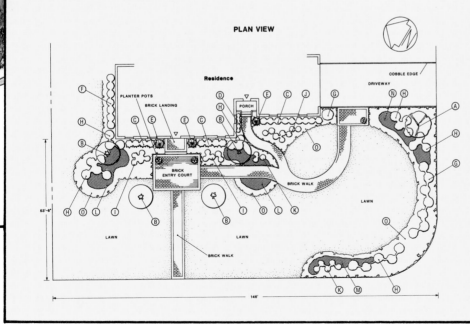

Landscape Plan L201 shown in autumn
Designed by Michael J. Opisso

Home Plan 2520

Highlighted by a pleasing front walk that incorporates several turns, a change in levels, and a charming white picket fence, the landscape design for this small property effectively transforms the house from ordinary to picture-perfect.

Cape Cod Cottage

Skillful landscaping transforms this ordinary, small Cape Cod house into a cozy, quaint cottage that has instant curb appeal. Relying on an exuberant mix of flowering shrubs and perennials, the design evokes the mood of a friendly country home whose bountiful gardens burst with colorful flowers.

Notice how the designer links the front walk to the driveway with a few pleasing turns and a change of levels rather than dissecting the small property with a front walk leading straight to the street. This layout adds visual interest to the small yard while making it seem broader. The white picket fence adds to the cottage-garden charm while giving the landscape some depth and a feeling of intimacy.

Massed together into several large planting beds, graceful trees, flowering shrubs, ground covers, and perennials border the house and entryway to create an ever-changing informal garden setting. Small boulders add a naturalistic character reminiscent of New England, and also provide a year-round structure to the beds. Planted along the base of the fence, perennials add color during the summer and soften the fence without hiding it. A deciduous shrub with strong spring color highlights the corner of the fenced garden, while evergreen flowering specimens brighten the corners of the house. To balance the weight of the entry bed and paving, the designer places a small tree and planting bed at the front corner of the driveway. These plants provide a colorful greeting as guests and family members approach the house.

Regionalized Plant Lists

Because climate and growing conditions vary greatly throughout North America, it is impossible to list here all the plants for this landscape plan that would do well everywhere on the continent. However, you can order a Blueprint Package with plant lists keyed to this plan and selected by expert horticulturists to thrive in your area.

The six-page Blueprint Package features a large-size version of this Plan View, plus a detailed regional Plant and Materials List. It also includes an illustrated list of hundreds of landscape plants suited to your region, in case you wish to make substitutions, as well as planting instructions and plant adaptation maps to ensure professional results with your new landscape.

See page 174 to order your regionalized Blueprint Package.

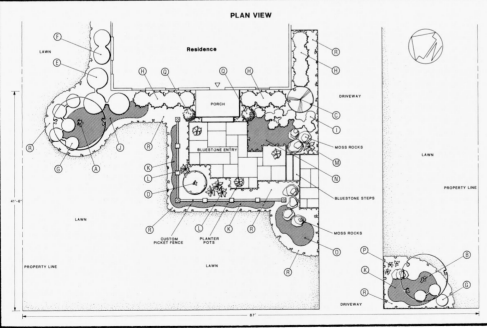

PLAN VIEW

Landscape Plan L202 shown in spring
Designed by Michael J. Opisso

Home Plan 2661

Gambrel-Roof Colonial

With two entries close to each other at the front of the house, it is imperative that the landscaping for this gambrel-roof Colonial define the formal or dominant entry—the one to which a visitor should go. While a similar problem with the Williamsburg Cape (see p. 42) was solved with a formal entry court and symmetrical planting, the design shown here accomplishes the same end by framing and blocking views.

Notice how small ornamental trees frame the large entry court that leads to the main door. The tree nearest the house blocks the view of the door leading to the family room while it also frames the walk and adds color and interest to the landscape. A low-growing evergreen hedge behind the tree aids in screening, so the visitor perceives only one walkway and one door. Access to the secondary door from the backyard, garage, or driveway is by a walkway at the back of this screen planting.

The weeping evergreen and summer-flowering shrubs bordering the outside of the front walkway direct the view up the walk and to the front door. This bed extends into a curving border of trees, shrubs, perennials, and ground covers, which is echoed on the other side of the property. These border plantings provide privacy from neighbors or a side street and—since one cannot see behind the house—further define the front garden.

Regionalized Plant Lists

Because climate and growing conditions vary greatly throughout North America, it is impossible to list here all the plants for this landscape plan that would do well everywhere on the continent. However, you can order a Blueprint Package with plant lists keyed to this plan and selected by expert horticulturists to thrive in your area.

The six-page Blueprint Package features a large-size version of this Plan View, plus a detailed regional Plant and Materials List. It also includes an illustrated list of hundreds of landscape plants suited to your region, in case you wish to make substitutions, as well as planting instructions and plant adaptation maps to ensure professional results with your new landscape.

See page 174 to order your regionalized Blueprint Package.

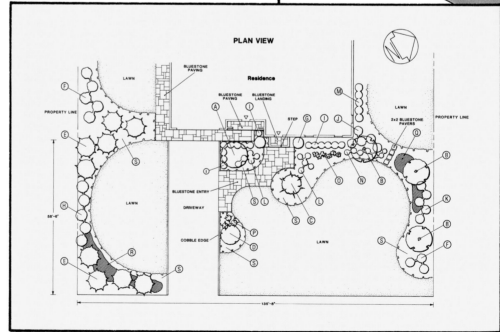

Landscape Plan L203 shown in spring
Designed by Michael J. Opisso

Home Plan 2131

The skillful placement of ornamental trees and shrubs in this landscape design frames the walk and front door, leading the eye and visitors past the secondary entrance and directly to the main entrance.

Center-Hall Colonial

Devoid of shutters and other ornamentation, this handsome center-hall Colonial could look austere without the right kind of landscaping. The design presented here uses soft-textured shade trees and a deep bed of shrubs accented with perennials and ground covers to alleviate any sense of starkness posed by this huge, formal home.

The straight driveway and front walk were designed to be functional as well as to match the clean lines of the home's architecture. To create interest and contrast with these straight lines, the brick entry court is circular. The brick inlay at the front of the driveway matches the brick paving on the walkway, defining the entrance to the driveway while unifying the design. Strong, curved planting beds and lawn shapes further relieve the symmetry and formality of house and walkway. Notice how the curving line of the lawn carries through to the foundation planting in front of the garage to complete the sweeping line. By mounding the soil in the front bed into a berm and planting a small ornamental tree on the berm, the designer adds height, interest, and a third dimension to the flat facade of the house. The lawn trees also soften the flatness of the house and partially block the view from the street, providing privacy and scale.

Regionalized Plant Lists

Because climate and growing conditions vary greatly throughout North America, it is impossible to list here all the plants for this landscape plan that would do well everywhere on the continent. However, you can order a Blueprint Package with plant lists keyed to this plan and selected by expert horticulturists to thrive in your area.

The six-page Blueprint Package features a large-size version of this Plan View, plus a detailed regional Plant and Materials List. It also includes an illustrated list of hundreds of landscape plants suited to your region, in case you wish to make substitutions, as well as planting instructions and plant adaptation maps to ensure professional results with your new landscape.

See page 174 to order your regionalized Blueprint Package.

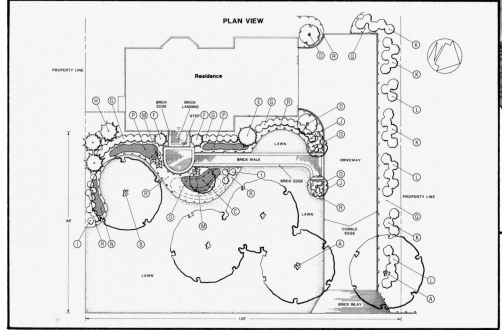

Landscape Plan L204 shown in summer
Designed by Damon Scott

Home Plan 2610

The landscape designer transforms this large, formal, straight-lined house into a warm, welcoming home with the artistic use of soft-textured trees and shrubs combined with colorful perennials in gracefully curving beds. The resulting landscape brings the house to life.

The uncomplicated sweeping lines of this front
yard reflect the tidy, neatly groomed appearance one expects to find in Colonial New England, while at the same time softening the
flatness and "salt-box" look of the house.

Classic New England Colonial

The success of this landscape design relies on using simple, clean lines and forms to balance the squareness and flat facade of this classic New England home. The foundation planting curves around and extends beyond the house, making it appear longer. The outlines of the shrub borders on both sides of the property transcribe a huge circle, enclosing a circular lawn area that perfectly balances the mass of the house. The curved walkway leading from the driveway provides a graceful entrance to the house, while the brick inlay at the front of the driveway announces the transition from public street to private residence.

Large trees situated in both the lawn and the planting borders integrate the two areas, soften the facade of the house, and provide privacy and cooling summer shade. Flowering deciduous and evergreen shrubs are used along both property lines for spring color. Rather than using an underplanting of ground covers to unify the planting beds, the designer chooses to dress up the beds with an organic mulch of wood chips, in keeping with a tidy, neatly groomed New England look.

Fencing on each side of the house separates the front yard from the backyard and helps to elongate the lines of the house. It is partly camouflaged by three small trees, which help to block the view beyond the front of the house and balance the visual weight of the garage.

Regionalized Plant Lists

Because climate and growing conditions vary greatly throughout North America, it is impossible to list here all the plants for this landscape plan that would do well everywhere on the continent. However, you can order a Blueprint Package with plant lists keyed to this plan and selected by expert horticulturists to thrive in your area.

The six-page Blueprint Package features a large-size version of this Plan View, plus a detailed regional Plant and Materials List. It also includes an illustrated list of hundreds of landscape plants suited to your region, in case you wish to make substitutions, as well as planting instructions and plant adaptation maps to ensure professional results with your new landscape.

See page 174 to order your regionalized Blueprint Package.

PLAN VIEW

Residence

Landscape Plan L205 shown in spring
Designed by Damon Scott

Home Plan 2731

Southern Colonial

The grand size of a traditional Southern Colonial home demands an equally grand landscape whose scale and style balance the house's imposing size and massive columns. The designer uses six tall shade trees to shelter the house and create a parklike setting for the home. The terrace at the front of the house creates a formal entry court that reflects the stateliness of the architecture, while planter pots positioned at each side of the courtyard provide a human scale to an otherwise large-scale house and landscape.

The large trees and planting bed at the entrance to the driveway buffer the view of the drive and the house and create a feeling of anticipation as one enters the property. The driveway splits, leading back to the side-entry garage and also swinging conveniently around front to deliver guests in style to the main entrance and a conveniently located parking bay. The canopy of trees at the entrance to the secondary driveway and the repeated semicircular lawn areas announce that this is the entry. Three decorative trees with colored foliage underplanted with low-growing shrubs screen cars parked in the parking bay from the street, while giving the entire entry area a sense of privacy and enclosure. For the convenience of family members, a brick walk, screened from view by a hedge, leads from the garage to the secondary entrance.

Regionalized Plant Lists

Because climate and growing conditions vary greatly throughout North America, it is impossible to list here all the plants for this landscape plan that would do well everywhere on the continent. However, you can order a Blueprint Package with plant lists keyed to this plan and selected by expert horticulturists to thrive in your area.

The six-page Blueprint Package features a large-size version of this Plan View, plus a detailed regional Plant and Materials List. It also includes an illustrated list of hundreds of landscape plants suited to your region, in case you wish to make substitutions, as well as planting instructions and plant adaptation maps to ensure professional results with your new landscape.

See page 174 to order your regionalized Blueprint Package.

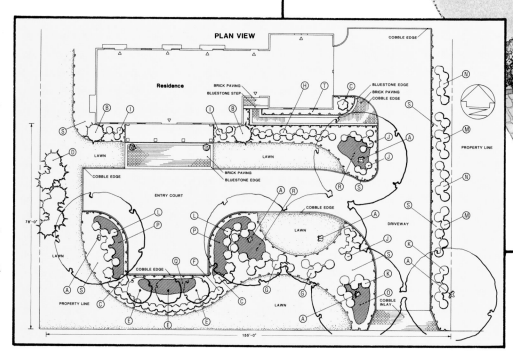

Landscape Plan L206 shown in summer
Designed by Damon Scott

Home Plan 2140

52

A massive house, such as this one, demands an equally impressive landscape to anchor it to its surroundings. The parklike setting and formal entry court created for this Southern Colonial balance the scale of the architecture in grand style.

Graceful trees, curving lines, and bursts of flowers blooming from spring through fall complement this comfortable country retreat. The friendly landscaping creates the perfect finishing touch that says here's a place to hang up a hammock and relax.

Country-Style Farmhouse

Set in a friendly and homey landscape brimming with flowers from spring through fall, this farmhouse's country atmosphere is now complete. Masses of perennials and bulbs used throughout the property create a garden setting and provide armloads of flowers that can be cut for indoor bouquets. But the floral beauty doesn't stop there; the designer artfully incorporates unusual specimens of summer- and fall-blooming trees and shrubs into the landscape design to elevate the changing floral scene to eye-level and above.

To match the informal mood of the house, both front walkway and driveway cut a curved, somewhat meandering path. A parking spur at the end of the driveway provides extra parking space and a place to turn around. Fieldstones, whose rustic character complements the country setting, pave the front walk. The stone piers and picket fence at the entrance to the driveway frame the entry and match the detail and character of the house's stone foundation and porch railing. The stone wall at the side of the property further carries out this theme.

Large specimen trees planted in the lawn set the house back from the road and provide a show of autumn color. One can imagine completing the country theme in this tranquil setting by hanging a child's swing from the tree nearest the front porch.

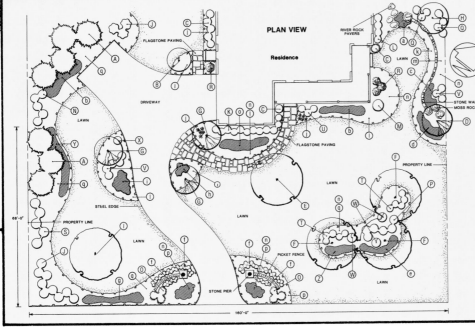

Landscape Plan L207 shown in summer
Designed by David Poplawski

Home Plan 2774

Regionalized Plant Lists

Because climate and growing conditions vary greatly throughout North America, it is impossible to list here all the plants for this landscape plan that would do well everywhere on the continent. However, you can order a Blueprint Package with plant lists keyed to this plan and selected by expert horticulturists to thrive in your area.

The six-page Blueprint Package features a large-size version of this Plan View, plus a detailed regional Plant and Materials List. It also includes an illustrated list of hundreds of landscape plants suited to your region, in case you wish to make substitutions, as well as planting instructions and plant adaptation maps to ensure professional results with your new landscape.

See page 174 to order your regionalized Blueprint Package.

In this landscape design, the country charm of the stone farmhouse is emphasized by creating an ample courtyard surrounded by a stone wall. The clean and simple lines of the wall and row of trees provide a sense of vitality and substance. Changing floral and foliage color throughout the seasons contrasts warmly with the gray stones.

Pennsylvania Stone Farmhouse

This Pennsylvania stone farmhouse evokes the strength and character of the large farming families that have for many years been the backbone of our country. In keeping with this theme, the landscape design is strong and clean, softening the rugged character of the house without competing with it.

The L-shape of the house lends itself perfectly to the creation of a courtyard, which provides for generous parking as well as a feeling of intimate enclosure. This space can double as a place for children to play games. By repeating the stone from the house in the courtyard wall, the designer gives strength and permanence to the landscape while reducing the massive scale of the house to a more human, friendly size. The visitor is immediately drawn to the front door and welcomed by a small purple-foliaged tree, which contrasts nicely with the subdued stone. While the tree serves as a focal point, it also unifies the courtyard and the home's entrance.

The repetition of formal trees planted on the inside of the wall and at the entrance to the driveway dresses up the landscape with bright spring flowers and fall foliage without making the scene busy or overpowering. The designer chooses to underplant the trees only with ground cover and perennials to keep the design simple and neat. In summer, the perennials provide color and a touch of country charm.

Regionalized Plant Lists

Because climate and growing conditions vary greatly throughout North America, it is impossible to list here all the plants for this landscape plan that would do well everywhere on the continent. However, you can order a Blueprint Package with plant lists keyed to this plan and selected by expert horticulturists to thrive in your area.

The six-page Blueprint Package features a large-size version of this Plan View, plus a detailed regional Plant and Materials List. It also includes an illustrated list of hundreds of landscape plants suited to your region, in case you wish to make substitutions, as well as planting instructions and plant adaptation maps to ensure professional results with your new landscape.

See page 174 to order your regionalized Blueprint Package.

PLAN VIEW

Residence

STONE WALL
STONE PIER
STONE PIER
STONE WALL
BLUESTONE PAVERS
COBBLE EDGE
ENTRY COURTYARD
BLUESTONE TERRACE
BLUESTONE LANDING
BLUESTONE STEP
LAWN
LAWN
STONE PIER
STONE WALL
DRIVEWAY
LAWN
LAWN
STONE PIER
STONE WALL
BLUESTONE PAVERS
LAWN

54'-0"
150'-0"

Landscape Plan L208 shown in spring
Designed by Michael J. Opisso

Home Plan 2542

In this plan, the landscape designer recreates the feeling of an earlier, simpler time that brings to mind cookies and milk on the porch and the sound of children's laughter. This bucolic setting is achieved by the simple lines of the traditional front walk, an overhead canopy of stately trees, and an open arrangement of flowering shrubs and perennials.

Raised-Porch Farmhouse

The style of this house with its raised and covered front porch is reminiscent of a time when streets were wide and children played beneath the shade of large, stately trees whose branches overhung the street. The symmetrical period design of this farmhouse calls for a straightforward, traditional landscape design. To reflect that period, the design for this corner lot uses a perimeter planting of large trees whose canopies frame the view of the house from overhead, providing a sense of tranquility.

A traditional front walk leads from the street to the steps and the front porch; the straightness of the walk is in keeping with the symmetry of the house and the clean lines of the landscape design. Low-growing, spreading shrubs frame the entrance to the front walkway along with fragrant, summer-flowering perennials, which offer a pleasing aroma to greet visitors.

The foundation planting features low-growing, flowering shrubs and perennials so that the handsome stone piers and latticework along the porch foundation remain visible. Taller spring- and summer-flowering shrubs provide easy-care beauty in the borders along the driveway and at the property line. To contrast with the tall trees around the perimeter of the property, small, informal trees soften the corners of the house near the side doors. At the other corner, a large tree balances the design. The entire landscape is unified with the same ground cover used throughout.

Regionalized Plant Lists

Because climate and growing conditions vary greatly throughout North America, it is impossible to list here all the plants for this landscape plan that would do well everywhere on the continent. However, you can order a Blueprint Package with plant lists keyed to this plan and selected by expert horticulturists to thrive in your area.

The six-page Blueprint Package features a large-size version of this Plan View, plus a detailed regional Plant and Materials List. It also includes an illustrated list of hundreds of landscape plants suited to your region, in case you wish to make substitutions, as well as planting instructions and plant adaptation maps to ensure professional results with your new landscape.

See page 174 to order your regionalized Blueprint Package.

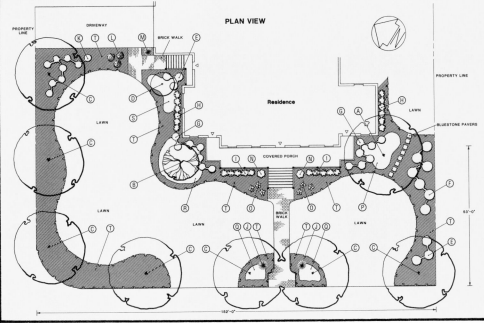

PLAN VIEW

Landscape Plan L209 shown in fall
Designed by Michael J. Opisso

Home Plan 2694

New England Barn-Style House

A charming flower court complete with fish pond is the highlight of this landscape design. Visible through two sets of sliding glass doors—one set leading from the dining room and the other from the playroom—the courtyard garden can be enjoyed even when the weather isn't fine enough to venture outdoors. When days are balmy, however, the courtyard makes a cozy spot in which to sit outside and relax in the afternoon sun. A board fence encloses the garden space and matches the architecture of the barn-style house. Planters set out on the terrace can be filled with colorful annuals and changed to match the seasons.

Because the courtyard is at the front of the house, it is screened from the driveway and front walk by a small flowering tree and shrubbery. Two additional flowering trees of the same type are located across the entry walkway from the first tree, casually marking the way to the front door. To match the informality of the house, the stone walkway is laid out in an irregular pattern, which allows a soft interplay with the ground-cover plants.

Four shade trees underplanted with shade-loving shrubs and ground cover frame the house near the street. Three of these trees are grouped in a free-standing bed whose gracefully curving outline invites one's eye to follow the lawn around to the side of the house. There one would expect to discover another pretty garden scene.

Regionalized Plant Lists

Because climate and growing conditions vary greatly throughout North America, it is impossible to list here all the plants for this landscape plan that would do well everywhere on the continent. However, you can order a Blueprint Package with plant lists keyed to this plan and selected by expert horticulturists to thrive in your area.

The six-page Blueprint Package features a large-size version of this Plan View, plus a detailed regional Plant and Materials List. It also includes an illustrated list of hundreds of landscape plants suited to your region, in case you wish to make substitutions, as well as planting instructions and plant adaptation maps to ensure professional results with your new landscape.

See page 174 to order your regionalized Blueprint Package.

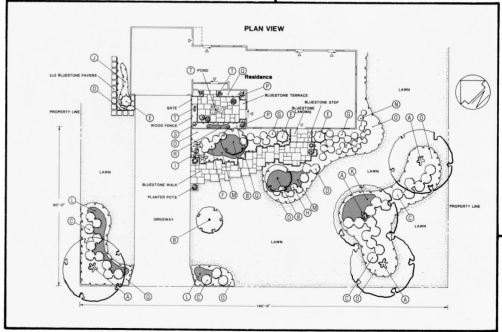

Landscape Plan L210 shown in spring
Designed by Damon Scott

Home Plan 2224

60

Curved planting beds, randomly laid paving stones, and skillfully placed trees and shrubs create an informal private setting for this barn-style home. Note the ornamental pond included in the courtyard garden.

Here the landscape designer offers an attractive way to provide ample parking space in front of the house by creating an entry court with inlaid cobblestones. The courtyard effect is reinforced by a border of ornamental trees, which can be enjoyed from a private garden encircled by a picket fence.

New England Country House

The layout of this L-shaped home presents several landscaping challenges. The landscape design must provide cars with easy access to the two-car garage and enough turnaround space so they needn't back out of the driveway. The home's three front entrances need to be distinguished one from another, and plantings should counter the elongated look of the house.

Though the driveway is large and comes close to the house, the inlaid cobblestones transform what could otherwise resemble a parking lot into an entry court that escorts visitors to the main entrance. A curving line of ornamental trees bordering the driveway leads the eye directly to the door, blocks headlights from glaring into the windows, screens the view into the front rooms, and camouflages the private entrance that leads from the master suite to the covered porch and private garden. A low picket fence keeps this lovely garden even more private. Though, of necessity, the driveway is up close to the house, the view from inside looking out is of beautiful flowering trees rather than asphalt.

A wide landing of bluestone paving further highlights the main entrance. Once on the landing visitors notice that the paving also leads to the service entrance beside the garage, which was hidden from direct view by a latticework trellis. Covered with a flowering vine, the lattice complements the home's country feeling.

Regionalized Plant Lists

Because climate and growing conditions vary greatly throughout North America, it is impossible to list here all the plants for this landscape plan that would do well everywhere on the continent. However, you can order a Blueprint Package with plant lists keyed to this plan and selected by expert horticulturists to thrive in your area.

The six-page Blueprint Package features a large-size version of this Plan View, plus a detailed regional Plant and Materials List. It also includes an illustrated list of hundreds of landscape plants suited to your region, in case you wish to make substitutions, as well as planting instructions and plant adaptation maps to ensure professional results with your new landscape.

See page 174 to order your regionalized Blueprint Package.

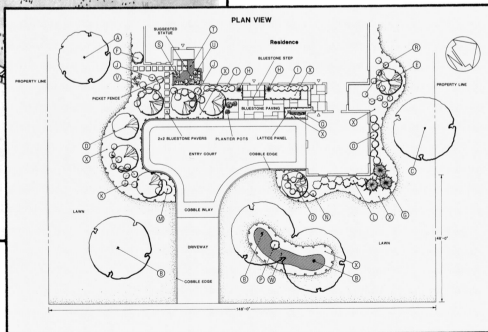

Landscape Plan L211 shown in spring
Designed by Michael J. Opisso

Home Plan 2615

Traditional Country Estate

The problem facing the landscape designer of this one-story home is to create intimacy and friendliness where a three-car garage near the front entrance necessitates a lot of pavement. The designer turns what could have been a barren driveway into a functional and attractive space by using trees and the sides of the L-shaped house as the walls of an airy entrance court. Cobble inlay marks the main garage and entrance to the home, and at the same time provides an interesting change in texture. The second garage is blocked from immediate view from both sides by a peninsular bed, which clearly separates it from the primary garage.

Enclosing a more intimate courtyard, a low picket fence and bluestone walk define the front door while bringing an informal, homey feeling to the setting. Small grassed areas within this doorstep garden, and in the semicircular area along the rest of the house, provide a green carpet that carries the perimeter lawn into the interior court. The small tree before the window of the master bedroom creates a pretty, ever-changing view through the window and blocks headlights from shining inside.

Graceful trees, masses of cheerful flowering perennials, and the flowing lines of the circular planting beds work together to create a friendly setting for this country home. It's simply pretty as a picture!

Regionalized Plant Lists

Because climate and growing conditions vary greatly throughout North America, it is impossible to list here all the plants for this landscape plan that would do well everywhere on the continent. However, you can order a Blueprint Package with plant lists keyed to this plan and selected by expert horticulturists to thrive in your area.

The six-page Blueprint Package features a large-size version of this Plan View, plus a detailed regional Plant and Materials List. It also includes an illustrated list of hundreds of landscape plants suited to your region, in case you wish to make substitutions, as well as planting instructions and plant adaptation maps to ensure professional results with your new landscape.

See page 174 to order your regionalized Blueprint Package.

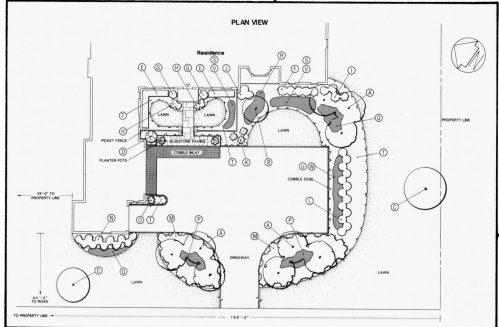

Landscape Plan L212 shown in spring
Designed by David Poplawski

Home Plan 2921

Skillful designing makes the most of this L-shaped house. A canopy of trees draws visitors inside the courtyard, and the doorstep garden outlined by a picket fence and carpeted in green provides a friendly greeting on an intimate scale.

French Provincial Estate

The formal and somewhat ornate appearance of the French Provincial style of architecture calls for an equally formal landscape design—one that can anchor the house and its traditional walled courtyard to its surroundings. The landscape solution presented here relies on large, symmetrically placed elements to answer the style and scale of the home. The front entrance features symmetrically placed evergreens and planter pots, which set off the home's architecture without detracting from it. Two large shade trees with uniform oval canopies frame the driveway and the line of sight straight to the front door. Around the inside of the courtyard wall stand oval-shaped flowering trees, which reflect the strength and scale of the house. The tree canopies enclose the courtyard above the wall, further secluding the home from the outside world.

The brick walls, which could look stark and forbidding if not properly landscaped, are softened here with a border of loosely formed flowering shrubs on the inside, creating a pretty scene within the walls. Groups of shrubs and ornamental trees carefully positioned in a bed of ground cover along the wall's exterior present a stunning picture to passersby. Swathes of flowering perennials and pots of summer annuals on the landing provide a long season of color and give the home the flavor of the French countryside, where flowers abound throughout the year.

Regionalized Plant Lists

Because climate and growing conditions vary greatly throughout North America, it is impossible to list here all the plants for this landscape plan that would do well everywhere on the continent. However, you can order a Blueprint Package with plant lists keyed to this plan and selected by expert horticulturists to thrive in your area.

The six-page Blueprint Package features a large-size version of this Plan View, plus a detailed regional Plant and Materials List. It also includes an illustrated list of hundreds of landscape plants suited to your region, in case you wish to make substitutions, as well as planting instructions and plant adaptation maps to ensure professional results with your new landscape.

See page 174 to order your regionalized Blueprint Package.

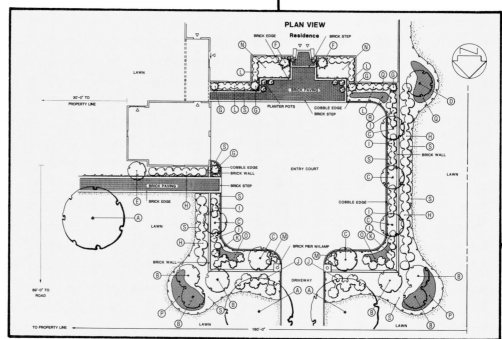

Landscape L213 shown in autumn
Designed by Damon Scott

Home Plan 1993

66

Reminiscent of a French chateau in the Loire Valley, this home achieves a warm, friendly atmosphere by means of adept landscaping. Tall shade and flowering trees provide privacy and a feeling of enclosure, while colorful shrubs, bulbs, annuals, and perennials create a changing color show.

Georgian Manor

The British have influenced more than one style of architecture, including this Georgian-style manor house. While many of these styles tend to be informal, the Georgian style appears formal and stately. Here the designer creates a beautifully symmetrical landscape that offers a dramatic parklike setting, perfectly suited to the country manor house of an English lord and lady.

Because of the vast size of the house and property, a circular driveway swings in front of the main entrance for easy access. The entry court, clearly defined by the brick inlay that matches the facade of the house, allows room to park several cars. This parking court is hidden from the street by a berm and an evergreen hedge; the hedge actually serves as a low privacy wall but appears more friendly than a brick wall would in the same position. Brick piers are placed on each end of the hedge and at each side of both driveway entrances to emphasize the symmetry of the design.

Majestic shade trees placed along the street and entry court create a transition from the public space to the home's private space. The large size of the trees also helps to scale down the size of the house, helping it to seem at home in its setting. Closer to the house, flowering trees in front of the large windows soften the facade and block the view into the house while providing those inside with a lovely sight in spring.

Regionalized Plant Lists

Because climate and growing conditions vary greatly throughout North America, it is impossible to list here all the plants for this landscape plan that would do well everywhere on the continent. However, you can order a Blueprint Package with plant lists keyed to this plan and selected by expert horticulturists to thrive in your area.

The six-page Blueprint Package features a large-size version of this Plan View, plus a detailed regional Plant and Materials List. It also includes an illustrated list of hundreds of landscape plants suited to your region, in case you wish to make substitutions, as well as planting instructions and plant adaptation maps to ensure professional results with your new landscape.

See page 174 to order your regionalized Blueprint Package.

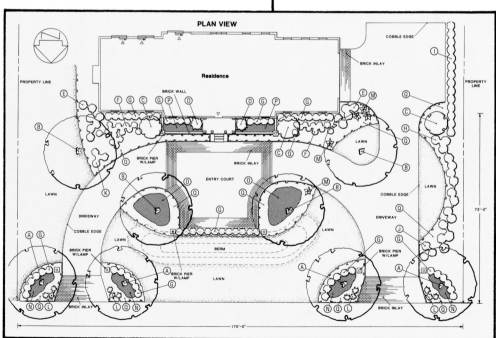

Landscape Plan L214 shown in spring
Designed by Damon Scott

Home Plan 2683

The symmetrical layout of this landscape design perfectly matches the character of the grand Georgian house. Overhanging trees create a quiet, private setting, while the circular drive-way and grassy berm hide the entry court from immediate view, revealing the full impact at the final moment.

Large evergreens and tall trees balance the scale of this grand-portico Georgian home. The plantings also provide screening from the street, enhancing the view of the house from the driveway and blocking the garage from immediate view.

Grand-Portico Georgian

The major challenge in designing the landscape for a large house with straight, rather symmetrical lines is to bring the scale and style of the architecture into the landscape while retaining a sense of human scale in the design. The four formally shaped flowering trees in front of the house achieve this goal, while defining the dominant area of the house and echoing the four columns supporting the portico. Colorful perennials and planters brimming with annuals achieve the second objective.

Because the garage is set at the side of the house, a circular driveway is designed to lead visitors directly to the front entrance in style. Brick inlay marks the space at the front door where cars should stop. Three large evergreens at the corner of the house block the view of the rear parking area and the garage, and they contrast in color and texture with the perennials planted under them. The secondary door can be reached by a walkway, which has a jog in it for added interest. Because of the skillful placement of trees, foundation plants, and paving, it is obvious to any visitor which door is the main entry.

An island bed in the lawn bordering the circular driveway contains large evergreens and a shade tree of grand proportions to provide needed privacy. Other evergreens along the street buffer the view of the house from the street and the driveway. The size of the island planting is balanced with the rest of the landscape by the bed on the left of the house, which sweeps around until it disappears out of sight.

Regionalized Plant Lists

Because climate and growing conditions vary greatly throughout North America, it is impossible to list here all the plants for this landscape plan that would do well everywhere on the continent. However, you can order a Blueprint Package with plant lists keyed to this plan and selected by expert horticulturists to thrive in your area.

The six-page Blueprint Package features a large-size version of this Plan View, plus a detailed regional Plant and Materials List. It also includes an illustrated list of hundreds of landscape plants suited to your region, in case you wish to make substitutions, as well as planting instructions and plant adaptation maps to ensure professional results with your new landscape.

See page 174 to order your regionalized Blueprint Package.

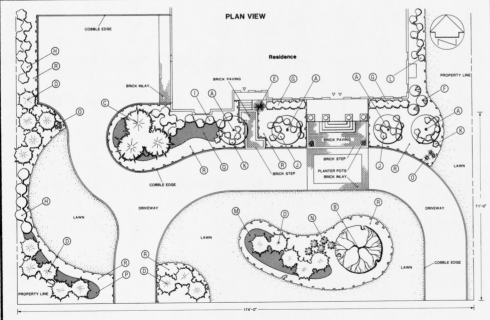

Landscape Plan L215 shown in summer
Designed by Michael J. Opisso

Home Plan 2889

Brick Federal

The architecture of the brick Federal house might remind you of a trip to Colonial Williamsburg, and so too does the formality and grandeur of the landscape design. The key to the success of this design, and its beauty, is its simplicity and symmetry, reflecting the symmetrical and repetitive lines of the house. If you fold the plan in half, it is, with the exception of the driveway, identical on both sides.

The symmetry is carried out in two ways. One is by mirror-imaging from left to right—note the placement of the large shade trees on either side of the house, the repetition of the foundation plants and the border plants, and the symmetrical paved area in front of the entry, flanked by two circular lawn areas. In the second way, the lines of symmetry go from the front of the land-scape to the back—note the repetition of the same trees on either side of the 2-foot-high wall, the use of brick in the wall to match the brick of the home, and the repetition of stone piers on each end of the wall. These, in turn, exactly line up with the stone piers at both sides of the entry, creating a feeling of a courtyard in the circular driveway.

The plants used in this design provide a graceful setting that gives the home a sense of permanence. Here and there, flowers, berries, and fall foliage provide spots of seasonal color, but the overall feeling is one of quiet, cool greenery. The elegance of this design matches the elegance of the house, reflecting well upon the good taste of the owners.

Regionalized Plant Lists

Because climate and growing conditions vary greatly throughout North America, it is impossible to list here all the plants for this landscape plan that would do well everywhere on the continent. However, you can order a Blueprint Package with plant lists keyed to this plan and selected by expert horticulturists to thrive in your area.

The six-page Blueprint Package features a large-size version of this Plan View, plus a detailed regional Plant and Materials List. It also includes an illustrated list of hundreds of landscape plants suited to your region, in case you wish to make substitutions, as well as planting instructions and plant adaptation maps to ensure professional results with your new landscape.

See page 174 to order your regionalized Blueprint Package.

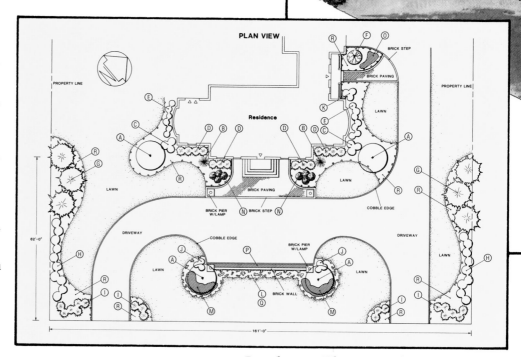

Landscape Plan L216 shown in spring
Designed by David Poplawski

Home Plan 2662

72

The success and beauty of this landscape design come from the clean lines and symmetry of the plantings, which reflect the formality of the brick Federal home both from left to right and from front to back.

The walled courtyard garden featured in this design creates a formal entrance in keeping with the elegant architecture. Sweeping lines used in the planting beds and driveway carry the eye past the house on either end, complementing the low lines of the house.

Country French Rambler

This country French home has elegant horizontal lines and a symmetrical facade that the designer accentuates with the long lines of the drive, lawn, and walkway. The elongated, narrow lawn panel in front of the house continues past the corner tree, giving the impression of a long, sweeping vista.

A circular driveway is not used in this plan, yet to make provision for adequate parking near the front door, a parking spur was added. An exquisite weeping tree accents the horizontal sight line from the parking spur and directs the eye toward the front door. This elegant tree is also the first thing one sees upon leaving the front door. Large evergreens screen the garage and rear parking areas as well as provide landscape interest, color, and texture. These are balanced at the other side of the house by a tall flowering tree, which is a surprise addition to the otherwise symmetrical planting scheme.

A small inner courtyard at the front door greets visitors and creates a transition from semi-public to private space. Defined by a low brick wall, the courtyard features symmetrically placed shrubs and a pair of ornamental trees, in keeping with the sophisticated ambience of the house.

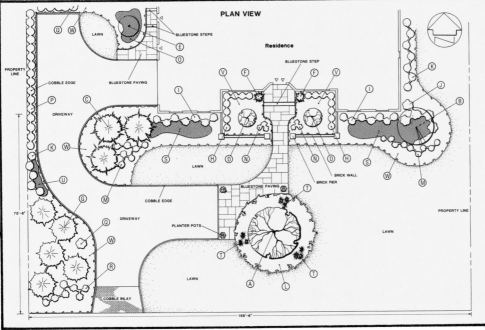

Landscape Plan L217 shown in summer
Designed by Michael J. Opisso

Home Plan 2779

Regionalized Plant Lists

Because climate and growing conditions vary greatly throughout North America, it is impossible to list here all the plants for this landscape plan that would do well everywhere on the continent. However, you can order a Blueprint Package with plant lists keyed to this plan and selected by expert horticulturists to thrive in your area.

The six-page Blueprint Package features a large-size version of this Plan View, plus a detailed regional Plant and Materials List. It also includes an illustrated list of hundreds of landscape plants suited to your region, in case you wish to make substitutions, as well as planting instructions and plant adaptation maps to ensure professional results with your new landscape.

See page 174 to order your regionalized Blueprint Package.

French Manor House

Designed with grand proportions and style, the front entrance to this French manor house demands landscaping that is equally substantial without being pretentious. Here, the designer creates a beautiful formal garden that sets the scene for this home, emphasizing the formality of the architecture and balancing the scale of the house. Four flowering trees mark and define the corners of the courtyard, which is enclosed by a traditional, neatly trimmed evergreen hedge. Surrounding the courtyard's paving, a summer-flowering ground cover creates a pattern of color and texture that contrasts pleasingly with the dark green hedge and red bricks. A sculpture, used as the focal point in the center of the garden, intersects the sight lines from both walks—the walk leading from the driveway and the walk leading from the front door.

Though a circular driveway could work well with this house, the designer chooses instead to devote the space to the lovely entrance garden; a parking spur brings visitors right up to the garden and directs them to the main entrance. The secondary entrance, recessed from the main part of the house, is made easily accessible by a brick walk, but is deemphasized by the prominence of the courtyard.

The formality of the house and garden extends to the driveway entrance, which is framed with two brick piers, flanked by spring-flowering trees, shrubs, and perennials. Tall shrubs and evergreens provide privacy along the property border, enhancing the aura of a substantial property worthy of any manor house.

Regionalized Plant Lists

Because climate and growing conditions vary greatly throughout North America, it is impossible to list here all the plants for this landscape plan that would do well everywhere on the continent. However, you can order a Blueprint Package with plant lists keyed to this plan and selected by expert horticulturists to thrive in your area.

The six-page Blueprint Package features a large-size version of this Plan View, plus a detailed regional Plant and Materials List. It also includes an illustrated list of hundreds of landscape plants suited to your region, in case you wish to make substitutions, as well as planting instructions and plant adaptation maps to ensure professional results with your new landscape.

See page 174 to order your regionalized Blueprint Package.

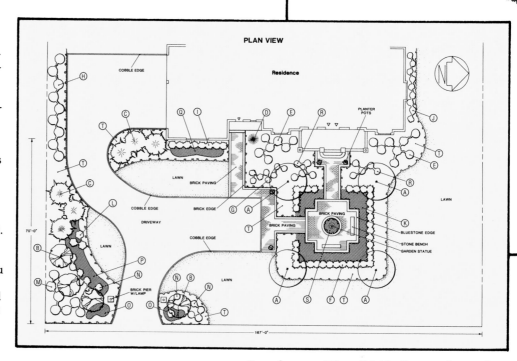

Landscape Plan L218 shown in spring
Designed by Michael J. Opisso

Home Plan 2543

To reflect the grandeur of this manor house, the landscape designer uses a sheared hedge to create a formal sculpture garden at the main entrance. Note how the changing brick patterns in the walks and courtyard direct visitors toward the entrance.

Elizabethan Tudor

The romance of the English countryside comes alive in this setting created for an Elizabethan Tudor home. The designer chooses rough stones for walls and walkway, reminiscent of the historical English landscape where stones and cobbles pave many roads and walks. The 16-inch-high retaining wall creates an outdoor vestibule where flowering shrubs, perennials, and a ground cover chosen for its dramatic color and texture delight the eye. The wall is circular to unify the many different angles and lines of the house and parallels the curved planting line of the trees surrounding the home. Repetition of curves throughout the design helps the entire landscape to flow easily to both sides.

The five formally shaped trees around the perimeter loosely define the boundaries of the design while separating the home from the road. Four clumped trees provide contrasting shape and texture. The designer places an ornamental flowering tree before the large window at the front of the house, which belongs to the guest bedroom, to provide privacy from the front walk. When in bloom, this showy tree becomes a focal point and creates a stunning view through the nearby window.

Designed for a corner lot, this plan provides access to the garage from the side street. Visitors parking in front are greeted by a walk with a broad entrance. To adapt this plan for a lot without a corner, swing the driveway toward the front and link the walk to it with a sweeping curve. Adapt the trees and shrubs to border the driveway.

Regionalized Plant Lists

Because climate and growing conditions vary greatly throughout North America, it is impossible to list here all the plants for this landscape plan that would do well everywhere on the continent. However, you can order a Blueprint Package with plant lists keyed to this plan and selected by expert horticulturists to thrive in your area.

The six-page Blueprint Package features a large-size version of this Plan View, plus a detailed regional Plant and Materials List. It also includes an illustrated list of hundreds of landscape plants suited to your region, in case you wish to make substitutions, as well as planting instructions and plant adaptation maps to ensure professional results with your new landscape.

See page 174 to order your regionalized Blueprint Package.

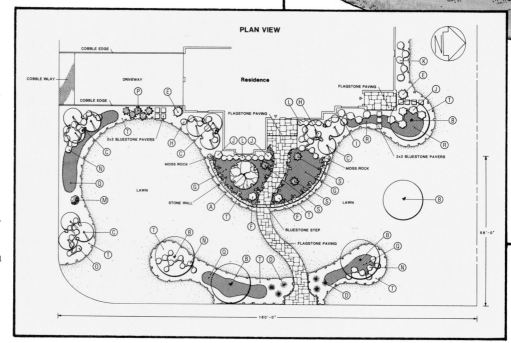

Landscape Plan L219 shown in spring
Designed by Michael J. Opisso

Home Plan 2356

The repetition of curves in this design successfully counteracts the angles of the architecture, while helping the landscape to flow easily from one side to another. Beautiful trees, shrubs, perennials, and ground covers provide an everchanging show of soft colors and textures throughout the year.

Although the circular driveway separates the lawn and planting borders into three distinct zones, these areas are visually linked because they sweep across the property in continuous lines. This visual trick unites the landscape, making the property appear much larger.

Tudor One-Story

The design for this charming Tudor-style home employs a repetitive theme of curved shapes throughout the landscape. Beginning with the circular driveway, the theme can be seen in the rounded outlines of the lawn areas before and on each side of the driveway, and in the curved edges of the front walk and bordering beds. These lines sweep across the design, playing up the horizontal lines of the one-story house.

The front walk, which branches toward the garage, is bordered by low-growing shrubs and flowering perennials and made even more intimate by decorative trees. This area offers a special welcome because it is intensely planted with plants that provide color throughout the year. The highlight of this garden is the ornamental tree, which is visible from the breakfast nook. It ties together the irregularly patterned paving leading to both segments of the driveway and camouflages the blank garage wall.

Drifts of flowering perennials located throughout the landscape provide friendly bursts of color during summer and well into fall. Fall too brings a stunning display of autumn foliage.

If for some reason a circular driveway would be undesirable, this plan is easily adapted without compromising any of the design elements. The circular part of the driveway can be eliminated and turned into a parking spur that ends in front of the entrance. The circular border to the left of the property can be merged into the front border to complete the curve, and lawn can fill in the rest of the area to create a picture-perfect design.

Regionalized Plant Lists

Because climate and growing conditions vary greatly throughout North America, it is impossible to list here all the plants for this landscape plan that would do well everywhere on the continent. However, you can order a Blueprint Package with plant lists keyed to this plan and selected by expert horticulturists to thrive in your area.

The six-page Blueprint Package features a large-size version of this Plan View, plus a detailed regional Plant and Materials List. It also includes an illustrated list of hundreds of landscape plants suited to your region, in case you wish to make substitutions, as well as planting instructions and plant adaptation maps to ensure professional results with your new landscape.

See page 174 to order your regionalized Blueprint Package.

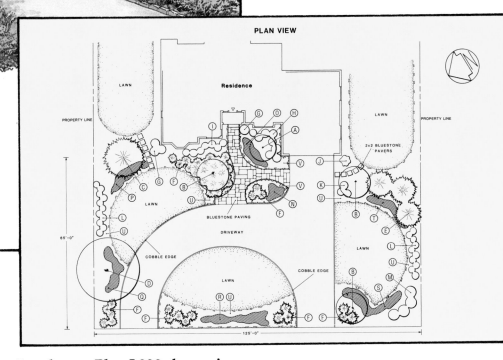

Landscape Plan L220 shown in summer
Designed by David Poplawski

Home Plan 2802

English-Style Cottage

Follow the examples set by the designer of this English-style cottage landscape, and you will learn several tricks about how to make a small property appear larger. Space is limited, but a small entry court was created at the end of the driveway; the paving that extends across the front of the house and the garage harmonizes with the house and unites the entire area. The bench and planter pots overflowing with flowers lend an informal atmosphere and extend the living space into the garden. The lawn sweeps around the side of the house, with curved lines defined by planting beds filled with masses of flowering shrubs and perennials. Pavers leading through the planting bed welcome visitors into the yard to enjoy the flowers. Although more pavers provide access to the backyard, the two areas are clearly separated, leaving the impression of greater space and creating curiosity about what lies beyond.

Narrow, upright evergreens placed at the corner of the garage balance and interplay with its low roof line and its strong horizontal lines. These are echoed and balanced by an evergreen screen on the right side of the property. Tall shade trees, chosen for their pleasing shape and seasonal color, form a garden ceiling. The trees towering over the one-story house give a woodsy feeling to the scene, enhancing its cottage charm and matching the rustic character of the home's natural wood siding.

Regionalized Plant Lists

Because climate and growing conditions vary greatly throughout North America, it is impossible to list here all the plants for this landscape plan that would do well everywhere on the continent. However, you can order a Blueprint Package with plant lists keyed to this plan and selected by expert horticulturists to thrive in your area.

The six-page Blueprint Package features a large-size version of this Plan View, plus a detailed regional Plant and Materials List. It also includes an illustrated list of hundreds of landscape plants suited to your region, in case you wish to make substitutions, as well as planting instructions and plant adaptation maps to ensure professional results with your new landscape.

See page 174 to order your regionalized Blueprint Package.

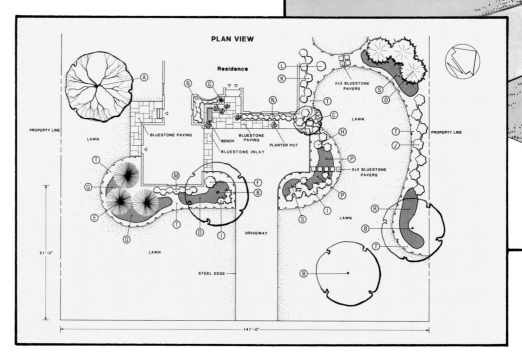

Landscape Plan L221 shown in summer
Designed by Michael J. Opisso

Home Plan 2606

The tall trees shading this property contrast with the size of the cottage, emphasizing its cozy appearance. A well-defined entry court, decorated with cheerful planters and a bench, further enhances the friendly atmosphere created by the landscape design.

Medieval Garrison

If ever a house took you back to your childhood and fairy-tale dreams of castles, knights, and ladies-in-distress, this one will. The landscape design, like the storybook character of the house, is both dramatic and whimsical. Drama is found in the long, curving walkway leading to the front door, which is accentuated by a low hedge that defines the area and complements the flow of foot traffic. Further drama comes with the repetition of circular beds at the corner of the house and before the driveway spur. The weeping tree, set just off-center in the corner bed, provides further whimsy because of its marvelous shape and gnarled branches. A path of pavers, which defines the circular center planting bed, continues around to the secondary door and branches toward the garage. Set within a bed of ground cover, this walk is clearly distinct from the main entrance.

Planting beds in front of the house are embellished with color from spring bulbs and summer perennials. The long, uninteresting roof line and the blank wall of the garage wing are decorated with four flowering trees, which soften the lines of the architecture. These trees could perhaps provide an escape route for a young maiden in distress being rescued from one of the high windows by her Prince Charming, who might carry her down the tree to flee along the driveway to a world of excitement beyond.

Regionalized Plant Lists

Because climate and growing conditions vary greatly throughout North America, it is impossible to list here all the plants for this landscape plan that would do well everywhere on the continent. However, you can order a Blueprint Package with plant lists keyed to this plan and selected by expert horticulturists to thrive in your area.

The six-page Blueprint Package features a large-size version of this Plan View, plus a detailed regional Plant and Materials List. It also includes an illustrated list of hundreds of landscape plants suited to your region, in case you wish to make substitutions, as well as planting instructions and plant adaptation maps to ensure professional results with your new landscape.

See page 174 to order your regionalized Blueprint Package.

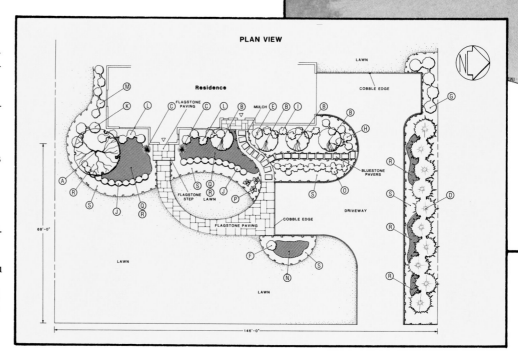

Landscape Plan L222 shown in spring
Designed by Michael J. Opisso

Home Plan 2191

Here is a neat, orderly, and simple landscape design that perfectly complements the unadorned facade and sharp angles of the house. Notice how rounded and weeping tree shapes, along with curved walks and planting beds, soften the architecture.

Queen Anne Victorian

This Victorian house ought to be the home of a large family where children delight in playing hide-and-seek and exploring its many nooks and crannies. The very large, all-wood house is of monumental scale and makes a significant presence on the property. In keeping with that, the designer presents a landscape plan that complements the uniqueness of the architecture and balances its weight and scale.

A circular driveway solves the problem of the garage being set so far to the back of the house and allows easy access to the front door. The driveway brings the visitor to a wooden platform that links the house to the drive and extends the wrap-around porch into the landscaping.

The smooth, flowing lines of the landscape extending around the house and to the street are clean and pleasing to the eye, while not competitive with the many angles of the house. Low-growing plants are chosen for the front of the house, in order not to hide the home's interesting architectural features. A large tree at the front right corner anchors the house and is repeated in three other areas to frame the view and balance the massive scale.

The uniqueness of the architecture demands that drama be carried through to the landscaping, which is accomplished with the pond and fountain on the outside of the driveway. Berms were added around the pond to enhance its setting. The weeping tree beside the pond also emphasizes the unique nature of the house and adds special interest.

Regionalized Plant Lists

Because climate and growing conditions vary greatly throughout North America, it is impossible to list here all the plants for this landscape plan that would do well everywhere on the continent. However, you can order a Blueprint Package with plant lists keyed to this plan and selected by expert horticulturists to thrive in your area.

The six-page Blueprint Package features a large-size version of this Plan View, plus a detailed regional Plant and Materials List. It also includes an illustrated list of hundreds of landscape plants suited to your region, in case you wish to make substitutions, as well as planting instructions and plant adaptation maps to ensure professional results with your new landscape.

See page 174 to order your regionalized Blueprint Package.

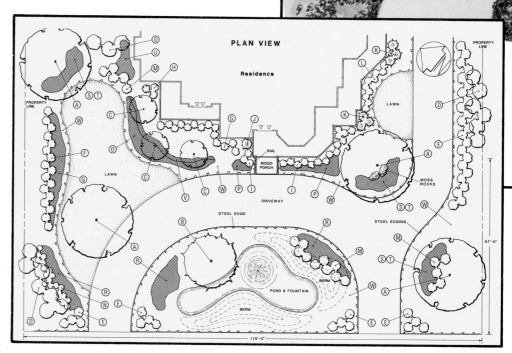

Landscape Plan L223 shown in spring
Designed by Damon Scott

Home Plan 2953

The massive size and drama of this Victorian house demand an equally dramatic landscape to balance it. This is achieved by framing the house with majestic trees and creating a dramatic approach. The entrance features a circular driveway leading in front of a garden pond and fountain nestled into a contoured mound of earth.

A vintage house, such as this one, looks best when landscaped in a simple style that doesn't compete with the architecture. This interesting design solution presents large venerable trees, a picket fence, and old-fashioned shrubs and perennials to recreate the romantic look of an actual turn-of-the-century home.

Gothic Victorian

This turn-of-the-century-style house demands a romantic-looking landscape to set it off to perfection. Decorative fencing, old-fashioned plants, and stately shade trees do just that. To get the most out of relaxing on the porch and enjoying the view of the lawn, only low-growing perennials and ground covers are planted in front. When summer breezes stir, the fragrance of the flowers planted among the ground cover perfumes the porch.

The driveway provides easy access to the garage and the extra parking area, while bringing guests directly to the front door. A weeping tree—a favorite Victorian specimen—obscures the service entrance in front from the main walk and drive, although it is easily accessible for deliveries by a narrow walk. Leading through the pretty planting bed in front of the garage, stone pavers allow family members to walk directly from the drive to the side door.

The semicircular garden bed in front of the circular driveway repeats the curves of the drive, walk, and porch. The designer intentionally leaves out lawn in this area in order to create a tapestry of colorful flowers and foliage from small shrubs, perennials, and ground cover. By using decorative fencing in this bed, and repeating it on both sides of the driveway, the designer skillfully carries the detail from the house's woodwork to the garden. For privacy, a screen of evergreen trees and tall flowering shrubs border the length of the driveway. The three large trees shading the house evoke the feeling of Main Street, U.S.A., just what you might expect if this house were an original Victorian.

Regionalized Plant Lists

Because climate and growing conditions vary greatly throughout North America, it is impossible to list here all the plants for this landscape plan that would do well everywhere on the continent. However, you can order a Blueprint Package with plant lists keyed to this plan and selected by expert horticulturists to thrive in your area.

The six-page Blueprint Package features a large-size version of this Plan View, plus a detailed regional Plant and Materials List. It also includes an illustrated list of hundreds of landscape plants suited to your region, in case you wish to make substitutions, as well as planting instructions and plant adaptation maps to ensure professional results with your new landscape.

See page 174 to order your regionalized Blueprint Package.

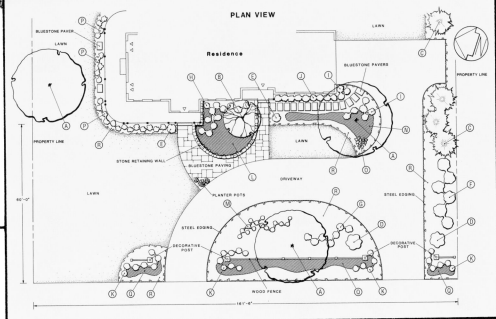

Landscape Plan L224 shown in summer
Designed by Michael J. Opisso

Home Plan 2645

Basic yet special, the landscaping for this ranch house fits it perfectly, creating a homey setting and making the property appear larger than it is because of the open design. Finished with a fence that echoes the clapboard siding, this house will stand out among similar homes in the neighborhood.

Basic Ranch

The basic ranch house with its clean, simple lines makes a perfect starter house, retirement retreat, or home for a small family. Its small size dictates an understated landscape design. In answer, the designer creates an attractive yet straightforward plan that sets it apart from similar ones in the neighborhood.

Access to the front door is easy and appealing by way of the curved brick paving—a more attractive choice than a straight walkway. The semicircular foundation planting creates a homey setting while extending the architecture forward, making the house appear larger than it is. Within this bed, a small flowering tree softens the corner while adding seasonal color. Because space is limited, an espalier grows flat against the wall near the entrance, providing sculptural interest and color while taking up minimal space.

Although the plan is asymmetrical, the informal repetition of forms on each side of the driveway balances the design. The brick walk leading to the front door is echoed by the walk leading to the back of the house. On each side of the driveway entrance, a decorative fence, whose horizontal boards respond to the horizontal siding on the house, ties the two sides of the design together. Along the property line, an elongated oval of lawn bordered by shrubs and flowering perennials creates an attractive alternative to the strip of lawn so commonly seen in side yards. This bed is picked up on the other side of the driveway and continued along the street, visually unifying the entire landscape.

Regionalized Plant Lists

Because climate and growing conditions vary greatly throughout North America, it is impossible to list here all the plants for this landscape plan that would do well everywhere on the continent. However, you can order a Blueprint Package with plant lists keyed to this plan and selected by expert horticulturists to thrive in your area.

The six-page Blueprint Package features a large-size version of this Plan View, plus a detailed regional Plant and Materials List. It also includes an illustrated list of hundreds of landscape plants suited to your region, in case you wish to make substitutions, as well as planting instructions and plant adaptation maps to ensure professional results with your new landscape.

See page 174 to order your regionalized Blueprint Package.

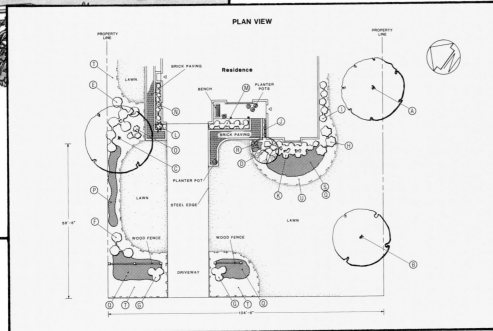

Landscape Plan L225 shown in spring
Designed by Michael J. Opisso

Home Plan 1920

The board fencing, repeated at three levels in
this landscape design, adds depth to the property while unifying the design. The fence sets off
the climbing roses, defines the entry courtyard—which accentuates an otherwise lost
front door—and unifies the plan by wrapping
around to the back of the property beside the
garage.

L-Shaped Ranch

This L-shaped ranch house has simple, clean lines and a small scale, leading the landscape designer to create a plan that, while not overdone, has charming interest. A small courtyard nestled into the L and defined by a board fence leads visitors to the front door, which is set back quite far. The courtyard presents a pleasant, more inviting entrance than would have been accomplished with a walkway, and creates a feeling of enclosure that extends the house. The courtyard is set off with a small ornamental tree whose foliage and branch outline adds color and sculptural interest all year.

The fence not only defines the courtyard, but also mirrors the horizontal lines of the house. A low hedge along the inside complements the fence, and a planting of fragrant perennials on the outside further heightens the invitation to step inside. The fence is repeated at the side of the house and along the front of the property, for unity, balance, and definition. Climbing roses adorn the fences in front, providing an excellent alternative to an extensive planting bed. The use of roses further adds a homey, welcoming feeling to the landscape.

The lawn tree to the right of the driveway, in addition to being a beautiful specimen, balances the weight of the courtyard planting and is itself balanced by the tree on the left. Together, they frame an inviting view of this simple ranch-style home.

Regionalized Plant Lists

Because climate and growing conditions vary greatly throughout North America, it is impossible to list here all the plants for this landscape plan that would do well everywhere on the continent. However, you can order a Blueprint Package with plant lists keyed to this plan and selected by expert horticulturists to thrive in your area.

The six-page Blueprint Package features a large-size version of this Plan View, plus a detailed regional Plant and Materials List. It also includes an illustrated list of hundreds of landscape plants suited to your region, in case you wish to make substitutions, as well as planting instructions and plant adaptation maps to ensure professional results with your new landscape.

See page 174 to order your regionalized Blueprint Package.

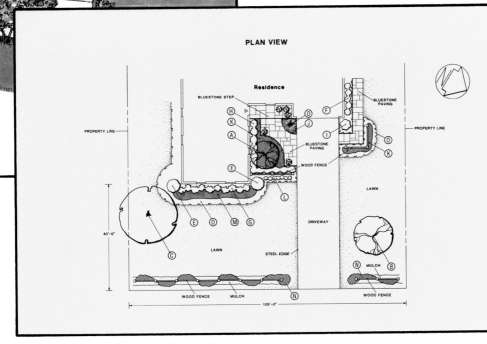

Landscape Plan L226 shown in summer
Designed by Michael J. Opisso

Home Plan 1343

Sprawling Ranch

To prevent this large sprawling ranch house from appearing intimidating and foreboding, the designer creates an informal courtyard in front. The courtyard fits naturally into the V-shape of the two house wings, repeating their form and scaling them down in size. Benches add to the feeling of welcome, creating a comfortable place to rest. The three small flowering trees on the right corner of the house, while acting as accents, also sustain the feeling of intimacy as they enclose the view from the courtyard, blocking the line of sight beyond the corner. Formally shaped trees enhance the courtyard with their neat oval shape and white flowers, while helping to define the court.

Upon entering the driveway, visitors clearly see the front entrance and are immediately oriented to their destination. Because it is a long walk from the garage to the front door, a parking spur is included to make access easier. The courtyard's stone paving, chosen to complement the stone facade on the house, borders the driveway spur.

Although the house is symmetrical and the landscaping is not, this design is clearly balanced. The mass of the large driveway and parking spur is balanced with the sweeping lawn and greater number of trees on the right side of the property. Large drifts of perennials planted along each wing add to the sense of balance while offering colorful accents. Located near the street, two shade trees complete the balancing scheme and also frame the entire front garden.

Regionalized Plant Lists

Because climate and growing conditions vary greatly throughout North America, it is impossible to list here all the plants for this landscape plan that would do well everywhere on the continent. However, you can order a Blueprint Package with plant lists keyed to this plan and selected by expert horticulturists to thrive in your area.

The six-page Blueprint Package features a large-size version of this Plan View, plus a detailed regional Plant and Materials List. It also includes an illustrated list of hundreds of landscape plants suited to your region, in case you wish to make substitutions, as well as planting instructions and plant adaptation maps to ensure professional results with your new landscape.

See page 174 to order your regionalized Blueprint Package.

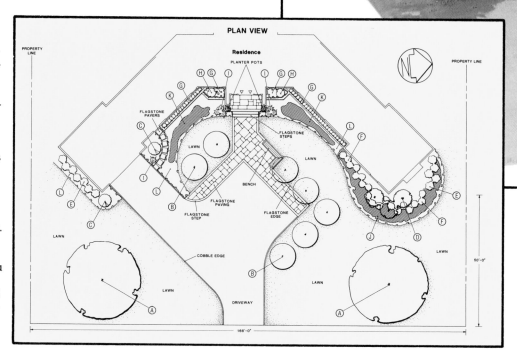

Landscape Plan L227 shown in spring
Designed by Damon Scott

House Plan 2534

The long symmetrical lines of this home could appear institutional if they were not softened and broken up by the oval canopies of trees lining the entryway. Providing eye-catching color with spring flowers and brilliant fall foliage, these lovely trees frame the main entrance and screen the front rooms from the driveway and walk.

Traditional Split-Level

The first step the landscape designer of this traditional split-level takes is to make the rolling grade of the property an asset rather than a liability. The designer creates a strong sense of entry with brick paving that is angled from the driveway to the front door. These angles do more than add interest to the squareness of the house—they also present a pleasing sequence of entry, transition, and arrival. This sequence is not only more visually appealing than a flat walkway coupled with a set of steps leading directly to the door, but also makes maneuvering from the driveway to the front door easier. The brick-and-timber combination for the walks and retaining walls offers a pleasing, informal quality that echoes the brick on the house.

Creating an entrance with various levels also allows the designer to extend one of the steps into a retaining wall, which defines a key planting area. The small, ornamental tree in this bed acts as a focal point and enhances the entry by providing privacy and enclosure. The sweeping bed lines, together with the three large shade trees, serve to unify the changes in height of both the house and the landscape.

Regionalized Plant Lists

Because climate and growing conditions vary greatly throughout North America, it is impossible to list here all the plants for this landscape plan that would do well everywhere on the continent. However, you can order a Blueprint Package with plant lists keyed to this plan and selected by expert horticulturists to thrive in your area.

The six-page Blueprint Package features a large-size version of this Plan View, plus a detailed regional Plant and Materials List. It also includes an illustrated list of hundreds of landscape plants suited to your region, in case you wish to make substitutions, as well as planting instructions and plant adaptation maps to ensure professional results with your new landscape.

See page 174 to order your regionalized Blueprint Package.

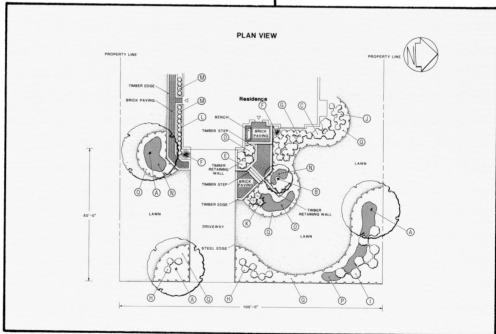

Landscape Plan L228 shown in spring
Designed by Michael J. Opisso

Home Plan 1981

A unique landscaping treatment can transform an ordinary split-level home into a showplace that stands out from its neighbor in a housing development. Here, a multilevel entrance deemphasizes the prominent garage, and a beautiful combination of plants creates a year-round gardenlike setting around the walkway.

The modern, angled architecture of this home is reflected in the angled brick paving, while the graceful weeping trees and the repetitive curves and circles of the planting scheme create a visual rhythm in the landscape.

Shed-Roof Contemporary

The landscape of this shed-roof contemporary leads visitors to the entry, which is set back quite far and hard to see at first. The outline of the pavement is a key factor in accomplishing this goal. The bricks not only attract the eye, they are laid out in such a way as to direct visitors to the left automatically, thus dictating which direction to follow to the entrance. The angles used in the brick paving respond to the contemporary architecture of the house and the bold roof line, and are mirrored and balanced by the brick inlay at the entrance to the driveway.

The large weeping evergreen planted at the corner of the garage further directs the view to the entrance by encouraging people to walk around it, heightening their sense of anticipation. The tree creates a focal point throughout the year because of its attractive shape. And its uniqueness gives the house an identity, which, along with the architecture, will not be forgotten.

The graceful trees framing the driveway are repeated and balanced on the left of the house by a grouping of the same trees. These trees soften the bold design, balance the projection of the garage, and answer the scale of the two-story height of the house.

This excellent landscape design, combining soft plant shapes with strong pavement angles, transforms this contemporary home into a dramatic showplace.

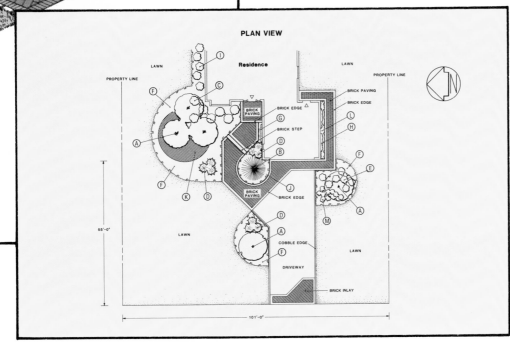

Landscape Plan L229 shown in autumn
Designed by Michael J. Opisso

Home Plan 2711

Regionalized Plant Lists

Because climate and growing conditions vary greatly throughout North America, it is impossible to list here all the plants for this landscape plan that would do well everywhere on the continent. However, you can order a Blueprint Package with plant lists keyed to this plan and selected by expert horticulturists to thrive in your area.

The six-page Blueprint Package features a large-size version of this Plan View, plus a detailed regional Plant and Materials List. It also includes an illustrated list of hundreds of landscape plants suited to your region, in case you wish to make substitutions, as well as planting instructions and plant adaptation maps to ensure professional results with your new landscape.

See page 174 to order your regionalized Blueprint Package.

In this landscape, the designer created an unusual angled landing and walkway leading to the front door to add visual excitement to the straight lines of the architecture. Combined with the sweeping curves of the planting beds and the soft textures of the evergreens, this treatment provides a most pleasing setting.

Wood-Sided Contemporary

A combination of sharp angles and circular and sweeping lines creates a dramatic setting for this wood-sided contemporary. The angled landing before the main entry looks more interesting than would a more typical squared-off walkway and entry. Angled as it is, the wooden landing becomes an extension of the modern architecture, projecting the house into the landscape.

In contrast to the angled paving and entry deck, sweeping curved lines are used in the planting beds across the front of the house. The designer maintains a flowing feeling while preventing the sprawling house from seeming longer than it is. Lawn areas placed on both sides of the walkway complete and unify this circular line, which is further strengthened by the circular planting bed that flows into the paving and integrates the softscape and hardscape features of the design.

Rather than employing a circular drive to bring visitors to the front of the house, a parking court is used instead to leave more room for plantings in the front of the house. To hide the asphalt leading to the garage, three large evergreens are placed at the corner of the house. These are repeated at the opposite corner for balance and they strengthen the front of the house by adding a vertical element to contrast with the horizontal lines of the architecture. More evergreens border the driveway to provide privacy and a windbreak. Soft in texture, these evergreens, together with the circular lines of the design, contrast nicely with the straight lines of the house and the angles of the landing and paving.

Regionalized Plant Lists

Because climate and growing conditions vary greatly throughout North America, it is impossible to list here all the plants for this landscape plan that would do well everywhere on the continent. However, you can order a Blueprint Package with plant lists keyed to this plan and selected by expert horticulturists to thrive in your area.

The six-page Blueprint Package features a large-size version of this Plan View, plus a detailed regional Plant and Materials List. It also includes an illustrated list of hundreds of landscape plants suited to your region, in case you wish to make substitutions, as well as planting instructions and plant adaptation maps to ensure professional results with your new landscape.

See page 174 to order your regionalized Blueprint Package.

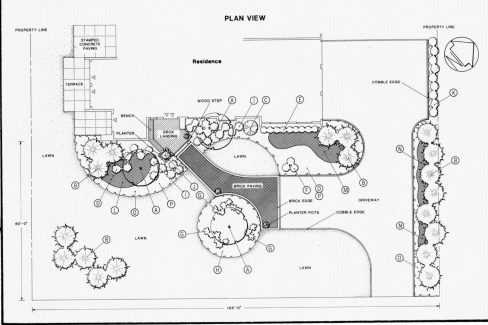

PLAN VIEW

Landscape Plan L230 shown in spring
Designed by Michael J. Opisso

Home Plan 2781

Hillside Contemporary

The layout of this house, which is designed to sit atop a steep hillside, presents a unique challenge to the landscape designer. Because the front door is immediately adjacent to the driveway, both entrances share the same space, and yet a feeling of separate use is needed. The solution is to create an attractive entry plaza that can function as both a front patio and a driveway. The entry plaza with its decorative brick inlay is built on concrete to take the weight of cars. The patterned brick design breaks up the large area and beautifies the expanse of pavement, while the inlay set in the perimeter of the parking court ties the driveway to the entry plaza and draws visitors toward the house.

A viewing garden borders the entry plaza. Enclosed by a free-standing, semicircular stone wall, which reflects the stone used in the house, the garden features brightly colored low-maintenance ground covers. Ringing the outside of the wall, six trees add vertical form that contrasts with the horizontal line of the wall.

To the right of the house, more stone walls act as retainers to the slope and lead the eye toward the side yard. Here a large curved lawn and privacy border balance the weight of the house and entrance court. The designer places the two stone piers asymmetrically, in answer to the contemporary design of the house, and to lead the eye from the driveway entrance into the plaza. With this creative landscape solution, the large windows and front door now look out onto a beautiful garden and plaza, rather than the more typical boring driveway.

Regionalized Plant Lists

Because climate and growing conditions vary greatly throughout North America, it is impossible to list here all the plants for this landscape plan that would do well everywhere on the continent. However, you can order a Blueprint Package with plant lists keyed to this plan and selected by expert horticulturists to thrive in your area.

The six-page Blueprint Package features a large-size version of this Plan View, plus a detailed regional Plant and Materials List. It also includes an illustrated list of hundreds of landscape plants suited to your region, in case you wish to make substitutions, as well as planting instructions and plant adaptation maps to ensure professional results with your new landscape.

See page 174 to order your regionalized Blueprint Package.

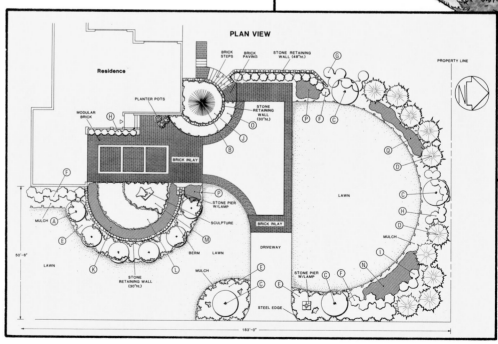

Landscape Plan L231 shown in autumn
Designed by David Poplawski

Home Plan 4334

What could have been a liability—a large space shared by the driveway and the entrance to the front door—has been turned into an asset. Here inlaid brick is employed to create an entry plaza that can double as a parking space and recreational area. The sculpture garden bordering the plaza can also be enjoyed from the upper floor of the residence as well as from the entrance.

Florida Rambler

Picture this house by the side of a Tampa canal, with the breezes blowing through the palm trees and the sound of a motorboat putting by. Because this house was planned for an area where outdoor living is the norm most of the year, it was designed with an informal, easy-to-live-in appearance—and the landscape design matches this style.

Because of the house's L shape, a cozy patio for sitting can be nestled into the front of the house to take advantage of the sun. This area is paved with stamped concrete, which is extended along the front of the house. The walkway unifies the design and provides access to the carport in the rear. A specimen tree planted in front of the patio acts as a buffer between the house and the street, adding beauty and fragrance while shading the patio.

Because the carport is set so far to the rear of the house, the designer creates a parking area in front of the house for guests and to make access to the front door easier for deliveries. To prevent this expansive driveway from heating up in the summer sun, graceful weeping trees line the side of the property, casting shade on the driveway throughout the day. Using gravel rather than concrete or blacktop for paving keeps the area cooler.

The home's architecture includes built-in planter boxes beneath the windows across the front of the house. To extend these planters into the landscape and effectively link the house and the garden, trailing plants cascade over the sides of the planters, and beds of low shrubs in the foreground further soften the walls.

Regionalized Plant Lists

Because climate and growing conditions vary greatly throughout North America, it is impossible to list here all the plants for this landscape plan that would do well everywhere on the continent. However, you can order a Blueprint Package with plant lists keyed to this plan and selected by expert horticulturists to thrive in your area.

The six-page Blueprint Package features a large-size version of this Plan View, plus a detailed regional Plant and Materials List. It also includes an illustrated list of hundreds of landscape plants suited to your region, in case you wish to make substitutions, as well as planting instructions and plant adaptation maps to ensure professional results with your new landscape.

See page 174 to order your regionalized Blueprint Package.

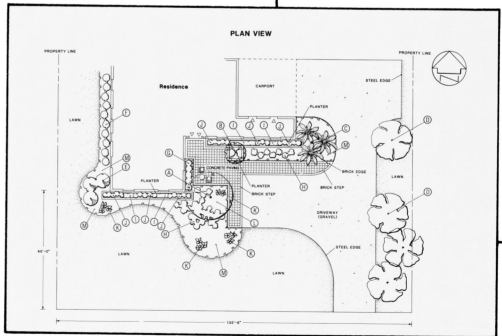

Landscape Plan L232 shown in spring
Designed by Michael J. Opisso

Home Plan 2268

This landscape, designed to accommodate the leisurely life of Florida, incorporates a small patio near the front entrance, where one can enjoy the sunshine as well as welcome guests. This informal entrance creates a warm, friendly first impression.

The Mediterranean influence reflected in this house, with its arches and balcony, is faithfully carried through in the landscape design. Featuring tall flowering trees for shade, an entry plaza, and a private courtyard, this home might be located on the sunny Spanish coast.

California Stucco

This house, with its traditional Spanish architecture, brings to mind the early California missionaries and the great influence they exerted on the region's culture—still evident today. The home's style is definitely Mediterranean, complete with arches, balcony, and a rear courtyard—perfect for a California hacienda. The landscape created for this stunning home matches the unique style of the house.

In keeping with the southern European style, a plaza is chosen for the front of the house instead of an asphalt driveway and separate walkway to the front entry. In effect, the driveway becomes part of the plaza. The attractive stamped and tinted concrete paving is carried through from one part of the plaza to the other, and the entire plaza is surrounded by brick inlay for unity and to heighten the Mediterranean effect. The brick inlay is repeated in the walkways leading to the street and to the courtyard in back.

The plaza is strengthened and anchored by a large tree situated in the center. The tree also shades the benches on the plaza and the covered porch. Terra-cotta planters placed on the plaza reflect the Mediterranean theme, and provide a splash of color when brimful of friendly flowers. Formally shaped trees outline the plaza the way trees lined the Appian Way in ancient Rome. By enclosing the plaza, these flowering trees provide privacy and create a more intimate feeling, while filling the plaza with white flowers in spring and russet foliage in fall.

Regionalized Plant Lists

Because climate and growing conditions vary greatly throughout North America, it is impossible to list here all the plants for this landscape plan that would do well everywhere on the continent. However, you can order a Blueprint Package with plant lists keyed to this plan and selected by expert horticulturists to thrive in your area.

The six-page Blueprint Package features a large-size version of this Plan View, plus a detailed regional Plant and Materials List. It also includes an illustrated list of hundreds of landscape plants suited to your region, in case you wish to make substitutions, as well as planting instructions and plant adaptation maps to ensure professional results with your new landscape.

See page 174 to order your regionalized Blueprint Package.

PLAN VIEW

PROPERTY LINE
PROPERTY LINE
STAMPED CONCRETE PAVING
Residence
BRICK PAVING
TERRACE
LAWN
BRICK INLAY
COVERED PORCH
BRICK EDGE
BALCONY
BENCH
ENTRY PLAZA
BENCH
BENCH
STAMPED CONCRETE PAVING
PLANTER POTS
LAWN
LAWN
DRIVEWAY
LAWN
BRICK INLAY
BRICK PAVING
59'-0"
110'-0"

Landscape Plan L233 shown in spring
Designed by Michael J. Opisso

Home Plan 2517

The modular character of this home is artfully reflected in the modular presentation of this landscape plan. Through the repeated use of brick walls, the designer has created a private entry court, and a side garden that serves as a quiet retreat.

Low-Gable Contemporary

To one approaching this house, the location of the front entrance might not be apparent were it not for the excellent landscaping. The design and layout of the pavement clearly point the way to the door, even though the entrance itself is out of sight. The brick inlay at the top of the driveway merges into the brick walkway leading to the recessed door. Brick serves well as the pavement material because it matches the brick facade of the house. The inlay before the garage is made wide to balance the weight of the landscaping on the left side of the residence.

Modular in its presentation, the walkway conforms with the modular architecture of the house, creating more interest than a straight walkway can do. Visitors approach the door by strolling between two trees and are then greeted by the soft shade of a third. An offshoot from the main walk extends the modular feeling and is defined by a brick wall. Within these walls the feeling of privacy and comfort is enhanced by the built-in benches.

Designed for a location on a well-traveled road, this home features only two large window panels in front, which admit light, and all other windows face the view to the rear of the property. To soften the stark facade, the three loose-textured trees in the entry area form a pleasing triangle while casting a light shade to soften the bold lines of the house. At the corner of the house, three tall evergreens accent the vertical lines and break up the blank wall. Toward the property line to the left, four larger evergreens block the view from the street and contain the landscape setting.

Regionalized Plant Lists

Because climate and growing conditions vary greatly throughout North America, it is impossible to list here all the plants for this landscape plan that would do well everywhere on the continent. However, you can order a Blueprint Package with plant lists keyed to this plan and selected by expert horticulturists to thrive in your area.

The six-page Blueprint Package features a large-size version of this Plan View, plus a detailed regional Plant and Materials List. It also includes an illustrated list of hundreds of landscape plants suited to your region, in case you wish to make substitutions, as well as planting instructions and plant adaptation maps to ensure professional results with your new landscape.

See page 174 to order your regionalized Blueprint Package.

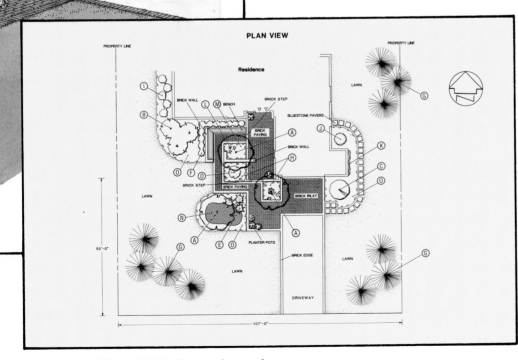

Landscape Plan L234 shown in spring
Designed by Michael J. Opisso

Home Plan 2729

Northern Brick Chateau

It would not be hard to imagine this picturesque home as the manor house of the family that controls the local vineyards. Large and strong, with many details, corners, and extensions, this house requires an equally strong landscape design that is straightforward and simple enough to complement the lines of the house without competing with them.

Because the property is large and the garage is located far to the rear, a circular driveway provides a grand entrance to the front door. Incorporating a courtyard in the driveway for parking creates an elegant setting that directs visitors to the paving leading to the front door. Cobble inlay around the courtyard enhances the manor-house mood while defining the space and creating a sense of welcome and arrival. Piers set at each side of the walkway provide strength and symmetry and also cast light for night viewing and security. The oval lawn areas between the driveway and courtyard are bermed to add interest and create a feeling of seclusion without closing in the space.

The low, curved walls contain planting beds that afford a transition between the house and the landscape. To the right, a decorative, spring-flowering tree adds color interest and creates a lovely garden to be viewed from the balcony above. The tall tree at the front right corner anchors the large house to the landscape, matching its scale, and serves to block some of the pavement leading to the garage. A band of small flowering trees adds color to the facade of the house and focuses attention on the entrance.

Regionalized Plant Lists

Because climate and growing conditions vary greatly throughout North America, it is impossible to list here all the plants for this landscape plan that would do well everywhere on the continent. However, you can order a Blueprint Package with plant lists keyed to this plan and selected by expert horticulturists to thrive in your area.

The six-page Blueprint Package features a large-size version of this Plan View, plus a detailed regional Plant and Materials List. It also includes an illustrated list of hundreds of landscape plants suited to your region, in case you wish to make substitutions, as well as planting instructions and plant adaptation maps to ensure professional results with your new landscape.

See page 174 to order your regionalized Blueprint Package.

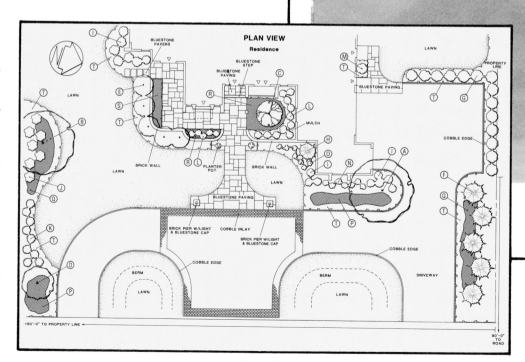

Landscape Plan L235 shown in spring
Designed by Michael J. Opisso

Home Plan 2952

In this landscape, the designer uses two lawn-covered berms to nestle the ample parking courtyard into its prominent setting. The berms also partially block the view of the property from the street, revealing the full view of the house and its lovely plantings only when one rounds the bend of the driveway.

Mission-Tile Ranch

The low, sprawling lines of this ranch house and its red-tile roof evoke the Spanish Mission style reminiscent of the easy-living, comfortable nature of Southwestern life. The landscape designer chooses both hardscaping and softscaping to complement the house and the climate. Exposed aggregate walks, simple yet attractive, lead to both main and secondary entrances, and blend well with the contemporary Southwestern architecture.

The bed bordering the walkway to the secondary entrance is bermed slightly to block the view of the walkway used by the homeowner, preventing the visitor from approaching the wrong door. The V-shaped driveway provides a convenient parking spur and the angles of the driveway create visual excitement in the design. Three flowering trees spaced out near the corners of the driveway reinforce the V-shape and provide welcome summer color. The tree on the right frames the entrance to the garage; the one on the left frames the view to the front door; and the one in the center buffers the view to the secondary entrance. Together, the three balance each other, forming a pleasing triangle.

The planting border running in front of the garage wing continues on the other side of the driveway, strengthening the lines of the bed and creating a transition between front and back. Without the continuation of the planting area, the landscaping would abruptly end; with it, the sight line gracefully continues. At the end of a second sight line, the small flowering tree at the left corner of the house creates a view for a visitor strolling up the walk.

Regionalized Plant Lists

Because climate and growing conditions vary greatly throughout North America, it is impossible to list here all the plants for this landscape plan that would do well everywhere on the continent. However, you can order a Blueprint Package with plant lists keyed to this plan and selected by expert horticulturists to thrive in your area.

The six-page Blueprint Package features a large-size version of this Plan View, plus a detailed regional Plant and Materials List. It also includes an illustrated list of hundreds of landscape plants suited to your region, in case you wish to make substitutions, as well as planting instructions and plant adaptation maps to ensure professional results with your new landscape.

See page 174 to order your regionalized Blueprint Package.

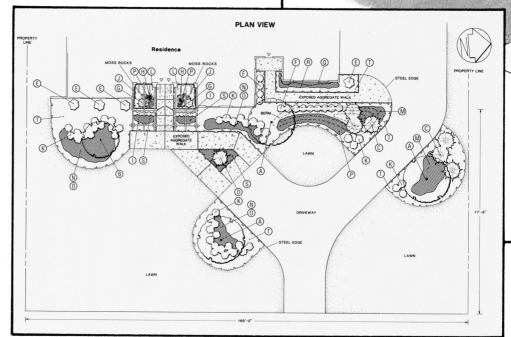

Landscape Plan L236 shown in summer
Designed by Damon Scott

Home Plan 2670

112

An effective landscape design matches the climate as well as the flavor of the home's architecture. Here, aggregate walkways, overhead trellising, and heat-tolerant plants work together to create a perfect cooling combination for a hot climate.

Designed to complement a desert environment, the earthtones of this landscape design are carried over from the adobe bricks to the rock outcroppings and two different hues of crushed stone. Interesting and colorful, this treatment also accommodates the intense heat and lack of water typical of this climate.

Adobe-Block Hacienda

When you fly over the Arizona desert into Tucson you observe that most of the color in the landscape comes from the blue water in the swimming pools—there is a noticeable lack of green. Because of the intense heat and lengthy dry season, many arid-climate homes do not have grassy lawns. The designer of this adobe-block hacienda follows this norm and designs the plan for this Southwestern-style home to feature crushed stone, instead of lawn, as ground cover. The driveway is also made of crushed stone in a contrasting earthtone to complement the desert setting.

The low-key architecture demands a simple landscape solution that blends well with the desert environment and uses a minimum number of high-maintenance plants. Only the plants used under the shady arbor at the front of the house require regular watering—all the others were chosen for their drought tolerance. Of course, in an arid environment even drought-tolerant landscape plants need regular irrigation until they are established.

The berm in the center of the property partially blocks the view to the main entrance, and contains boulders to enhance further the naturalistic look of the crushed stone. A second berm and boulder to the right of the house balances the first berm and gives needed dimension to an otherwise flat piece of property, which no doubt looks out on a mountain view in the distance.

Regionalized Plant Lists

Because climate and growing conditions vary greatly throughout North America, it is impossible to list here all the plants for this landscape plan that would do well everywhere on the continent. However, you can order a Blueprint Package with plant lists keyed to this plan and selected by expert horticulturists to thrive in your area.

The six-page Blueprint Package features a large-size version of this Plan View, plus a detailed regional Plant and Materials List. It also includes an illustrated list of hundreds of landscape plants suited to your region, in case you wish to make substitutions, as well as planting instructions and plant adaptation maps to ensure professional results with your new landscape.

See page 174 to order your regionalized Blueprint Package.

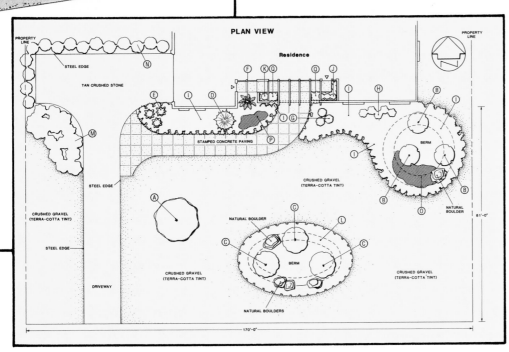

Landscape Plan L237 shown in spring
Designed by David Poplawski

Home Plan 2231

Courtyard Patio Home

The architect originally designed this house with the entrance to the front walled walkway leading from the upper corner of the driveway; the wall across the front was solid, hiding the front door from view. To make the vista of the home more open, the landscape designer modifies the original entry and opens up the wall in front. With the addition of two decorative gates, there is now a direct sight line down the corridor to the front door, yet the home still appears private and secure.

The narrow corridor has limited planting space. Shrubs that grow in a somewhat flat plane and could easily be espaliered against the walls of the house are employed to take best advantage of the layout. Stamped concrete paving is used in the driveway and is repeated in the walkways to match the character of the surrounding stucco walls. At each side of the driveway entrance, a 3-foot stucco wall mirrors the wall around the house, unifying and strengthening the design. Flowering trees soften the walls near the house and driveway, providing a burst of summer color; these trees are underplanted with a flowering ground cover.

The private courtyard, which provides a beautiful outdoor living space, is viewed through sliding doors from the master suite, living room, and dining room. Shrubs, vines, and perennials offer a changing palate of color to be enjoyed close at hand from the patio or at a distance through the windows.

Regionalized Plant Lists

Because climate and growing conditions vary greatly throughout North America, it is impossible to list here all the plants for this landscape plan that would do well everywhere on the continent. However, you can order a Blueprint Package with plant lists keyed to this plan and selected by expert horticulturists to thrive in your area.

The six-page Blueprint Package features a large-size version of this Plan View, plus a detailed regional Plant and Materials List. It also includes an illustrated list of hundreds of landscape plants suited to your region, in case you wish to make substitutions, as well as planting instructions and plant adaptation maps to ensure professional results with your new landscape.

See page 174 to order your regionalized Blueprint Package.

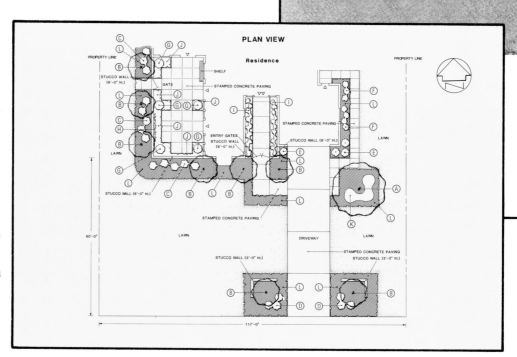

Landscape Plan L238 shown in summer
Designed by Michael J. Opisso

Home Plan 2386

The decorative stucco walls at the driveway entrance have several functions. They frame the entrance and help to unify the landscape by repeating the walled theme of the entrance and courtyard. Stamped concrete walks and driveway match the walls and are appropriate to a warm climate.

Center-Court Contemporary

The challenge facing the designer of this landscape was to minimize the depth of the house from front to back without making the distance from the driveway to the front door seem longer than it is. This is accomplished by integrating the walkway with the entry court and adding a central planting bed and benches to create an inviting, intimate feeling. The 2-foot-high brick wall around the front right corner of the entry court defines its boundaries, complements the house, and ties the house to the landscaping. The brick wall and piers defining the courtyard are repeated in the front of the property to carry out further this goal. Though the landscape design would work without the wall near the street, this wall reinforces the entry court and balances its weight. Vase-shaped shade trees also mark the space and frame the house.

The modular brick paving extends across the front of the driveway to the depth of the court, extending the entry and unifying the area while easily leading visitors toward the front door. A little more than halfway along the courtyard, two tall piers signal arrival.

Intended as a home to be situated on a well-traveled road, this house lacks front windows as a way to create privacy and reduce traffic noise. This leaves a rather stark facade, which the designer uses as a backdrop to display a group of striking evergreens.

Regionalized Plant Lists

Because climate and growing conditions vary greatly throughout North America, it is impossible to list here all the plants for this landscape plan that would do well everywhere on the continent. However, you can order a Blueprint Package with plant lists keyed to this plan and selected by expert horticulturists to thrive in your area.

The six-page Blueprint Package features a large-size version of this Plan View, plus a detailed regional Plant and Materials List. It also includes an illustrated list of hundreds of landscape plants suited to your region, in case you wish to make substitutions, as well as planting instructions and plant adaptation maps to ensure professional results with your new landscape.

See page 174 to order your regionalized Blueprint Package.

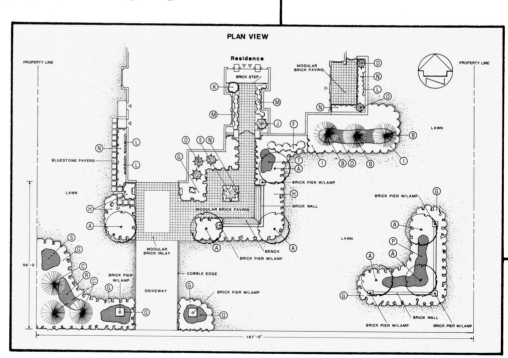

Landscape Plan L239 shown in summer
Designed by David Poplawski

Home Plan 2857

Here is a solution appropriate for a busy street. The layout of the house and landscape effectively screens out traffic noise and provides privacy through the skillful use of walls and plant materials.

Chapter 3

Livable Backyard Landscape Designs

Here Is a Selection of Beautiful Backyard Designs to Suit Most Families' Needs for Outdoor Living Space

The landscape designs included in this chapter reflect a variety of different themes and family needs. There are several designs featuring swimming pools and large decks and patios, suitable for entertaining on a grand scale. Avid gardeners might be inspired by the edible landscape design, or the rose or cottage garden. By browsing through these pages and examining the plot plans and the accompanying illustrations, you are sure to discover the backyard that is perfect for your needs.

The landscape paintings show the design a few years after installation, when the new plantings have filled in and matured a bit. A plant list is not included along with the plot plan in the book because few plants adapt to all regions of the country. For any of these designs, you can order a full-sized, highly detailed blueprint package, which includes a plant list especially selected to perform well in your area of the country. (See p. 174 for ordering information.) The painting for each landscape shows the plants recommended for the Mid-Atlantic region. Similar-appearing plants are selected for other regions, where possible.

Notice how the gray stones in the patio match the gray stain on the wooden arbor and deck, creating a beautifully decorated setting for an inviting swimming pool.

Designed for families who love outdoor living,
this backyard features a deck and patio combination that is perfect for entertaining. It features separate areas for cooking and dining,
intimate conversations, and relaxing in the sun.

Deck and Terrace for Entertaining

The perfect setting for an outdoor party or for simply relaxing with family and friends—this backyard features an elegant wooden deck and brick patio that run the length of the house. The deck area on the right acts as an outdoor kitchen, featuring a built-in barbecue, serving cabinet, and space enough for a dining table and chairs. For those who opt to mingle with the other guests, rather than kibitz with the cook, a separate area has been provided at the other end.

Built at the same level with the house, and easily accessible from inside, the deck extends the interior living space to the outdoors. Three lovely flowering trees shade the deck and house, while creating a visual ceiling and walls to reinforce further the idea that these areas are outdoor rooms.

Down a few steps from the deck, the brick terrace makes a transition between the house (and deck) and the garden. Open on two sides to the lawn, this sunny terrace feels—and is—spacious and open, creating a great place in which people can mingle and talk during a cocktail party or sunbathe on a Saturday afternoon. From here, one can enjoy the garden setting close at hand. The plantings around the perimeter of the yard feature several kinds of tall evergreens to provide privacy. In front of the evergreens, large drifts of flowering perennials are perfectly displayed against the green background. Between the evergreens, masses of shrubbery provide a changing color show from early spring through fall.

Regionalized Plant Lists

Because climate and growing conditions vary greatly throughout North America, it is impossible to list here all the plants for this landscape plan that would do well everywhere on the continent. However, you can order a Blueprint Package with plant lists keyed to this plan and selected by expert horticulturists to thrive in your area.

The six-page Blueprint Package features a large-size version of this Plan View, plus a detailed regional Plant and Materials List. It also includes an illustrated list of hundreds of landscape plants suited to your region, in case you wish to make substitutions, as well as planting instructions and plant adaptation maps to ensure professional results with your new landscape.

See page 174 to order your regionalized Blueprint Package.

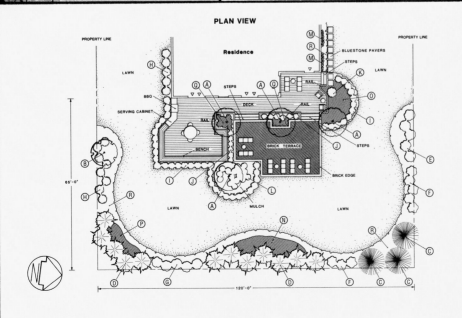

Landscape Plan L240 shown in spring
Designed by Michael J. Opisso

Japanese-Style Garden

When a busy couple desire a garden that is distinctive and requires little maintenance, the Japanese-style garden and backyard pictured here are a perfect solution. The essence of a Japanese garden lies in emulating nature through simple, clean lines that do not look contrived. The low, tight hedges underscore the planting behind them, while providing a contrast in form. Looking straight out from the deck, the perimeter planting is a harmony of shades of green, with interest provided from contrasting textures. Plants throughout require little fuss.

Paving stones border the deck, because, in the Japanese garden, every element has both an aesthetic and a functional purpose. The stones alleviate the wear that would result from stepping directly onto the lawn from the deck, and provide a visual transition between the man-made deck and the natural grass. The pavers act as more than a path; they also provide a sight line to the stone lantern on the left side of the garden.

The deck, like the rest of the landscape, has clean, simple lines, and provides the transition from the home's interior to the garden. It surrounds a viewing garden, one step down. In the Japanese tradition, this miniature landscape mimics a natural scene. The one large moss rock plays an important role—it is situated at the intersection of the stepping-stone paths that lead through the garden; here a decision must be made as to which way to turn. The stone water basin, a symbolic part of the Japanese tea ceremony, is located near the door to the house, signaling the entrance to a very special place.

Regionalized Plant Lists

Because climate and growing conditions vary greatly throughout North America, it is impossible to list here all the plants for this landscape plan that would do well everywhere on the continent. However, you can order a Blueprint Package with plant lists keyed to this plan and selected by expert horticulturists to thrive in your area.

The six-page Blueprint Package features a large-size version of this Plan View, plus a detailed regional Plant and Materials List. It also includes an illustrated list of hundreds of landscape plants suited to your region, in case you wish to make substitutions, as well as planting instructions and plant adaptation maps to ensure professional results with your new landscape.

See page 174 to order your regionalized Blueprint Package.

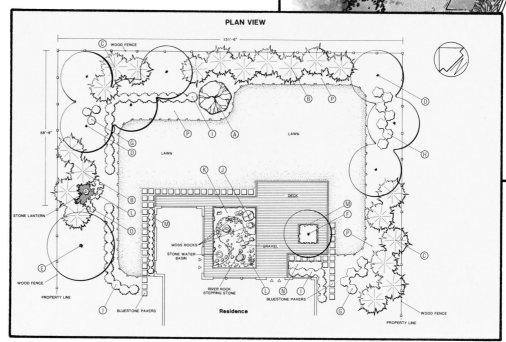

Landscape Plan L241 shown in spring
Designed by Michael J. Opisso

124

This beautiful Japanese-style garden provides space for outdoor living and entertaining in a tranquil setting. Featuring straight, simple lines, a small lawn, a large deck, and extensive plantings of ground covers and evergreens, the garden practically cares for itself.

Shade Garden

Woe to the gardener who has to deal with established tall trees that cast a great deal of shade—a beautiful, colorful backyard is out of the question. Right? Wrong! Nothing could be further from the truth, as demonstrated by this artfully designed shade garden. The key to working with large existing trees is in using the shade as an asset, not as a liability, and in choosing shade-loving plants to grow beneath them. If the trees have a very dense canopy, branches can be selectively removed to thin the trees and create filtered shade below.

In this plan, the designer shapes the lawn and beds to respond to the locations of the trees. Note that all but one of the trees are situated in planting beds, not open lawn. Placing a single tree in the lawn helps to integrate the lawn and planting beds, creating a cohesive design. At the right, the deep planting area is enhanced by pavers, a bench, and a birdbath, creating an inviting shady retreat. Near the house, a small patio provides a lounging spot; its curving shape echoes the curving form of the planting beds.

Throughout the garden, perennials, woody plants, and ground covers are arranged in drifts to create a comfortable and serene space. The garden is in constant but ever-changing bloom from early spring through fall as its special plants—ones chosen because they thrive in just such a shady setting in their native habitats—go in and out of bloom. And fall brings big splashes of foliage color to complete the year-long show. To provide the finishing carpet to this beautiful and cool shade garden, choose a grass-seed variety selected to tolerate shade.

Regionalized Plant Lists

Because climate and growing conditions vary greatly throughout North America, it is impossible to list here all the plants for this landscape plan that would do well everywhere on the continent. However, you can order a Blueprint Package with plant lists keyed to this plan and selected by expert horticulturists to thrive in your area.

The six-page Blueprint Package features a large-size version of this Plan View, plus a detailed regional Plant and Materials List. It also includes an illustrated list of hundreds of landscape plants suited to your region, in case you wish to make substitutions, as well as planting instructions and plant adaptation maps to ensure professional results with your new landscape.

See page 174 to order your regionalized Blueprint Package.

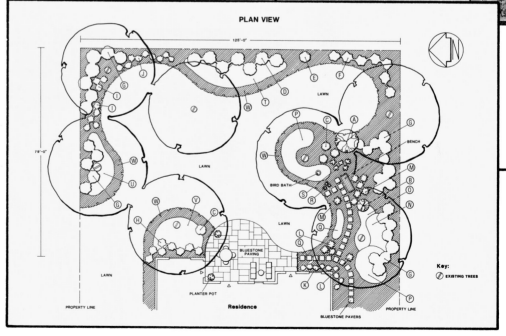

Landscape Plan L242 shown in spring
Designed by Michael J. Opisso

Shaded yards need not be dark and dull, as this backyard design demonstrates. Here, beneath the shadows of seven mature trees, a colorful collection of shade-loving shrubs, perennials, and ground covers flourishes.

Formal Garden for Entertaining

Want to play a role from the Great Gatsby? Then close your eyes and imagine being a guest at a large party in this magnificent garden designed for formal entertaining. Imagine standing in the house at the French doors, just at the entrance to the paved area, and looking out at this perfectly symmetrical scene. The left mirrors the right; a major sight line runs straight down the center past the fountain to the statue that serves as a focal point at the rear of the garden. Three perfectly oval flowering trees on each side of the patio frame the sight line, as well as help to delineate the pavement from the planted areas of the garden.

The flagstone patio along the house rises several steps above the brick patio, giving it prominence and presenting a good view of the rest of the property. The change in paving materials provides a separate identity to each area, yet by edging the brick with bluestone to match the upper patio, the two are tied together.

Pink and purple flowering shrubs and perennials provide an elegant color scheme throughout the growing season. A vine-covered lattice panel, featuring royal purple flowers that bloom all summer long, creates a secluded area accessible by paving stones at the rear of the property. What a perfect spot for a romantic rendezvous!

Regionalized Plant Lists

Because climate and growing conditions vary greatly throughout North America, it is impossible to list here all the plants for this landscape plan that would do well everywhere on the continent. However, you can order a Blueprint Package with plant lists keyed to this plan and selected by expert horticulturists to thrive in your area.

The six-page Blueprint Package features a large-size version of this Plan View, plus a detailed regional Plant and Materials List. It also includes an illustrated list of hundreds of landscape plants suited to your region, in case you wish to make substitutions, as well as planting instructions and plant adaptation maps to ensure professional results with your new landscape.

See page 174 to order your regionalized Blueprint Package.

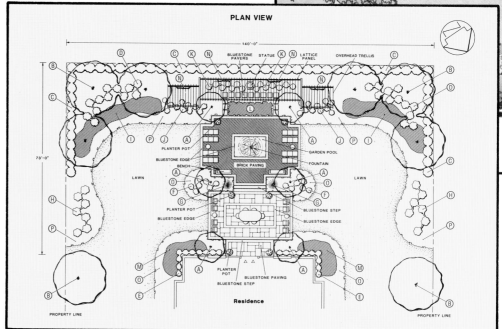

Landscape Plan L243 shown in summer
Designed by Michael J. Opisso

128

This formal garden provides a perfect setting for romantic outdoor parties or for simply relaxing in the sun on a Saturday afternoon.

Children's Play Yard

If there's one thing that can be said about children's play areas, it's that their function usually far outweighs their attractiveness. However, this backyard design presents an excellent solution to a functional children's play yard that is still pleasing to look at. The backyard includes all the fun elements a child would love. On one side of the yard are grouped a play structure for climbing and swinging, a playhouse, and a sandbox enclosed in a low boardwalk. A play mound—a perfect place for running, leaping, and holding fort—rises from the lawn on the side of the other yard.

These play areas are integrated into the landscape by their circular form, which is repeated in the sandbox, play mound, boardwalk, and the sand areas under the playhouse and play structure. The curved brick patio and planting border carry through the circular theme. The stepping stones leading to the play areas also follow a circular path—a playful pattern that invites a child to "follow the yellow brick road."

From the house and patio, the views of both the garden and the play areas are unobstructed, affording constant adult supervision from both indoors and out. The border surrounding the yard creates a private setting that offers a changing show of flowers from the masses of shrubs and perennials. Beyond the play structure, a large tree shades the area, providing landscape interest, and perhaps even a place for adventurous young feet to climb.

When the children are grown, this design can be adapted as a playground for older folk by removing the playhouse and play structure and planting lawn, or a flower or vegetable garden.

Regionalized Plant Lists

Because climate and growing conditions vary greatly throughout North America, it is impossible to list here all the plants for this landscape plan that would do well everywhere on the continent. However, you can order a Blueprint Package with plant lists keyed to this plan and selected by expert horticulturists to thrive in your area.

The six-page Blueprint Package features a large-size version of this Plan View, plus a detailed regional Plant and Materials List. It also includes an illustrated list of hundreds of landscape plants suited to your region, in case you wish to make substitutions, as well as planting instructions and plant adaptation maps to ensure professional results with your new landscape.

See page 174 to order your regionalized Blueprint Package.

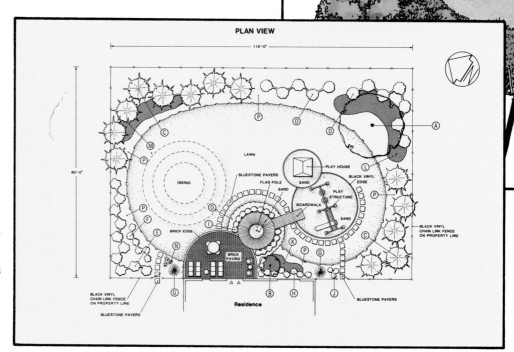

Landscape Plan L244 shown in summer
Designed by Michael J. Opisso

Here is a special backyard designed for both children and adults. The yard offers youngsters their own place to escape into a world of imagination and discovery without compromising the attractiveness of a garden setting.

Nature lovers will delight in the abundant birds that will flock to this beautiful garden. An attractive collection of berried plants and evergreens offers food and shelter for the wildlife, while creating a handsome, pastoral setting.

Garden to Attract Birds

There is no better way to wake up in the morning than to the sound of songbirds in the garden. Wherever you live, you will be surprised at the number and variety of birds you can attract by offering them a few basic necessities—water, shelter, nesting spots, and food. Birds need water for drinking and bathing. They need shrubs and trees, especially evergreens, for shelter and nesting. Edge spaces—open areas with trees nearby for quick protection—provide ground feeders with foraging places, while plants with berries and nuts offer other natural sources of food.

The garden presented here contains all the necessary elements to attract birds to the garden. The shrubs and trees are chosen especially to provide a mix of evergreen and deciduous species. All of these, together with the masses of flowering perennials, bear seeds, nuts, or berries known to appeal to birds. The berry show looks quite pretty, too, until the birds gobble them up. Planted densely enough for necessary shelter, the bird-attracting plants create a backyard that's enjoyable throughout the seasons.

The birdbath is located in the lawn so it will be in the sun. A naturalistic pond provides water in a more protected setting. The birdhouses and feeders aren't really necessary—though they may be the icing on the cake when it comes to luring the largest number of birds—because the landscape provides abundant natural food and shelter. Outside one of the main windows of the house, a birdfeeder hangs from a small flowering tree, providing up-close viewing of your feathered friends.

Regionalized Plant Lists

Because climate and growing conditions vary greatly throughout North America, it is impossible to list here all the plants for this landscape plan that would do well everywhere on the continent. However, you can order a Blueprint Package with plant lists keyed to this plan and selected by expert horticulturists to thrive in your area.

The six-page Blueprint Package features a large-size version of this Plan View, plus a detailed regional Plant and Materials List. It also includes an illustrated list of hundreds of landscape plants suited to your region, in case you wish to make substitutions, as well as planting instructions and plant adaptation maps to ensure professional results with your new landscape.

See page 174 to order your regionalized Blueprint Package.

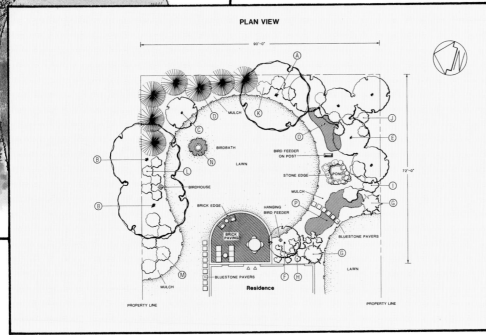

PLAN VIEW

90'-0"

MULCH

BIRDBATH

BIRD FEEDER ON POST

LAWN

STONE EDGE

POND

BIRDHOUSE

MULCH

BRICK EDGE

HANGING BIRD FEEDER

BLUESTONE PAVERS

BRICK PAVING

BLUESTONE PAVERS

Residence

MULCH

LAWN

PROPERTY LINE

PROPERTY LINE

72'-0"

Landscape Plan L245 shown in autumn
Designed by Michael J. Opisso

Low in maintenance requirements, high in natural appeal, this garden of ornamental grasses delights the senses all year with subdued foliage colors, sparkling flower plumes, and rustling leaves.

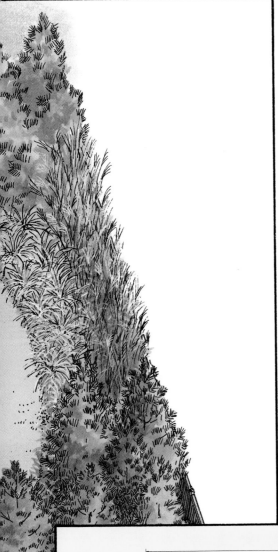

Naturalistic Grass Garden

Many cultures seem to have an identifiable garden style—there are formal Italian fountain gardens, French parterres, English perennial borders, and Japanese contemplation gardens. For many years, we didn't have an American-style garden. Now, a new trend has arisen, which the originators have dubbed the "New American Garden." This style of landscaping is naturalistic and relies on sweeps of ornamental grasses to create the feel of the prairies that once dominated much of the American landscape.

The backyard garden presented here follows that theme. The grasses used vary from low-growing plants hugging the borders to tall plants reaching 6 feet or more. Some of the grasses are bold and upright; others arching and graceful. When the grasses flower, they produce plumes that dance in the wind and sparkle in the sun. Foliage colors include bright green, blue-green, variegated, and even blood-red. During autumn, foliage and flowers dry in place, forming a stunning scene of naturalistic hues in varying shades of straw, almond, brown, and rust. Most of the grasses remain interesting to look at all winter, unless heavy snow flattens them to the ground. In early spring, the dried foliage must be cut off and removed to make way for new growth—but this is the only maintenance chore required by an established garden of ornamental grasses!

The design includes a large realistic-looking pond, which can be made from a vinyl-liner or concrete. At the end of the path leading from the bridge, a small seating area provides a retreat.

Regionalized Plant Lists

Because climate and growing conditions vary greatly throughout North America, it is impossible to list here all the plants for this landscape plan that would do well everywhere on the continent. However, you can order a Blueprint Package with plant lists keyed to this plan and selected by expert horticulturists to thrive in your area.

The six-page Blueprint Package features a large-size version of this Plan View, plus a detailed regional Plant and Materials List. It also includes an illustrated list of hundreds of landscape plants suited to your region, in case you wish to make substitutions, as well as planting instructions and plant adaptation maps to ensure professional results with your new landscape.

See page 174 to order your regionalized Blueprint Package.

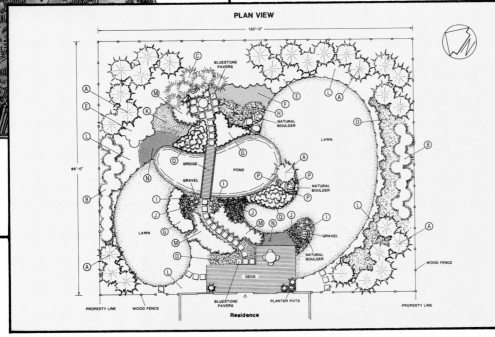

PLAN VIEW

Landscape Plan L246 shown in summer
Designed by Damon Scott

Pool and Deck Garden

Take the usual rectangular backyard and place in it a simple rectangular swimming pool and the result, more often than not, is boring! Not so with this effective landscape design. By situating the pool along the diagonals of the property, the designer creates an exciting view that juxtaposes the angles of the hardscape with the curves of the planting areas, making the property appear larger and visually interesting.

The steps leading into the pool are placed on the outside of the rectangle to alleviate some of the straight lines; however, the theme still remains angular. This is reinforced by the lines of the wooden decking surrounding the pool. At the end of the pool, hedges not only complete the angular design, they also screen the pool's filter and heater. The line of the hedge is strengthened by two flowering trees positioned at each end; these also terminate the sight line along the pool's length.

Three planters play important roles in the planting design—they serve as pockets of color to break up the large expanse of wood. One brings color to the poolside; a second links the poolside deck with the upper deck off the house; the third wraps around the upper deck and defines the seating area. Notice how the boards change direction from one deck level to the next. Besides being visually interesting, this helps to distinguish the two areas. When guests arrive, they can clearly distinguish the different use areas of the decking. The area closest to the house offers a perfect place for cooking, dining, and entertaining, while the lower deck beckons one to swim and relax in the sun.

Regionalized Plant Lists

Because climate and growing conditions vary greatly throughout North America, it is impossible to list here all the plants for this landscape plan that would do well everywhere on the continent. However, you can order a Blueprint Package with plant lists keyed to this plan and selected by expert horticulturists to thrive in your area.

The six-page Blueprint Package features a large-size version of this Plan View, plus a detailed regional Plant and Materials List. It also includes an illustrated list of hundreds of landscape plants suited to your region, in case you wish to make substitutions, as well as planting instructions and plant adaptation maps to ensure professional results with your new landscape.

See page 174 to order your regionalized Blueprint Package.

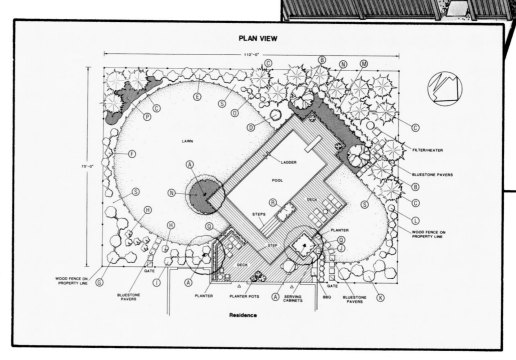

Landscape Plan L247 shown in summer
Designed by Michael J. Opisso

136

Is it possible to start with the same ingredients and combine them into a different recipe? Yes, by angling a rectangular pool, breaking up the large expanse of deck with planters, and mixing in gracefully curving shrub borders, this pool and deck garden becomes a gourmet treat.

Naturalistic Swimming Pool

If you look at this landscape design and ask yourself, "Is that really a swimming pool?" then the designer is to be congratulated because he has succeeded in his intention. Yes, it is a swimming pool, but the pool looks more like a natural pond and waterfall—one that you might discover in a clearing in the woods during a hike in the wilderness.

The designer achieves this aesthetically pleasing, natural look by employing several techniques. He creates the pool in an irregular free-form shape and paints it "black," actually a very dark marine-blue, to suggest the depths of a lake. Large boulders form the waterfalls, one of which falls from a holding pond set among the boulders. River rock paving, the type of water-worn rocks that line the cool water of a natural spring or a rushing stream, surrounds the front of the pool. The far side of the pool is planted right to the edge, blending the pool into the landscape. If you want to make a splash, you can even dive into this pool—from a diving rock rather than a diving board.

Although the pool is the main attraction here, the rest of the landscape offers a serene setting with abundant floral and foliage interest throughout the year. For security reasons, a wooden stockade fence surrounds the entire backyard, yet the plantings camouflage it well. The irregular kidney shape of the lawn is pleasing to look at and beautifully integrates the naturalistic pool and landscaping into its man-made setting.

Regionalized Plant Lists

Because climate and growing conditions vary greatly throughout North America, it is impossible to list here all the plants for this landscape plan that would do well everywhere on the continent. However, you can order a Blueprint Package with plant lists keyed to this plan and selected by expert horticulturists to thrive in your area.

The six-page Blueprint Package features a large-size version of this Plan View, plus a detailed regional Plant and Materials List. It also includes an illustrated list of hundreds of landscape plants suited to your region, in case you wish to make substitutions, as well as planting instructions and plant adaptation maps to ensure professional results with your new landscape.

See page 174 to order your regionalized Blueprint Package.

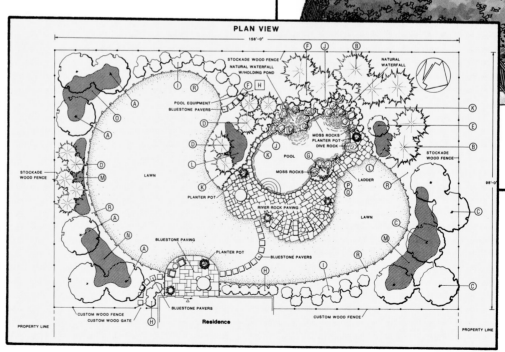

Landscape Plan L248 shown in summer
Designed by Damon Scott

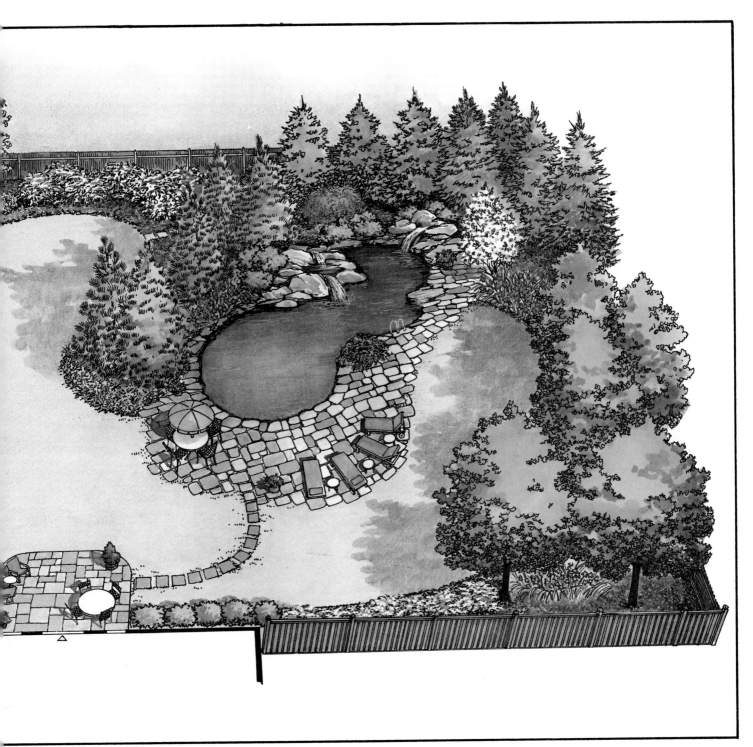

Resembling a tranquil country pond high in the mountains, this swimming pool, with its waterfalls, river-rock paving, and border planting, brings a wonderful, natural setting to your own backyard.

High above the rest of the garden, this second-story deck affords a beautiful view of the grounds. And the deck looks beautiful too, because latticework and soft plantings integrate it into the landscape.

Second-Story Deck

A second-story deck can be the answer to many different landscaping problems. Sometimes it is built at a mother-daughter house to provide a private deck for a second-story apartment. Where a house is built on sloping property, which cannot accommodate a ground-level deck, a raised deck is the answer. With split-level or raised-ranch houses, where the kitchen is often on the second level, a second-story deck right off the kitchen eliminates carrying food and dishes up and down stairs.

Even though a deck is high, it can have two levels and therefore two separate use areas, as the designer accomplishes with this deck. The upper area features a built-in barbecue, service cabinet, and space for dining. The lower area invites family and guests to lounge and relax in the sun. Because the deck is high enough off the ground that an accidental fall could be dangerous, a railing and planters that double as a railing ensure safety. Filled with masses of annuals, the planters bring living color above ground.

Without screening, the underside of the deck would be an eyesore when viewed from the yard. The designer solved this problem by enclosing the void beneath the deck with latticework and using a hedge to soften the effect. If the area beneath the deck is to be used as storage, a door can be added to the latticework. The triangular shape of the deck is far more pleasing than a square or rectangular design. Three flowering trees at the corners of the deck anchor this triangular shape and further serve to bring color and greenery up high. Tall evergreens help to screen the deck from the neighbors.

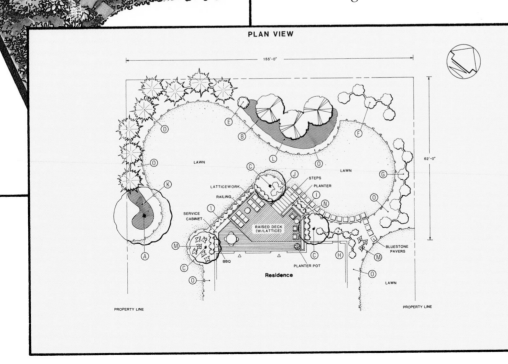

Landscape Plan L249 shown in summer
Designed by Michael J. Opisso

Regionalized Plant Lists

Because climate and growing conditions vary greatly throughout North America, it is impossible to list here all the plants for this landscape plan that would do well everywhere on the continent. However, you can order a Blueprint Package with plant lists keyed to this plan and selected by expert horticulturists to thrive in your area.

The six-page Blueprint Package features a large-size version of this Plan View, plus a detailed regional Plant and Materials List. It also includes an illustrated list of hundreds of landscape plants suited to your region, in case you wish to make substitutions, as well as planting instructions and plant adaptation maps to ensure professional results with your new landscape.

See page 174 to order your regionalized Blueprint Package.

Cottage Garden

The English cottage garden, beloved for its romantic, old-fashioned, homey appeal, is the kind of country garden to have again these days—whether or not you actually live in a cottage. The backyard design pictured here includes a cottage garden of easy-care, mixed perennials enclosed by a quaint picket fence. Suitable for many types of homes, from cottage to Colonial, this garden offers intimate scale and small spaces to create a comfortable backyard in which family and friends can feel at home. And there are plenty of flowers to cut all summer long for making indoor arrangements.

Paving stones lead from the front of the house to the backyard, where an arbor beckons visitors into the cozy patio and garden. Straight ahead, in the midst of the flower garden, a sundial acts as a focal point, drawing the eye right across the patio and into the garden beyond. A picket fence encloses the informal patio and flower garden, while defining the patchwork quilt of flowers inside it. Walk through the garden gate and down the path, and you will discover a garden swing nestled in the shade—a perfect spot for a romantic interlude or for whiling away the hours on a lazy afternoon.

Not to be outdone by the garden itself, the shrub borders edging the property offer an ever-changing arrangement of flowering shrubs backed by a privacy screen of tall evergreens. The trees located at each corner of the house balance and unify the patio and flower garden, while framing the garden when viewed from a distance.

Regionalized Plant Lists

Because climate and growing conditions vary greatly throughout North America, it is impossible to list here all the plants for this landscape plan that would do well everywhere on the continent. However, you can order a Blueprint Package with plant lists keyed to this plan and selected by expert horticulturists to thrive in your area.

The six-page Blueprint Package features a large-size version of this Plan View, plus a detailed regional Plant and Materials List. It also includes an illustrated list of hundreds of landscape plants suited to your region, in case you wish to make substitutions, as well as planting instructions and plant adaptation maps to ensure professional results with your new landscape.

See page 174 to order your regionalized Blueprint Package.

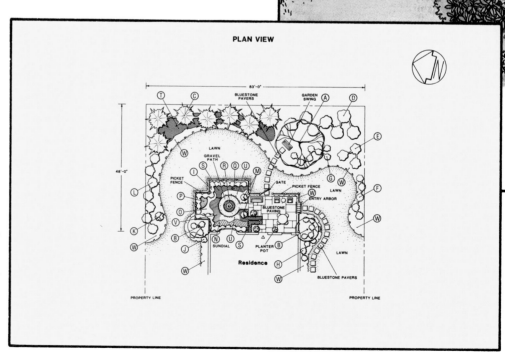

PLAN VIEW

Landscape Plan L250 shown in summer
Designed by Michael J. Opisso

It isn't necessary to live in a cottage to have a cottage garden. Almost any informal home would be enhanced by this charming backyard with its effervescent color, secluded retreats, and cozy spaces—all wrapped up in a white picket fence.

Raised Perennial Border

The yard and garden pictured here would delight any flower lover, since it is designed to bloom from early spring until fall. During spring, flowering trees and shrubs, which border part of the property, provide seasonal color. The main feature of the property, however, is a dramatic perennial border designed to bloom from summer through fall. The key to creating a successful display of flowering perennials lies in choosing and combining a selection of plants that bloom together and in sequence, so the garden is never bare of flowers. When so orchestrated—as this one is—the border displays a fascinating, ever-changing collection of colors. The perennials grow in large drifts to create the most impact when viewed from across the lawn.

The planting beds surround an irregular, bow-shaped lawn, a pretty way to add interest to an uninspiring squared-off property. A low stone wall raises the planting beds several steps up, bringing the flowers closer to eye level and emphasizing the contours of the design. The low retaining wall also provides an attractive way to deal with a sloping property so the lawn can be level. If your property is flat, the wall can be eliminated without altering the basic design. Behind the perennial garden, evergreens form a background that sets off the colors in summer.

When sitting on the patio of this beautiful yard, one's eye is drawn toward the gazebo, which is located two steps up from the lawn. Accessible by a stepping-stone walk, the gazebo makes a wonderful place to sit and relax in the shade while enjoying the beauty of the perennials from a different perspective.

Regionalized Plant Lists

Because climate and growing conditions vary greatly throughout North America, it is impossible to list here all the plants for this landscape plan that would do well everywhere on the continent. However, you can order a Blueprint Package with plant lists keyed to this plan and selected by expert horticulturists to thrive in your area.

The six-page Blueprint Package features a large-size version of this Plan View, plus a detailed regional Plant and Materials List. It also includes an illustrated list of hundreds of landscape plants suited to your region, in case you wish to make substitutions, as well as planting instructions and plant adaptation maps to ensure professional results with your new landscape.

See page 174 to order your regionalized Blueprint Package.

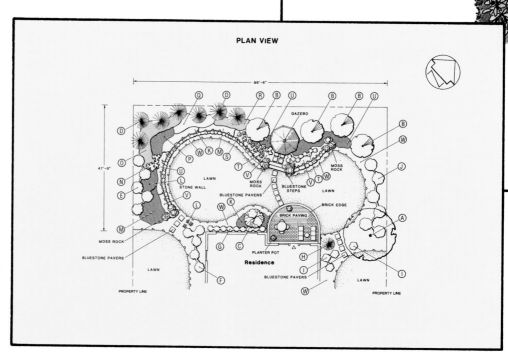

Landscape Plan L251 shown in summer
Designed by Michael J. Opisso

Here is a yard that is alive with flowers from spring through fall. In winter, the pretty stone wall, shrubs, and evergreen trees and ground covers keep the yard looking bright and beautiful.

Edible Landscape

The suburban food gardener needn't worry about turning the backyard into unattractive rows of vegetables when following this innovative design. Here is a backyard that looks good enough to eat! It is designed to produce abundant, fresh, home-grown produce and still be a beautiful spot for relaxing and entertaining. Though the main feature of the property is a central vegetable garden, many of the landscape plants used in the border plantings and along the house produce edible fruit as well. These plants were especially chosen because they can perform double duty, acting both as ornamentals and as food-producers.

The vegetable garden is accessible by way of a short path across the lawn. The garden is designed in a round form for greater interest, and has gravel paths dissecting it for ease of working and harvesting. Even in winter, when bare of plantings, this garden will be attractive to look at because of its geometrical layout. The designer has left the choice of vegetables up to the gardener and chef, but there is plenty of space to grow the family's favorite choices. Off to the side, a storage shed provides needed space for storing wheelbarrow, hoe, and other gardening paraphernalia. A compost pile is conveniently located out of sight behind the shed.

The outdoor kitchen area on the brick patio contains a barbecue, a sink, and a serving cabinet that doubles as a bar. Covered with an overhead lattice to set off the chef's culinary preparation area, this part of the patio provides a comfortable spot in which to lounge and dine out of the sun. For sunning, one can move out from under the lattice and soak up the rays.

Regionalized Plant Lists

Because climate and growing conditions vary greatly throughout North America, it is impossible to list here all the plants for this landscape plan that would do well everywhere on the continent. However, you can order a Blueprint Package with plant lists keyed to this plan and selected by expert horticulturists to thrive in your area.

The six-page Blueprint Package features a large-size version of this Plan View, plus a detailed regional Plant and Materials List. It also includes an illustrated list of hundreds of landscape plants suited to your region, in case you wish to make substitutions, as well as planting instructions and plant adaptation maps to ensure professional results with your new landscape.

See page 174 to order your regionalized Blueprint Package.

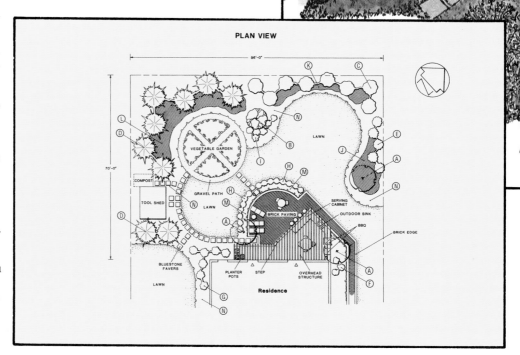

Landscape Plan L252 shown in summer
Designed by Michael J. Opisso

146

A cook's garden, this backyard provides everything the family needs to eat except for the hamburgers and buns. The vegetable garden is integrated into the yard in a manner infinitely more attractive than usual vegetable gardens, and the attractive shrub borders feature berry plants and fruit trees.

Water Garden

There are few places more tranquil, more relaxing, or more cooling on a hot summer day than a garden with a view of the water—even if the water is no more than a garden pool. In the garden pictured here, two ponds filled with water lilies are used as focal points and integrated with plantings and paving to create a tranquil setting. The first pond is situated near the house, where it is visible from indoors. The deck is cantilevered over the pond to enhance the closeness of the water, and is covered with an overhead trellis, which ties the two areas together. The trellising also frames the view of the pond from the deck, and of the deck from the garden area.

A second, smaller pond is set into the corner of the garden and has a backdrop of early-spring flowering trees, ferns, and shade-loving perennials. This intimate retreat is made complete by setting a bench and planter pots beside the pond.

Throughout the property, river-rock paving enhances the natural feeling of the water and provides a sitting area nearby where one can literally reflect upon the water. Moss rocks, placed in strategic places in the garden, further carry out the naturalistic theme, as do most of the landscape plants. The shrubs and perennials bordering the undulating lawn provide the needed soft-textured, informal look that makes both ponds seem natural and right at home.

Regionalized Plant Lists

Because climate and growing conditions vary greatly throughout North America, it is impossible to list here all the plants for this landscape plan that would do well everywhere on the continent. However, you can order a Blueprint Package with plant lists keyed to this plan and selected by expert horticulturists to thrive in your area.

The six-page Blueprint Package features a large-size version of this Plan View, plus a detailed regional Plant and Materials List. It also includes an illustrated list of hundreds of landscape plants suited to your region, in case you wish to make substitutions, as well as planting instructions and plant adaptation maps to ensure professional results with your new landscape.

See page 174 to order your regionalized Blueprint Package.

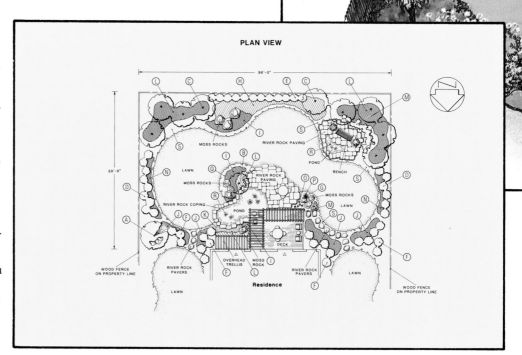

PLAN VIEW

Landscape Plan L253 shown in summer
Designed by Michael J. Opisso and Damon Scott

This backyard features not one, but two, ponds in which to dip your toes during summer's heat. If you choose to keep your shoes on, sit on the patio near the large pond or on the bench by the small one to cool off in the reflection of the colorful surroundings.

Formal Rose Garden

The grandeur of a European palace or estate garden comes alive in the formality and scale of this landscape design, which features a formal rose garden. In creating this mood, the designer makes the landscape completely symmetrical. Both sides of the garden are exact mirror images of each other, with extensive lawn areas on each side that can be used for relaxing or entertaining.

In the tradition of the formal rose garden, neat crisp evergreen hedges outline the rose plantings, providing interest and structure even during the off-season when the roses have been cut back to near the ground. The straight lines of the stepping-stone paths form a strong cross shape in the center of the garden. Each arm of the cross begins with a formal tree rose and ends at the edge of the garden in a strong focal point. The sight line looking up the horizontal arms, which is emphasized by the overhead trellises and pergolas, terminates in groups of oval-shaped trees backed by lattice panels. Flowering vines adorn the trellises.

From the bluestone paving at the house, a sight line leads along the paving stones, past the sundial in the center of the rose garden, and culminates with a reflecting pool situated in a paved area at the far end. Note that, although the same paving material was used in the front and back areas, the pattern is formal near the house and more informal at the back. Within the strong geometrical space of the rose garden, an early-spring flowering perennial provides a blanket of color until the roses burst into their summer-long show. The rose arbor and gate at each side of the house feature climbing roses, echoing the main theme of the garden.

Regionalized Plant Lists

Because climate and growing conditions vary greatly throughout North America, it is impossible to list here all the plants for this landscape plan that would do well everywhere on the continent. However, you can order a Blueprint Package with plant lists keyed to this plan and selected by expert horticulturists to thrive in your area.

The six-page Blueprint Package features a large-size version of this Plan View, plus a detailed regional Plant and Materials List. It also includes an illustrated list of hundreds of landscape plants suited to your region, in case you wish to make substitutions, as well as planting instructions and plant adaptation maps to ensure professional results with your new landscape.

See page 174 to order your regionalized Blueprint Package.

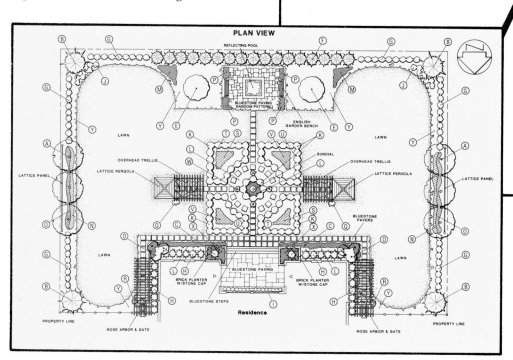

Landscape Plan L254 shown in summer
Designed by Jim Morgan

150

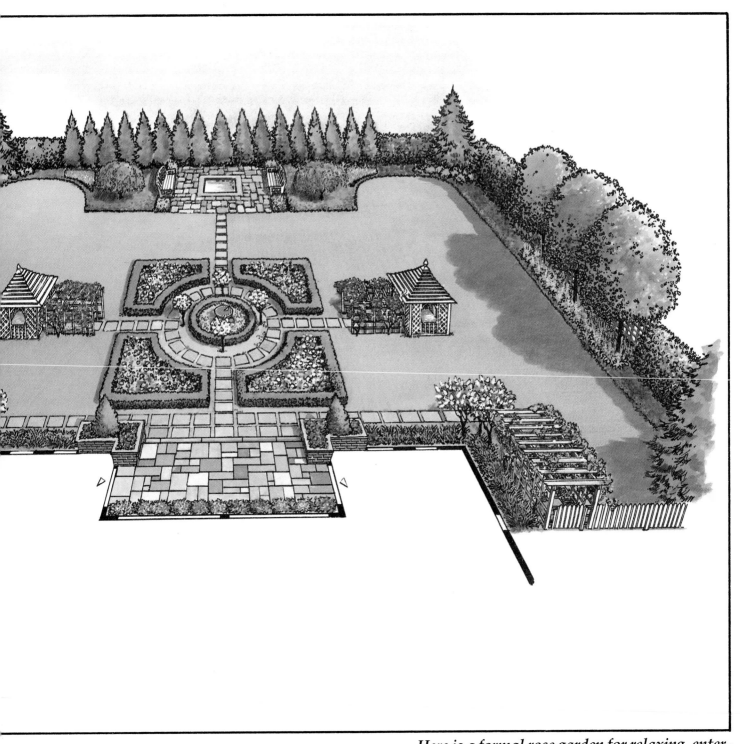

Here is a formal rose garden for relaxing, entertaining, or just enjoying the scent of nature's most beloved flower. Strong in line and impact, the garden is softened with overhead flowering vines and rose arbors, which provide enticing views in all directions.

Chapter 4

Installing Your Landscape

It's Easy to Adapt Any of These Landscape Designs to Suit Your Property—Here's How to Do It

The plans in this book were designed to assist you in landscaping your home—in making the landscape as professional looking, as beautiful, and as special as it can be. There are several ways the plans included here can help to make your dream landscape a reality. If your home's size and style matches one of the designs, you can use that design exactly or almost as it appears on these pages. Where there are slight variations in the size or layout of your home, the plans are easily adapted—this chapter will tell you how. Or you might want to follow the plans as a basic recipe, using your own imagination and creativity to customize the plan to your home.

If you've never designed a landscape, it's understandable that you may not feel comfortable about how to begin. You may be concerned that you lack the necessary creativity, knowledge, or experience. If this is in the back of your mind, don't worry, for it is relatively simple to adapt the designs presented in chapters 2 and 3. Study the plans and the renderings in these two chapters, considering those that might look attractive with your property. Select one or two with the style of architecture closest to your home and the landscaping style you like most, and then proceed with any necessary adjustments, as outlined below.

The plans in the book show the layout and placement of plants and hardscape, but do not detail the exact name or variety of plants used to carry out the design. This is because landscape plants are adapted to different climates and most are not suited to all parts of the country. Even though the plans shown do not indicate the exact plants to use, you can read the template to tell where the designer chose to place different trees, shrubs, evergreens, and perennials. (See illustration on next page.) And you can individualize the plans by carrying out the design with your favorite plants. The plan itself solves the design problem of artistically laying out the landscape by balancing sizes and shapes to complement the house and in figuring out how to direct people and cars gracefully to the house and garage. This basic layout will remain the same regardless of the particular plants you choose to

A pleasing combination of restful greenery and bright masses of floral color creates an inviting setting for this impressive home.

153

include, as long as the plants are in keeping with the spirit of the landscape design as shown in the color illustration.

You can select the plants to carry out the landscape design yourself, using the advice of a knowledgeable nurseryman or landscape designer if need be. There are many excellent reference books on trees and shrubs that can also guide and inspire you. Or, for any of the plans pictured here, you can order a complete set of construction and installation blueprints with a plant list selected specifically to do well in your region (see p. 174).

MAKING PLANS

A landscape plan is a drawing that depicts the three-dimensional aspects of a house, property, and planting scheme in two dimensions. It is impossible to say enough about the importance of drawing an accurate plan, and of laying out everything fully on paper before one tree is removed or one new shrub is planted. Just as an interior plan would have told you that the new table was going to be too large for the dining room, a landscape plan will aid you in visualizing existing features, developing new ideas, and finally guiding you when you are installing the landscape. Whether you are adapting a plan from this book or creating your own plan, you will need to do some planning and drawing.

The time taken to put the plan on paper will pay off later. You will, like any professional designer, be able to see if everything fits without crowding, and blends well together. You will know that paths and driveways will be in logical places, that the new tree won't block the view from the picture window, and that your family's private outdoor living space is screened from the neighbors' inquisitive eyes.

Before purchasing anything at the nursery or garden center, your next purchase—unless you have school-age children whose math and art classes have loaded the closets with some necessary tools— should be at an art supply store. Make sure your shopping list includes large sheets of graph paper and tracing paper, pencils, an eraser, a T-square, a right-angle triangle, a compass, a scale-rule, and a template. The template, which is used by landscape architects, allows you to easily draw symbols for trees and shrubs. The compass allows you to draw circles of a size different from those on the template. Once fully equipped to draw, you will be able to continue with the design process.

The graphic symbols shown here are ones commonly used on professional landscape designs to indicate different types of plants. Size indicates mature size.

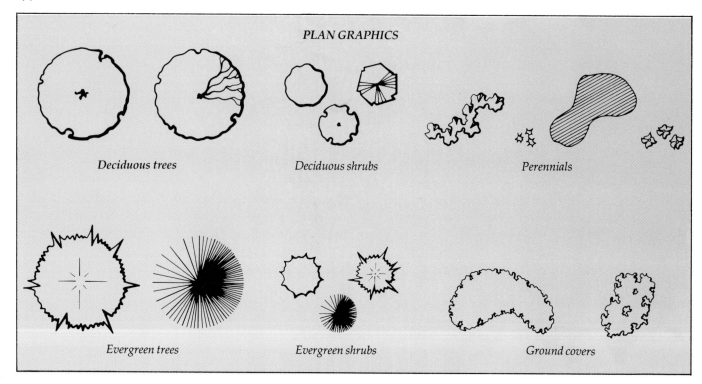

PLAN GRAPHICS

Deciduous trees *Deciduous shrubs* *Perennials*

Evergreen trees *Evergreen shrubs* *Ground covers*

Begin with a Survey

A plot plan is of no use unless it is drawn to scale. You must therefore start with an accurate drawing of your existing property. One of the easiest ways to do this is to use your property survey as a guide. If you don't have one, the building department of your town or county should have one on file. If a survey doesn't exist, you can measure your property yourself or have it professionally surveyed.

Use whatever scale for drawing your plot plan that you feel most comfortable with, allowing each square on the graph paper to equal a fixed dimension, such as 1 foot, 5 feet, or 10 feet, depending on the size of your paper and the size of your property. If you are going to order a set of blueprints from this book, use a scale of 1 inch equals 8 feet, since the blueprints are drawn to that scale on paper measuring 18 by 24 inches. (Landscape plan L202 is drawn to a scale of 1 inch equals 4 feet.) You can also draw directly on tracing paper, using a scale rule to help you get the dimensions correct. The triangular ruler offers nine different scales, which gives you a wide choice.

You may first want to make one overall plan for the entire property, selecting a small scale so it will fit on one piece of paper. Later you can create separate drawings for the front yard or the backyard in a larger scale so they can show more details.

If your survey is the right size and scale, simply trace it onto tracing paper to create a plot plan with which to work. If it is not a workable size, redraw it in a larger scale, using the scale rule to assist you. Add all existing and permanent features, such as sidewalk, driveway, patio, or deck if they are not on the survey. Then draw in all existing trees, shrubs, and garden areas. Don't guess when you do this; go outside, and with a 50- or 100-foot tape measure, measure everything exactly, as a professional would do.

Look back over the plans in this book and notice how the locations of the houses' doors and windows appear on the plans. Add your home's doors and windows to the plan. Using a directional arrow, mark which way is north. When the drawing is complete, make Xerox copies to work from and keep the original safe so you won't have to redraw the basic property lines, location of the house, and permanent features as you are experimenting.

Tracing It

Now it is time to design your home's new landscape. If you wish to adapt a plan from this book or from one of the blueprints you've ordered, you need a tracing-paper copy to put on top of your existing plot plan. Copy the plan from the book onto tracing paper, using the same scale as your existing plot plan; the scale rule will be helpful here when enlarging the plan. If starting with a blueprint, you need only make an exact-size copy by tracing it, since you should have drawn your existing plot plan to the same scale.

Lay the tracing paper copy of the new plot plan over the copy of the existing site and see how good a fit you have. Place a third piece of tracing paper over the other two—you can use small pieces of tape to keep them all aligned—and then begin to make any needed adjustments in the layout.

ADAPTING THE BOOK OR BLUEPRINT PLANS TO YOUR HOME

You may feel as though you received a gift from heaven if your house and the size of your property exactly matches one of the plans in this book. But if it doesn't, don't feel that you have been left out in the cold. With a little imagination and a few guidelines, you can easily adjust any of these plans to your property while maintaining the professional design quality of the landscape. Here's where your third sheet of tracing paper comes in. Trace the basic outlines of your house and property lines and any other softscape or hardscape that won't be changed. Now, shift around the paper over the plan that you wish to adapt, tracing the planting bed or walkway in your preferred new location. Examples of how to make specific adjustments are described below.

Adjusting for Different Lot Sizes and Shapes

Your property may be a bit longer, a bit narrower, or a bit larger than the average-sized properties for which these designs are created. To get a proper fit, a few easy adjustments can be made. For example, study the designs for the traditional Cape Cod on page 40 and the gambrel-roof Colonial on page 46. If you intend to use one of these basic designs on a larger property, there are several options available. Where the property line is further to the left, keep the planting bed at the left the same size, and simply redraw it along the edge of the property line, making up for the difference by increasing the size of the lawn. The bed itself could be made slightly deeper, but not so deep that it would be hard to maintain or would be out of scale to the rest of the design. Widening the lawn area instead of increasing the number of shrubs is also a more economical approach to adjusting the design. To use either of these designs on a much larger property, you might choose to keep the planting beds just about where they are shown in the plan and use a backdrop of tall evergreen trees for additional privacy.

Moving a planting bed over to the left or right to accommodate a larger property often leaves a gap in the planting. Fill this gap in at a suitable point, such as where it curves around toward the house, by adding more plants of the same type; for example, plant five yews instead of three. Where even larger areas need to be filled in, repeat an entire group of plantings, which might include another tree of the same type along with additional shrubs and ground cover.

A professional designer does not regard the lawn area as a catchall to solve leftover space, and neither should you. The size and shape of the lawns on these plans represents an important part of the overall design. The lawn is used as a sculptural element; it guides views and circulation around the property. Maintain the shape of the lawn and its relationship with the rest of the plantings as much as possible when making adjustments in scale. This may mean enlarging island beds or including an additional tree or two to maintain balance on a larger property; conversely, on a smaller property you might wish to scale down the size of island beds and remove one or more trees from a group.

When lawn areas as specified on these plans need to be reduced in size, keep in mind that a lawn area that is less than 6 to 8 feet wide serves little design purpose and is difficult to maintain. In this instance, substitute ground cover or paving for the lawn. Large trees and shrubs that border a lawn area will be out of proportion if the size of the lawn is greatly reduced. When this occurs, substitute smaller trees and shrubs in place of the larger ones to scale down that entire portion of the design. Conversely, increasing the size of the lawn significantly would call for larger trees and shrubs at its perimeter.

The size of an entry court can be adjusted when necessary to make a design smaller. For example, the entry court at the French Provincial estate house (p. 66) can be made less deep and the plantings around the sides adjusted by eliminating one grouping of the repeating pattern of trees and shrubs on the interior of the wall. The plantings on the outside of the wall can be shortened in the same way. Conversely, the entry court could be made longer or wider by adding another of the groupings of trees and shrubs to its perimeter as long as the symmetry of the design is maintained and vehicular circulation is not restricted.

It is not difficult to adjust a design when the space between the house and the property line is not as great as indicated on the plan. Consider the design for the New England barn-style house (p. 60). If the distance to the right side of the

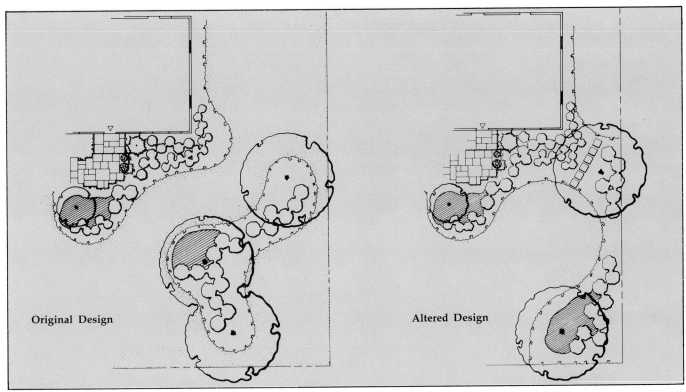

If the size of your property is smaller than that indicated on the plot plan, it is an easy matter to adapt the design to fit your lot. The original design (left) employs three trees and an island bed to the side of the yard. The altered design (right) uses the same plants but rearranges them to fit the smaller space by eliminating one of the trees and some of the shrubs and extending the ground cover bed into an appealing arc.

property line is smaller than on the plan, include only one or two trees with its underplantings instead of three, and make the lawn area smaller as necessary. If this leaves a lawn area on the side of the house that is only a few feet wide, replace the lawn in this section with ground cover. (See illustration.)

You will note throughout this book that professional designers usually work with odd numbers. You may see one specimen tree, or a planting of three, five, or seven shrubs, but you will rarely see two, four, or six of a particular plant. When making adjustments, follow professional design techniques and try to work with odd numbers.

Adjusting for a Different House Layout

Are you saying "That's my house—almost"? Perhaps the layout of your house resembles one that appears in this book, but with some minor differences that will affect the landscape design. For example, you may be landscaping a basic ranch house similar to the one on page 90, but somewhat longer. This can be easily accommodated by extending the length of the paving and the foundation shrubs across the front of the house. Nothing else needs to be done to retain the

professionally designed look.

Or, with the same house, you might have a situation where the house does not have the slight L configuration as shown on the plan. Here, the vine on the wall of the L would be eliminated, and the shrub planting and seasonal-color bed shifted back toward the house. The ornamental tree can be located in the same area, far enough away from the house so its branches will not rub against the walls of the house or the roof, or interfere with the entry.

You might have a traditional split-level such as the one on page 96, but yours is longer across the front, or has a mother-daughter addition built onto it. If this is the case, leave the large shrub planting at the corner as it is indicated, and increase the number of smaller shrubs across the front. If the addition makes the front of the house twice as large as shown on the plan, the grouping of small and large shrubs can be repeated, or a tree of the same type as planted on the left corner can be planted on the right corner for balance.

If your house is a mirror-image of one shown here, the solution is simple: trace the plot plan and then flip the paper over. *Voilá,* you have an instant landscape plan.

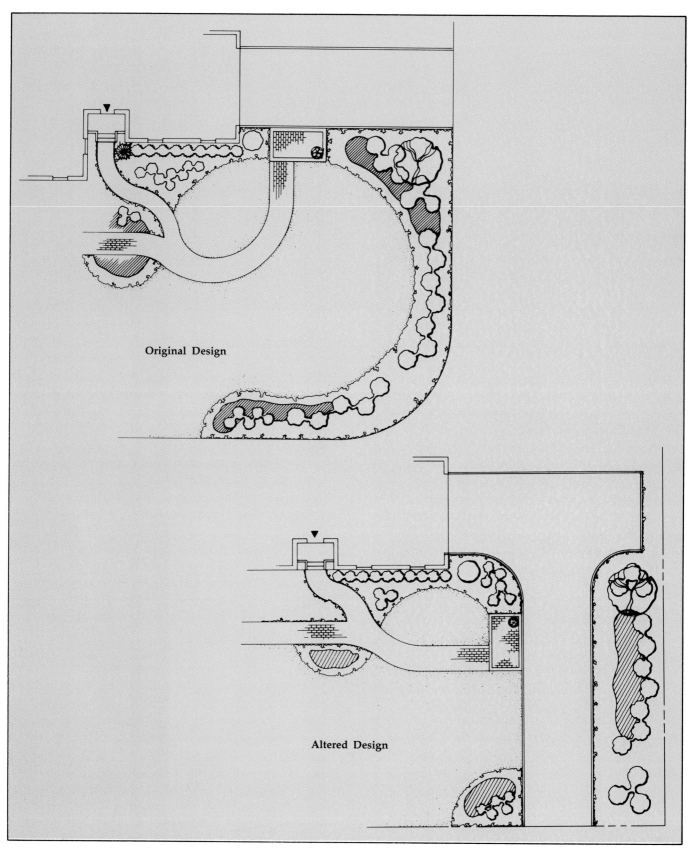

Original Design

Altered Design

A plan designed for a corner lot and a recessed garage can be easily adapted to fit an interior lot and a house with a flush garage. The original design (top) shows the driveway extending to the side street, with plantings camouflaging the garage entrance and driveway. The altered design (bottom) uses the same plants and bed designs in slightly different shapes and positions to accommodate a garage that is flush with the front of the house and a driveway that swings forward to meet the street.

158

Garages in the house plans in this book are often set forward or behind the rest of the house. Some repositioning is all that is needed if your garage is flush with the front of the house. Study the plan for the Williamsburg cape (p. 42) where the garage is recessed. If it were flush, the entire planting in front of the garage could be moved forward, adjusting the position of the walk with it. The planting area in front of the garage could be slightly scaled down, and the lawn area could be reduced, or eliminated if it is too small. If it is eliminated, fill in the area by extending the ground cover. This is also an excellent place to consider placing seasonal flowers. (The illustration on page 158 shows this plan adapted to an interior lot with a flush garage.)

Conversely, if the plan shows a garage that is extended in front of the line of the main house, but the garage you are dealing with is flush or recessed, realign the plantings backward and extend the lawn or ground cover as desired.

Whenever an adjustment is made for a different house layout, remember that the professional designer used certain principles when creating the landscape plan. Any adjustments you make must be done with those principles in mind. For example, the planting beds around the right wing of the sprawling ranch house on page 94 are balanced by the driveway and parking court on the left wing. Any changes to one side will need balancing changes on the other side. Remember too that balance does not necessarily dictate symmetry. If you are not sure how to accomplish this, it would be best to consult a professional designer.

Adjusting for Corner or Interior Lots

Some designs in this book, such as the raised-porch farmhouse (p. 58) and the Williamsburg cape (p. 42), are designed for corner lots where the driveway enters the garage from a side street. If you are following one of these designs but your house is located in the middle of the block, all you need do is move things around a little bit. Swing the driveway toward the front and trace the shrub borders and lawn into a workable position. (See illustration on opposite page for an adaptation of the Williamsburg cape.)

With the raised-porch farmhouse, redraw the driveway so it enters from the main street and swings into the garage on the outside of the trees. If space does not permit this, locate the driveway through the lawn area, shifting the trees as necessary, and eliminating the tree at the front and the shrubs at the back where the new driveway will be. The contour of the lawn that will be adjacent to the driveway will need to be straightened out or replaced with ground cover so you are not left with small patches of grass. The same principle can be followed with the Elizabethan Tudor (p. 78), if it is not on a corner, by adjusting the location of the driveway and the plantings as necessary to serve an interior lot.

The country-style farmhouse on page 54 can be adjusted for a corner lot by relocating the driveway or by adding a second curb-cut on the side street. To add to the unity, a picket fence and stone piers that match those situated at the entrance to the driveway can be repeated and possibly extended at the corner. The large trees at the left of the property line can be eliminated or replaced with smaller shrubs unless their function is to provide screening. Depending on your local laws, you might have to substitute lower plantings at the corner.

A border planting of tall evergreens and colorful flowering trees and shrubs along a corner property provides privacy from the street.

Shrub borders and decorative fences or walls can also be added to any plan to provide extra privacy on a corner property. You can extend a foundation planting over to and along the property line, or erect a wall or fence along the property border, choosing a material that matches the character of the house.

Adjusting Driveway Shape

Several of the homes in this book feature circular driveways, such as the Georgian manor on page 68, and the grand-portico Georgian on p. 70. If space does not permit a circular driveway, or if local regulations prohibit a second curb-cut, the circular portion of the driveway can be narrowed into a walkway from the main driveway to the house, and the plantings moved forward. The space for the driveway can also be converted into a lawn area. Or the driveway can end near the front door, as in the design on page 114, which provides an ideal space for guest parking.

Circular driveways, often elegant and formal-looking, are not necessarily suited only to grandiose houses—they can fit more modest houses as well. For example, look at the plan for the Tudor one-story (p. 80). The property is small, yet the circular driveway effectively enhances the design and traffic flow without being out of proportion to the home or property.

If your existing driveway has a different configuration from the one on the plan, you can make compromises in the landscape design rather than alter the driveway if the latter is too costly. For example, if the driveway of the traditional Cape Cod on page 40 were straight instead of curved, eliminate the tree situated at the left of the driveway entrance and increase the size of the planting bed to the right of the driveway. Shift the right-hand tree to the left to keep it adjacent to the driveway.

Your driveway might pose the problem of being in a different location from the one on the plan. The garage of the southern Colonial (p. 52) faces the side of the property. If it faced the front, as is shown in the classic New England Colonial on page 50, the landscape design can be manipulated a bit. Study the two plans side by side to see how the treatment differs. It may be as simple as eliminating the plantings directly in front of the garage where the driveway will be and making minor adjustments in the placement of the trees so that they do not overhang the driveway enough to interfere with cars.

ADJUSTING FOR GRADING AND DRAINAGE

Sometimes it seems that the grass really is greener on the other side. Those people who live where the land is flat find it dull and uninteresting, and they go out of their way to create height and contours in the garden. Those who live on sloped property often try to flatten it out so they can play volleyball or avoid the problem of getting up the driveway when it is covered with ice and snow.

Even property that seems flat may not really be perfectly flat. Almost every property has some grade (slope) or dips and rises. The "grade" of a property should not be confused with "grading," which is the term used to describe changing the

The grade in this garden was made less steep by adding a retaining wall and steps to create two levels, sparing the apple tree's roots from suffocation.

existing slope. You should assess the variations in grade existing on your property and consider any needed or desired grade changes before finalizing your landscape design.

Grading needs may be minimal or extensive. You may need to flatten an area for a patio or a ground-level deck. Your lawn may need grading so that it will slope evenly away from the house toward the street. Some plans call for adding mounds of earth, known as berms, for effectively screening a view or adding interesting height on an otherwise flat property. Changes of grade can also be used to separate one activity area of the landscape from another.

The grade should not be changed around the drip line of a large tree because this can either expose or bury the roots, eventually killing the tree. If it becomes necessary to raise the grade around an existing tree, construct a well around the tree to avoid burying the roots.

Drainage and Soil Considerations

Grading and drainage are interdependent. It is best to grade your property so that water will drain away from structures and will not collect in beds, borders, and paved areas. Proper grading prevents having to pump water out of the basement after heavy rains. It will eliminate low areas where water and snow collect rather than draining away properly. Water must quickly drain from paved areas so the pavement does not become icy, creating a safety hazard, or remain unusable for hours after a rain storm.

Paved areas should maintain a minimum pitch of ¼ inch per foot. If located next to the house, a patio should slope slightly away from the structure. In instances where a patio is located in a lower area of the landscape, where water cannot run off because a wall or higher ground surrounds the paving, drains and drain pipes will be necessary to channel water away. This should be discussed with a professional designer to ensure a practical and economical solution.

It is wise to know how well your soil drains before planning on grade changes. Professionals have a simple way to test drainage, which you can do yourself. Dig a hole 3 feet deep and fill it with water. Let it drain for a day and fill it again. If it is empty or less than one-third full by the next day, there are no drainage problems. If it is still two-thirds or more full, drainage problems are severe and drainage pipes or tiles may need to be installed. If the hole is between one-third and two-thirds full, you may be able to correct the drainage problems by amending the soil.

Consider your soil structure. Will changing the grade expose areas with poor soil and bury good topsoil? It may be necessary when changing grade to do it in a two-step process. The topsoil may need to be removed and retained, the grading done, and the topsoil replaced. You may also need to purchase soil to complete a grading project, which will affect your budget. Soil is expensive, so if possible fill in low areas of your property by moving soil into it from a higher level.

Any soil that is purchased should be as close as possible in texture and composition to the existing soil. Placing a fast-draining soil over a heavy, poor-draining soil will cause subsurface drainage problems that could drown plants growing above. Removing trees and shrubs when changing the grade may also alter the drainage pattern, sometimes for the better, sometimes not.

Consultation with the utility companies may be necessary to determine the location of underground pipes and cables. The feasibility of changes in grade may be determined by whether pipes and cables will be exposed or make access to them or their meters impossible by the grade change.

You cannot just move soil around the garden or pave large areas without thinking of the consequences. Before attempting any major changes of grade or paving large areas near the house, consult with a professional to ensure that your plan

Retaining walls look most appealing when planted with cascading plants, such as moss phlox and candytuft.

won't cause drainage problems. A professional can help you to determine whether some type of drainage tiles or pipes need to be installed, or how to change the grade to avoid potential problems.

If your property is relatively flat and the soil is naturally fast-draining, you will not need to be too concerned about drainage. Follow the principles already outlined for changing grade, ensuring that any new structures or paved areas have proper drainage. If, on the other hand, heavy soil dictates drainage problems, consult with a professional regarding the installation of drainage pipes.

Adjusting Plans to Sloped Property

The landscapes illustrated in chapters 2 and 3 were created for relatively flat pieces of property or for properties with a slight slope away from the house. If your property is more sloped, you can adjust many of these plans to fit by regrading or working with the existing terrain and adding a series of steps and landings or even retaining walls. However, any more than a slight change of grade may require the services of a professional designer to ensure that the walls and steps are located where they best fit the contour of the land.

Retaining walls are often used by professional designers to create several flat levels out of steeply sloped ground. Not only are the walls functional, they look attractive too. Build walls out of landscape timbers, bricks, or stones that match your home's architecture. You can regrade and incorporate retaining walls into many of the designs shown here using the same basic plot plan. If the retaining wall intersects a walkway, include steps and perhaps a landing in the walk to accommodate the change in levels. When planning a retaining wall, include drainage pipes at the base of the wall to prevent water buildup behind the wall.

INSTALLING THE LANDSCAPE

Whether you plant the shrubs and trees and construct the driveway, walkways, and patio yourself or hire a contractor to do all or part of the work, certain facts ought to be kept in mind.

Construction Regulations

Many communities have rules that may affect how you install your landscape. It is important in the design process to discover and understand any regulations regarding construction and planting. Town officials normally enact such rules for good reasons, whether they be safety precautions, to ensure a pleasing community appearance, or to guarantee that new construction is properly designed and executed. It is your responsibility to find out if any regulations govern your landscape design.

If you are planning to install new plants only, you probably will not need a permit, but it is worth checking. For safety, shrubs at the property line may have height restrictions if they block the view of cars entering an intersection. For aesthetic reasons, there are often height restrictions for fences.

Local laws usually require that swimming pools be enclosed by walls or fences. Here, a low wall borders the patio, but the tall security wall is softened with foreground plantings.

Concrete or aggregate is the favored pavement choice in hot climates, where other materials, such as asphalt, heat up excessively.

Landscape design: Margaret West

Landscape design: John Harlow, Jr.

Building permits are often needed for permanent structures such as decks; raised decks may need to be a certain distance from the property line unless a variance is secured. It may be a requirement that any construction done on your property not block the view or be displeasing to a neighbor. Swimming pools almost always require enclosure by a fence to prevent small children from accidentally wandering into the area. The building inspector may need to sign off on construction at different stages of the work.

Some communities require that construction materials fit the style of the neighborhood in order to retain a certain flavor or charm. Others may not allow trees to be planted in the strip between the sidewalk and the street, or they may not allow you to cut down trees without permission. Permits are often required to change curbcuts and the location of the driveway. It is also possible that electrical and plumbing work must be done by a licensed contractor.

If you are doing deep digging, the utility company may need to be consulted to determine where underground pipes and cables are located. If you will be installing a new driveway, check with the utility company to make sure you are not covering existing pipes and cables. Also, be sure you know where sewer pipes and cesspools are located. Some utility companies will not let you plant a tree that will grow into overhead electrical or telephone lines. This may sound like a lot of "do's and don'ts," but it is better to know in advance than be forced later to take down a fence or to redo your landscape.

Find out in advance if you need a building permit and what type of drawings are needed to complete your landscape construction. Some communities require that plans have an architect's stamp on them before permits will be issued for construction. If your community is one of these, you can hire an architect to review and approve your plan or one of the plans purchased through this book. This will be more economical than having the architect redraw the entire plan.

Plant Selection

The final step in the design process is the selection of plants to carry out your design. If you order one of the blueprint sets from this book, it comes with a list of plants coded to the landscape design and selected to perform well in your region. Each plan is available with customized plant lists for up to eight regions, with regional plant selection based on a number of climatic factors, including winter hardiness, summer temperatures, and drought resistance. Plants will also match the exposure on the plan and provide interest and beauty throughout the year. Most plans include plants that bloom in spring, summer, and fall and others with beautiful fall foliage or evergreen leaves.

You can, however, choose the plants to carry out the design yourself. If you are an avid gardener, you probably already know which plants perform well in your part of the country. You can plant your favorites, selecting trees and shrubs for specimen use or mass planting as indicated on the plan. If you need help, a high-quality local nursery is a good source of information. Browsing through several garden books, such as those published by Ortho or HPBooks, can provide inspiration as well as solid information about particular species of landscape plants.

Begin your selection by making a list of plants that are hardy in your area. Then match them to your specific needs for sun or shade, soil type, and drought- or heat-resistance. When this list is finalized, choose those plants that best meet your design needs for creating shade or screening, or for providing a particular plant shape, flower color, texture, or season of bloom. When selecting plants and positioning them, also keep in mind their mature size and shape. How many people do you know who planted shrubs in front of the house, only to discover ten years later that they dwarfed the house and had to be removed?

Selecting Paving

Selection of paving materials will vary with the climate. The landscape blueprints include suggested paving materials and amounts needed to carry out the design. You may choose to substitute a similar locally available stone for the sake of economy. Concrete is the most flexible paving material, followed by brick. Bluestone and flagstone are usually not used in hot climates because of the heat the stones give off, preventing you from running outside in summer in your bare feet. In these areas, aggregate is more often used. On the other hand, concrete pavers are not always wise in very cold climates, because the freezing and thawing that occurs during winter can heave them from the ground.

Color Your Plans

When you are satisfied with your design, make four copies of the plan, borrow your children's crayons or Magic Markers, and color the four

These beautiful summer-flowering shrubs have reached their mature heights and will never grow too large for their setting.

plans, one for each season. Show the color of the blossoms in the appropriate season of bloom. In the other seasons use green for foliage or brown for winter when the plant is leafless. If a plant is evergreen it should be colored green whenever it is not in bloom. If a deciduous plant develops notable fall foliage or bright berries, color it the appropriate color in the fall plan. While flowers may be the primary source of color, this coloring exercise will point out how beautiful the red, gold, and orange tones of autumn can be, that some colorful berries remain all winter, and that evergreen foliage provides year-round interest. If after coloring all four plans you find the colors are not harmonious, or that one season lacks color accent, you can choose other more complementary plants.

Exposure Considerations

All the plans in this book have been marked with a north arrow so you can determine the exposure that the landscape will receive. You did this on your own plan for the same reason, to determine exposure and make final plant selections based on sun or shade conditions. If you have ordered a blueprint set for one of the designs in this book and are adapting that plan for a different exposure, some adjustments in plant material might need to be made.

Usually foundation plants chosen for the east, west, and south side of a building can be interchanged, as long as the site isn't shaded all day by trees. The north side of a building usually receives little direct sun and needs to be landscaped with plants chosen for their ability to tolerate shade. The south-facing side of a building

often receives all-day sun, requiring heat-tolerant plants. It's best not to use those plants listed for the south side on the north side and vice versa. Instead, rework the plant selection for that exposure. Consult reference books, your county agent, or your nursery for suggested substitutions.

Usually the plant recommendations for shrub borders, island beds, and ornamental or shade trees are not influenced by exposure. These are planted out in the open, away from the shadow of the house and will receive the proper amount of sunlight if planted as the plan indicates.

Where your property includes large shade trees that you may not wish to remove, you can follow many of these landscape designs by making plant substitutions. Make adjustments by substituting a shade-tolerant ground cover for lawn, or by using shade-tolerant shrubs where sun-loving ones were indicated. Many flowering perennials and ferns thrive in the shade, and these can be substituted for those that prefer sun.

Scheduling

Have you ever said to yourself, "Gee, I didn't think it would take that long"? If you have never installed a landscape before, you will probably be surprised to find that it takes longer than you thought. This will be especially true if you try to get the job done after work or on Saturday afternoons. So, once your plans are completed, and before you start the installation, make a workable schedule.

First, obtain any necessary permits, especially if you need a variance, because securing one can take time. Some permits expire if work is not completed within a certain time period, and you would need to apply for a second permit if you do not finish on time.

Installing a landscape involves several steps. First is site preparation, which includes demolition, grading, and drainage. Next, the hardscape is constructed, including patios, decks, walkways, driveways, walls, and fences. Shrubs and trees go in next, followed by irrigation and lighting systems, if any, and finally by ground covers, lawn, and perennials. Then the patio furniture can be set out and the landscape is ready to be enjoyed.

Landscape plants are best transplanted in spring or fall in most climates. At these times of year, the weather is cool and rainfall plentiful. If you are going to plant in the fall, plan to have the job finished well before the ground freezes, and mulch the soil around small plants to prevent their roots from being heaved out of the ground. This could be as much as two months after the first actual frost, depending on location.

Container-grown and balled-and-burlaped landscape plants can be successfully planted in summer if given extra care. Since summer often subjects plants to heat stress and drought conditions, extra care will be needed. Lawns are best seeded in spring or fall—summer seeding rarely succeeds. Sod can be laid down in spring, summer, or fall, as long as it is cared for properly.

Schedule the work in a logical sequence. You might wish to begin installing the hardscape in spring or summer and finish the planting in fall. Electrical cables and irrigation pipes obviously need to be installed before the lawn. Pools cannot be used comfortably until walkways, paving, and fences are in place. You obviously would not plant first and build the patio later. Leave enough time to complete all work before it gets too cold in the fall to work outside.

One of the major activities at a large landscape contracting office is scheduling. You need to do this on a smaller scale. Your schedule should include projected and feasible starting and completion dates for each phase of the project. In northern areas, you will have to work around the weather, as asphalt and concrete cannot be laid in the winter, nor can planting be done once the ground freezes. Make a list of the supplies you will need, and order them to allow enough time for delivery but not so far in advance that you will have storage problems.

If you are doing the work yourself, block out dates you cannot work because of vacation and other commitments. Make arrangements with subcontractors as early as possible. You know how frustrating it is to try to get someone to come to your house to do work, only to be told they will not be available for weeks or months. Delays like that could set you back a year.

PREPARING THE SITE

You do not put in new carpeting before you take out the old, and neither can you start your new landscape until the floors are bare, so to speak. The first thing you need to do is clear away all existing structures and plants that are not being retained. If this will be an excessive amount of debris, plan first on some method of disposing of it. You may need to rent a dumpster or hire a carting company to remove a large amount of wood and plants.

If the renovation is extensive and you are planning on doing it in stages, clear away only the area that will be immediately worked on. Removing large numbers of trees or shrubs or a large grassed area may cause runoff and erosion problems until the area is replanted, and you will wind up tracking mud into the house.

If you are redoing a fence, deck, or other wooden structure, you will have to take the old one apart first, so keep a woodpile in your disposal plans. And be careful not to injure yourself on the nails, even if your tetanus booster is up to date. Old concrete walkways and patios will have to be broken up with a sledge hammer or a jackhammer into pieces small enough to be easily carted away. Fieldstones, bluestones, bricks, and other paving materials can be saved and reused if they are carefully removed and stored.

After all the existing features have been removed, take one last look at your property and compare it to your plan. The absence of a large tree or structure may change your thoughts about the best place for your new patio, deck, or entry garden. You may want to make a few last-minute changes.

Transplanting and Removing Shrubs

In many cases, existing shrubs can be dug up and transplanted from inappropriate sites into better sites in the new landscape. If you are moving and transplanting shrubs from one area of your property to another, it is easier if the area to which they will be moved is readied first. Then you can dig up the shrubs and replant them right away. Otherwise, you have the problem of storing and caring for the plants, and perhaps tripping over

Shrubs growing where they are not wanted can be dug up and moved. A: First root prune the plant several months before digging. B: Lift the rootball with a board used as a lever. C: Wrap the rootball in burlap to protect it during moving. D: Slide a heavy plant on a board set on rollers.

them, instead of spending your time in a productive way.

It is usually possible to remove shrubs yourself, although you can hire a professional, or even a few high school students looking for extra money, if the shrubs are large or if you feel you have better things to do with your time. If the shrubs are to be discarded, they can be dug up in their entirety or cut away in pieces. The stems can be bundled and placed for trash collection or taken to the local dump. Roots can be removed or left in place; again, it depends on what you plan to put in where the shrubs had been planted.

It is easier to remove deciduous shrubs (with the possible exception of the roots) during the winter when there is no foliage on them, as there is less debris to discard. This also leaves time during warmer weather to perform those tasks that cannot be done during the winter. Deciduous shrubs are also best moved when they are dormant and have no foliage. This can be done in early spring, as soon as the ground can be worked, or in late fall. Although they should still be pruned back by about one-third to compensate for root loss and damage, shrubs will undergo less transplanting shock if they have no foliage.

When shrubs are being transplanted, they must be dug with care to preserve as much of the roots as possible. To ensure greater success, root prune the shrubs with a spading fork several months before digging them up, if scheduling allows. This encourages new roots to develop in a more confined ball, which is easier to dig and move. When deciduous shrubs are moved while in full leaf, use extra care to dig up the roots intact.

Water the roots and mist the foliage often after transplanting until the plant becomes established.

Evergreens should be moved in mid-spring or early fall so roots have a chance to grow and become established while weather is most favorable. Although you can move a shrub during high summer heat, it will take a lot of TLC to keep it alive—and you have a good chance of saying "Sayonara" the following year, if you don't kill it immediately. If the shrub is in flower when it is moved, removing the flowers will aid it to grow roots and become established more quickly.

When moving a shrub, have the new planting hole already dug so the shrub will be out of the ground for as short a time as possible. Lift the roots with a shovel or spade and wrap them in burlap or plastic to protect them and keep the soil from falling off during moving. If shrubs cannot be planted immediately, the roots must be enclosed and tied in burlap or placed in a container and the plant kept out of sun and wind until it can be planted.

Large trees should be removed by a nursery or a professional arborist, who will haul away the wood unless you want it for firewood. The arborist can also turn much of the wood into wood chips, which you can use for a decorative landscape mulch. Before you keep any for firewood, be sure it is a type of wood that burns well, and consider how long it will need to be cured before it can be burned. You may or may not have the room to store it. The stump may be yanked out or left in place and ground to the soil level, depending on what need you have for the spot. If a tree is being removed to build a deck, the stump can be left in place. Some trees will resprout if the roots are left in the ground; these can be pruned away or treated with an herbicide. Be careful when using an herbicide not to spray any on plants that are left in the landscape.

Nurseries or professional arborists are also capable of moving large trees with specialized equipment. Consult with them first as to cost, the value of the tree, and whether or not the tree is in good health. It would be ridiculous to spend a lot of money to move a valueless tree such as a silver maple, or a tree whose life expectancy is too short.

Removing Lawn

There are several ways to remove an existing lawn where new beds and borders, walkways, or a patio will go. The lawn can be stripped away just below the roots with a spade, or you can rent a power sod cutter. Sod that is stripped off can be saved and transplanted where it is needed. If you have no need for the sod, use it as fill or add it to the compost pile. When building a ground-level deck, don't bother removing the lawn under it, because the grass will soon die for lack of light. Lawns can also be killed with herbicides such as glyphosate, but be careful not to spray these chemicals accidentally on desirable plants, or you will kill them too.

If a lawn is being removed and a new lawn being installed in the same area, take advantage of the situation and improve the soil. Both seeded and sodded lawns will be healthier and need less care for years to come if the soil has been improved. Till organic matter into the soil, level the ground, and then roll it after seeding or sodding. Keep seed and sod moist until well established.

Transferring Your Plan

Once the area to be landscaped has been cleared, transfer your plan to your property. Using a measuring tape, accurately measure the location of all new walkways, structures, and plants. Place markers at the various points of major construction and planting—the location of walkways, entry court, patio, deck, pool. Mark the sites of major trees and the outline of planting beds and borders. You can use wooden or metal stakes, and run strings between them to show clearly where everything will be located. A garden hose or clothesline works well to outline beds and borders.

Stand on the site of the proposed deck and double-check its location and the views. Note if trees are properly located. Walk from the driveway to the various doors to make sure the walkways are in the most logical place. Walk out to the street and see what a first-time visitor will see. Go inside, and look at your landscape from the living room or family room. When you are pleased with all aspects of the design, then you can start to put your plan in action.

PLANTING TIME

Even though fall is a perfect planting time, it is unlikely that you can go to a garden center or nursery in the fall and select exactly what you want. Many plants may be sold out by then. On the other hand, you won't want to take delivery of trees and shrubs in the spring if you cannot plant them until fall. Follow the procedure used by professional contractors when selecting plants. After you have completed your plant list, visit nursery dealers and select the plants needed for your landscape. You may be able to deal directly with a grower and get wholesale prices, if there is one in your area and if you are buying a large quantity. Purchase the plants and have them tagged "Sold." Then, when the ground is prepared and you are ready to plant, the delivery can be made.

Professional landscapers know that the soil must be well prepared before planting to ensure the health and longevity of expensive landscape plants. You should do the same thing to ensure that your new landscape will thrive.

When starting a new planting bed where lawn is growing, first strip off the sod with a spade, then turn over the soil. This prevents the grass from returning as weeds.

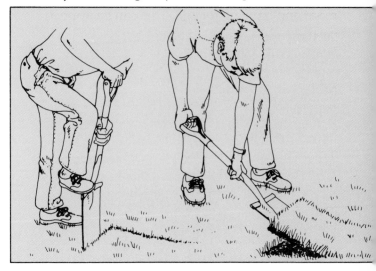

The best way to start is with a soil test. This can be done by your County Extension Service or, for a more detailed analysis, by a soil-testing lab. The analysis will report on the structure of your soil, its pH, and its fertility. This will aid you in knowing what soil amendments are necessary, if the pH is too low or too high, and what types of soil amendments and fertilizers are needed.

The next thing is to ensure that the soil can be worked. If soil is turned over too early in spring, when it is still wet, the clay particles may compact and form hard lumps that will interfere with drainage. Dry soil also can be difficult to work, repelling your shovel and becoming dusty.

To test your soil for workability, take a handful of it and squeeze it hard. It should break apart easily. If the soil forms a solid mass, it is too wet. Allow it to dry and test again. If it totally crumbles in your hand, the soil is too dry. Water it well and try again the next day.

Your soil should have already been tested for drainage (see p. 161). Depending on the severity of the problem, if you have one, you may have already installed drainage pipes, or you may be able to correct the drainage at this point.

Almost all garden soils benefit from the addition of organic matter, which improves drainage and aeration, and increases biological activity in the soil. Organic matter may be compost, peat moss, leaf mold, rotted manure, or dried grass clippings. Depending upon the condition of the soil, spread 2 to 6 inches of organic matter across the top of the bed and work it into the soil, using a spade or power equipment, to a depth of at least 12 inches, preferably more.

All-purpose fertilizer such as 5-10-5 or 10-10-10 should be worked into the soil before planting. If your soil analysis showed that the soil was deficient in one or more major or trace elements, the amount and type of fertilizer can be adjusted to compensate for this. Plants also benefit from having a good supply of phosphorous in the soil at root level, so professionals recommend adding superphosphate at planting time.

Fertilizer should be spread over the soil and worked in thoroughly. This can be done at the same time that organic materials are added. It is important that fertilizer not come into direct contact with roots, as this can damage them, so complete mixing is necessary.

If soil pH needs to be altered, the adjustments must be made several weeks before any fertilizer is added. Sulfur is used to lower alkaline pH, and lime is used to raise acidic pH. Dolomitic lime is recommended because it contains trace amounts of magnesium, necessary for plant growth. Agricultural lime can be used; it can burn roots, however, so it must be used in advance of planting.

Most plants don't grow well in heavy soil. To avoid this disappointment where soil is heavy, you can include several other amendments in addition to organic matter to lighten the soil and improve its drainage. These include perlite, vermiculite, and coarse sand. Gypsum will also work to condition the soil. It contains calcium, as lime does, but will not alter the pH the way lime will.

Planting Trees and Shrubs

Plants for the landscape are available as bare-root, balled-and-burlaped (B&B), or containerized plants. Bare-root plants were dug from the nursery where they were grown and the soil removed from the roots. They are perishable and should be planted while still dormant. Balled-and-burlaped plants were dug from the nursery, severing some roots, and their rootballs wrapped with burlap for protection. As long as the roots are kept moist, the plants suffer little stress. Containerized plants were usually grown right in the container. Their rootballs are completely intact and can be transplanted with little or no shock. However, if the plant has grown too large for the container, the roots may be tangled and growing in circles, preventing the plant from establishing itself in the garden.

Before planting a bare-root plant, trim off any broken, damaged, or extremely long roots and soak the plant overnight in a bucket of water to restore any moisture that might have been lost. To plant a bare-root tree or shrub, dig a hole in the prepared planting bed large enough to accommodate the roots without crowding them. Make a cone-shaped mound of soil in the bottom of the hole, and spread the roots evenly around the mound so that the plant is at the same depth at which it had been grown. Fill the hole halfway with soil, tamp it down gently, and fill the hole with water. After the water has drained, fill the hole completely with soil.

To plant a B&B or a containerized tree or shrub, dig a hole that is several inches wider on all sides and slightly deeper than the root mass of the plant. Place enough improved soil in the bottom of the hole to enable the plant to rest at the same depth at which it was grown.

For a B&B plant, place the plant in the hole with

Balled-and-burlaped shrubs are easy to plant. Top left: Dig a hole larger and wider than the rootball. Improve the backfill by mixing in peat or compost, returning some soil to the bottom of the hole. Top right: Place the plant in the hole so it is level with the soil surface. Bottom left: Fold back the burlap, fill the hole part way and water. Bottom right: Fill hole to the top, gently press the soil in place, then form a ring of soil over the rootball to hold water.

A tree should be staked only if it cannot stand upright by itself. Tie the trunk loosely to 2 or 3 stakes driven alongside the rootball.

the burlap intact. Rotate the plant so that its best side faces forward, and make sure it is standing straight in the hole. Then untie the strings that hold the burlap in place and pull the burlap away from the trunk, exposing about one-third of the rootball. Bury the burlap in the backfill; in time, it will disintegrate. Some B&B plants have a plastic sheeting over the burlap; although the burlap can remain, the plastic must come off. Backfill the hole halfway with soil and fill the hole with water; after the water drains, fill the hole to the top with soil.

Containerized plants cannot survive in a metal or a plastic can for very long, but it is surprising how many people fail to remove the plants from their containers before planting them. Before you remove the plant from the container, make sure the medium in the container is moist enough to hold the rootball together. If it is not, water the plant. Holding the plant by its base, turn the con-

tainer upside down and gently lift off the container. Place the plant in the hole, positioning it as you did with the B&B plants. If the roots are matted or heavily encircling the rootball, loosen them, heading them outward, before refilling the hole. Backfill halfway, water, and complete the planting as with B&B plants.

If a tree cannot stay upright by itself, it should be staked for a year to prevent it from whipping around in the wind and to keep it growing straight and tall. Trees whose trunks have been allowed to sway in the breeze actually grow stronger wood, so don't tie trees too tightly or leave them staked for years. Place two or three stakes around the tree's rootball before filling the hole. Tie the stakes to the tree with pieces of tubing, soft cloth, or other material that will not damage the trunk.

Newly planted trees and shrubs can suffer greatly from lack of water, because they do not

A

B

C

D

have an established root system that can reach deep down to bring up water from the soil. Make a shallow ring of soil over the rootball of all new plants to hold water and direct it into the root zone until the plant is well rooted and growing.

Planting Ground Covers and Lawns

Ground covers are often sold in flats or packs, the same way most flowering annuals are sold. Space them at equal distances in the area to be covered. For quick coverage, five pachysandra, three vinca (myrtle), three English ivy, or three ajuga are used for every square foot. For the sake of economy, you can use fewer plants, but complete coverage will take longer.

Before planting, make sure both the bed and the flats are well watered. Dig a hole slightly larger than the rootball in the prepared planting bed, carefully separate the plants from the flats by cutting apart individual plants, if need be. Put them in place and gently tamp the soil around them and then water gently. Keep the plants moist until established.

New lawns are usually started by seeding or sodding. A sod lawn is most expensive but provides instant gratification. A seeded lawn can be just as picture perfect and perhaps even healthier, but it takes longer before it looks good and erosion can be a problem until the grass fills in. Whether seeding or sodding, the choice of grass variety depends upon your climate and particular site. There are many different species and improved varieties available, making the choice confusing. Mixes of different species usually perform best. A knowledgeable nurseryman or your county agent can advise you about which variety or mix will thrive on your particular site.

You can install sod yourself or have it done professionally. Sod comes in several standard widths based on the size of the cutting tool, but the thickness of the sod should be between 1/2 and 1 inch—thicker pieces may not establish well. Sod is often stacked or rolled but should not be kept this way for more than twenty-four hours

A handy do-it-yourselfer can put down a sod lawn. A: Unstack sod and keep it shaded and moist until you need it. B: Begin by laying the sod along the longest straight edge of the lawn space, butting the ends together. C: Lay subsequent rows in a staggered bricklike pattern, using a board to support your weight so the sod pieces will stay in place. D: Lastly, go over the sod with a roller to press the roots into the soil.

because heat buildup can injure the grass. After delivery, unroll or unstack pieces of sod and lay them out in the shade if you cannot plant them immediately. Be sure to keep them moist.

Soil should be well prepared by tilling it and enriching it with organic matter. Rake it smooth and level, and water before planting the sod. Begin by installing the sod along the longest edge of the area to be sodded. Butt the ends together, but lay the individual pieces in a staggered brick-like pattern. Cut pieces to fit curves with a serrated knife. While working, it is best to walk on a board laid across the sod to prevent the pieces from slipping.

Once the sod is laid, roll it at right angles with a heavy roller to press the roots into the soil. New sod requires watering several times a week for the first month or two. You can mow as soon as required but don't fertilize until the next season.

Seed can be sown successfully only in early spring or fall; fall sowing is usually more successful in any climate. Prepare the soil as described above. Spread seed evenly across the soil using a drop spreader. Divide the total amount of seed needed by half and spread it by walking across the area twice, making the second pass at right angles to the first. (The rate of seeding—number of pounds of seed per 100 square feet—varies with grass variety.) Roll the soil to press the seed into the soil. Water every day with a light mist, which won't wash out seed, to keep the soil surface moist until seeds germinate—in about ten days. Continue watering regularly until the grass is established.

HIRING A CONTRACTOR

The advantage of using one of the landscape plans in this book, or its blueprint and regionalized plant list, is that you have a professional design without the professional price tag. If you are a handy do-it-yourselfer, you can plant and build the entire landscape yourself; but you may choose to contract parts of the work. You may want to have a mason do the brick work or a carpenter build the deck and then plant the trees and shrubs yourself, or you may prefer to contract the entire job.

If your property has difficult aspects, such as large changes of grade or is simply too different from those in this book, you may wish to hire a landscape designer or architect to redraw the plans for you. If the project is more straightforward, you may be able to use the plans in this book with only minimal adjustment and not need another set of drawings.

A contractor will need a planting plan, and may need grading plans and irrigation plans if changes in contour are planned or if an automatic irrigation system is being installed. Grading plans show existing and proposed contours, and show how the site will drain. This is important if drainage problems exist and need to be corrected; unless you are expert in this area, a professional should be consulted. Irrigation plans show location of pipes, sprinkler heads, and control panels. Irrigation plans can be drawn by landscape architects or by irrigation consultants at the firm you have hired to install the irrigation. Construction plans will be needed for decks, patios, steps, and walls. A separate lighting plan may be needed, or lighting can be incorporated into the master plan.

There are some tasks involved in installing a new landscape that might be impossible for you to achieve yourself. These include excavation and building of an in-ground pool, or extensive changes of grade. You might want to hire a contractor to perform other tasks, even if you are capable of performing them yourself. One added advantage of hiring one general contractor is that he will coordinate all aspects of the job for you, relieving you of having to deal with separate excavators, carpenters, bricklayers, electricians, plumbers, nurseries and workers to do the planting, and a lot of headaches.

One of the best ways to engage a contractor is from the recommendation of someone who has used the firm. If you don't know anybody who has used a landscape contractor, you can consult several national professional landscape organizations located in the Washington, D.C. area, who can provide a listing of their members in your area. There is a lot to be said for a firm that is an active member of its industry organization. These organizations include the American Society of Landscape Architects, the Associated Landscape Contractors of America, and the National Landscape Association. Look also for contractors who have won awards. There is no greater recommendation than being recognized as performing superior work by a jury of your peers. There may also be a local chapter of one of these associations or a local nurserymen's association that you can contact for a listing of their members.

Once you have made up a list of reliable contractors, call them and ask them for price quotes. Get quotations from at least three firms, which will give you an accurate idea of what the job should cost and what is reasonable to pay in your area. Show the contractor your plan or one of the plans from this book and ask for a written quote to execute it exactly as it is designed. Professionals may help you adapt the plan to your property, but you will not be able to compare prices unless they are given for exactly the same job. Obtain a basic price, so you can compare apples to apples, and then a separate price to deviate from the plan as outlined. Estimates should include details as to construction materials and their quality, and the size of the plants that will be installed. Size and quality of the components of the landscape must be the same to compare prices.

Ask about scheduling—when the installation will start and how long it will take. You must be prepared for delays due to bad weather, but start with knowing what time period the contractor expects the job to take. If the landscaping must be finished by a certain date, such as for a garden party or a wedding, make sure this is understood in advance, and allow more time than is needed so you are not disappointed.

Once you have decided on a contractor, written contracts should be drawn that detail all aspects of the installation. Many of these will be the same items as outlined on the estimate. Also ask for a completion date. Many municipalities and counties require that work be completed within a certain time after the estimated completion date, or a penalty can be legally imposed.

Contracts will outline payment schedules, which generally include a down payment and then a percentage as the job is one-third done, two-thirds done, and completed. Down payments may be higher than 25 percent of the total when the contractor needs to buy a large amount of building materials in advance. Final payment should never be made until the job is completed to your satisfaction.

An extra safeguard that some communities require of a contractor when a building permit is issued is that he post a construction bond, which is returned to him after the building inspector has done his final inspection. Under no circumstances should you post the bond for the contractor. This bond is your assurance that any problems found by the inspector will be corrected. If electrical work has been done, there should also be an inspection by the local electrical board, done as much for insurance purposes as for anything else.

Keep copies of all plans, building permits, certificates of occupancy, and inspections after the work is completed. You will need them when you sell the house.

Working Within Your Budget

To determine how much your landscape will cost and whether you want to complete it in one year or spread it over several years, you will need to come up with a complete budget. Consider how the work will be done. Will you do it all yourself, do the planting yourself and hire a contractor to do the construction, or hire a contractor to do everything including construction and the supplying and installation of all plants? You may want to work out price figures for all three possibilities and compare costs.

An extensive landscape can be installed over several years to spread out the cost. Here, the pool and patio were professionally installed first to provide immediately usable outdoor living areas. Later, the homeowner will plant shrub borders and flower beds around the property's perimeter.

It's impossible to place a dollar figure on the amount of enjoyment a beautiful landscape brings to your family; however, real estate professionals estimate that landscaping can add as much as 40% to the resale value of your home.

If you choose the last possibility, you will know up front what the total landscape will cost. The other two possibilities need more work on your part. You will have to get estimates from a number of different subcontractors, such as bricklayers, electricians, and carpenters. You will have to price materials and plants.

Be aware that there are many hidden costs to consider before making a decision. To the price of plants, you must add the cost of peat moss or other soil amendments. To the cost of brick for a patio, you must add the cost of sand or concrete and the material needed for the subgrade. To determine the cost of a lawn, you must add the cost of soil amendments, lime, and fertilizer to the cost of the seed or sod. You may also need to purchase or rent tools or power equipment.

Keep in mind that landscaping adds from 10 to 40 percent to the value of your property. Will you be investing more in your property than you are likely to get back? To a great extent this depends on average real estate values in your neighborhood. Only you can decide if a high investment is worth the pleasure you will derive if your landscaping costs are out of proportion to the value of your home. However, any well-planned and executed improvement that is in keeping with the house and the neighborhood is sure to be a good investment.

If the estimated costs are higher than your budget, there are several steps you can take. The easiest is to spread the cost of the landscaping over several years, doing, for example, the entryway one year and the backyard the next. Major construction, such as deck and driveway, can be done one year, in the fall, and the major planting done the next spring so the property does not lie unplanted for too long a time. You can modify your plans by making the patio or entry court smaller to save on the cost of construction materials, or by using less-mature plants.

You can do some or all of the work yourself to save money, but remember that your time has value as well. You may not be as satisfied if the job takes several years instead of one, or does not look professional when finished. Ask yourself honestly if you are capable of doing the work yourself.

Your professional contractor can give you suggestions as to how to cut costs if you are over budget. One possibility when renovating an older landscape is to remove the landscape yourself, cutting costs in that area, and leave your budget dollars for a professional installation. Another alternative is to hire contractors to do the work you are least able to do yourself, such as electrical, plumbing, or carpentry jobs, and save costs by doing your own planting.

When it is all finished, and the time has come to invite the family and friends to relax with you and enjoy your new surroundings, you will have a new look that you can be proud of for many years to come. You won't need to invite the neighbors over to show off your new landscape, however. They will have been watching every step of your work, and probably doing so with great envy and admiration!

173

Ordering Landscape Plans

The Landscape Blueprint Package

The Landscape Blueprint Package available from Home Planners includes all the necessary information you need to lay out and install the landscape design of your choice. Professionally designed and prepared with attention to detail, these clear, easy-to-follow plans offer everything from a precise plot plan and regionalized plant and materials list to helpful sheets on installing your land-scape and determining the mature size of your plants. These plans, together with the information in Chapter 4 on adapting the design to your lot, will help you achieve professional-looking results, adding value and enjoyment to your property for years to come.

Each set of blueprints is a full 18" x 24" in size with clear, complete instructions and easy-to-read type. Consisting of six detailed sheets, these plans show how all plants and materials are put together to form an exciting landscape for your home.

Frontal Sheet. This artist's line sketch shows a typical house and all the elements of the finished front-yard landscape when plants are at or near maturity. This will give you a visual image or "picture" of the design and what you might expect your property to look like when fully landscaped.

Plan View. Drawn at 1/8" equals 1'-0", this is an aerial view of the property showing the exact placement of all landscape elements, including symbols and callouts for flowers, shrubs, ground covers, walkways, walls, gates, and other garden amenities. This sheet is the key to the design and shows you the contour, spacing, flow, and balance of all the elements in the design, as well as providing an exact "map" for laying out your property.

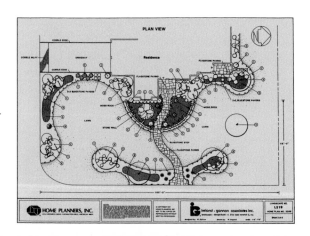

Regionalized Plant & Materials List. *Keyed to the Plan View sheet, this page lists all of the plants and materials necessary to execute the design. It gives the quantity, botanical name, common name, flower color, season of bloom, and hardiness zone for each plant specified, as well as the amount and type of materials for all driveways, walks, walls, gates, and other structures. This becomes your "shopping list" for dealing with contractors or buying the plants and materials yourself. Most importantly, the plants shown on this page have been chosen by a team of professional horticulturalists for their adaptability, availability, and performance in your specific part of the country.*

Planting and Maintaining Your Landscape. *This valuable sheet gives handy information and illustrations on purchasing plant materials, preparing your site, and caring for your landscape after installation. Includes quick, helpful advice on planting trees, shrubs and ground covers, staking trees, establishing a lawn, watering, weed control, and pruning.*

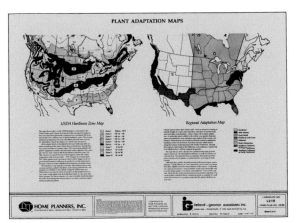

Zone Maps. *These two informative maps offer detailed information to help you better select and judge the performance of your plants. Map One is a United States Department of Agriculture Hardiness Zone Map that shows the average low temperatures by zones in various part of the United States and Canada. The "Zone" listing for plants on Sheet 3 of your Plant and Materials List is keyed to this map. Map Two is a Regional Adaptation Map which takes into account other factors beyond low temperatures, such as rainfall, humidity, extremes of temperature, and soil acidity or alkalinity. This map is the key to plant adaptability and is used for the selection of plant lists in your plans.*

Plant Size & Description Guide. *Because people often have trouble visualizing plants, this handy regionalized guide provides a scale and silhouettes to determine the final height and shape of various trees and shrubs in your landscape plan. It also provides a quick means of choosing alternate plants in case you do not wish to install a certain tree or shrub or if you cannot find the plant at local nurseries.*

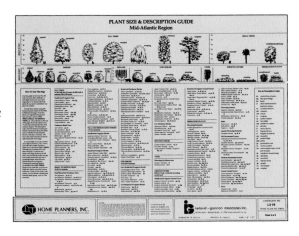

To order, see page 176.

Landscape Plans Price Schedule and Index

To order your plans, simply find the Plan Number of the design of your choice in the Plans Index below. Consult the Price Schedule at right to determing the price of your plans, choosing the 1-, 3-, or 6-set package and any additional or reverse sets you desire. To make sure your Plant & Materials List contains the best selection for your area, refer to the Regional Order Map below and specify the region in which you reside. Fill out the Order Coupon on the opposite page carefully and mail to us for prompt fulfillment or call our Toll-Free Order Hotline for even faster service. (If you want to order blueprints for any of the houses in this book, please turn to page 200.

Landscape Plans Price Schedule

Price Group	X	Y	Z
1 set	$35	$45	$55
3 sets	$50	$60	$70
6 sets	$65	$75	$85

Additional identical sets $10 each
Reverse sets (mirror image) $10 each

Regional Order Map

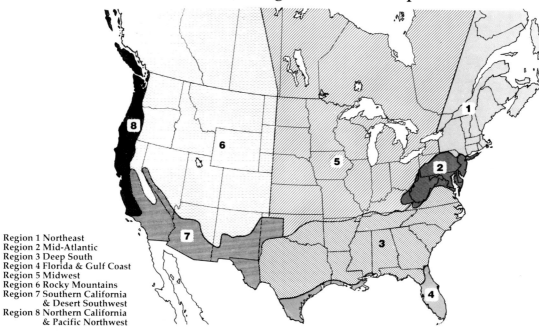

Region 1 Northeast
Region 2 Mid-Atlantic
Region 3 Deep South
Region 4 Florida & Gulf Coast
Region 5 Midwest
Region 6 Rocky Mountains
Region 7 Southern California
    & Desert Southwest
Region 8 Northern California
    & Pacific Northwest

Landscape Blueprint Order Form

To order, just clip the accompanying order blank and mail with your check or money order. If you prefer, you can also use a credit card or order C.O.D. (Sorry, no C.O.D. shipments to foreign countries, including Canada.) If time is of the essence, call us Toll-Free at 1-800-521-6797 on our Blueprint Hotline. If your call is received by 5:00 p.m. Eastern time, we'll ship your order the next business day. If you use the coupon, please include the correct postage and handling charges.

Our Exchange Policy

Because we produce and ship plans in response to individual orders, we cannot honor requests for refunds. However, you can exchange your entire order of blueprints, including a single set if you order just one, for a set of another landscape design. All exchanges carry an additional fee of $15.00, plus $8.00 for postage and handling if they're sent via surface mail; $20.00 for priority air mail.

About Reverse Blueprints

If you want to install your landscape in reverse of the plan as shown, we will include an extra set of blueprints with the Frontal Sheet and Plan View reversed for an additional fee of $10.00. Although callouts and lettering appear backwards, reverses will prove useful as a visual aid if you decide to flop the plan.

How Many Blueprints Do You Need?

To study your favorite landscape plan or make alterations of the plan to fit your site, one set of Landscape Blueprints may be sufficient. On the other hand, if you plan to install the landscape yourself using subcontractors or have a general contractor do the work for you, you will probably need more sets. Because you save money on 3-set or 6-set packages, you should consider ordering all the sets at one time. Use the checklist below to estimate the number you'll need:

Blueprint Checklist

_____ **Owner**
_____ **Landscape Contractor or Subcontractor**
_____ **Nursery or Plant Materials Supplier**
_____ **Building Materials Supplier**
_____ **Lender or Mortgage Source, if applicable**
      Community Building Department for Permits
_____ **(sometimes requires 2 sets)**
_____ **Subdivision Committee, if any**
_____ **Total Number of Sets**

Blueprint Hotline

Call Toll-Free 1-800-521-6797. We'll ship your order the following business day if you call us by 5:00 p.m. Eastern Time. When you order by phone, please be prepared to give us the Order Form Key Number shown in the box at the bottom of the Order Form.

CANADIAN CUSTOMERS: For faster, more economical service, Canadian customers may now call in orders on our Toll-Free line. Or, complete the order form at right, and mail with your check indicating U.S. funds to:

Home Planners, Inc.
3275 W. Ina Road, Suite 110
Tucson, AZ 85741
Phone: (800) 848-2550

 HOME PLANNERS, INC.
3275 WEST INA ROAD, SUITE 110
TUCSON, ARIZONA 85741

Please rush me the following Landscape Blueprints:

_____ Set(s) of Landscape Plan _____
(See Index and Price Schedule) $ _____

_____ Additional identical blueprints
in the same order @ $10.00 per set $ _____

_____ Reverse blueprints @ $10.00 per set $ _____

Please indicate the appropriate region of
the country for Plant & Material List
(See Map on opposite page):
[ ] Region 1 Northeast
[ ] Region 2 Mid-Atlantic
[ ] Region 3 Deep South
[ ] Region 4 Florida & Gulf Coast
[ ] Region 5 Midwest
[ ] Region 6 Rocky Mountains
[ ] Region 7 Southern California & Desert Southwest
[ ] Region 8 Northern California & Pacific Northwest
SALES TAX: (Arizona residents add 5% sales tax;
   Michigan residents add 4% sales tax) $ _____

POSTAGE AND HANDLING

CARRIER DELIVERY—Must have street address - No P.O. Boxes		
•Ground Service Allow 4-6 days delivery	❏ $6.00	$_____
•2nd Day Air Allow 2-3 days delivery	❏ $12.00	$_____
•Next Day Air Allow 1 day delivery	❏ $22.00	$_____
POST OFFICE DELIVERY— If no street address available. Allow 4-6 days delivery	❏ $8.00	$_____
OVERSEAS AIR MAIL DELIVERY Note: All delivery times are from date Blueprint Package is shipped.	❏ $30.00 ❏ Send COD	$_____

TOTAL IN U.S. FUNDS $ _____

YOUR ADDRESS (please print)

Name _____

Street _____

City _____ State _____ Zip _____

Daytime telephone number (____) _____

CREDIT CARD ORDERS ONLY

Fill in the boxes below

[| | | | | | | | | | | | | | |]
Credit card number

[| | | |]
Exp. Date: Month/Year

Check one: ❏ Visa   ❏ Mastercard   ❏ Discover

_____
Signature

About Our Home Plans

The Home Planners' Advantage

For over forty years, Home Planners, Inc. has been supplying quality home plans and construction blueprints to consumers and builders across the United States and Canada. The company's impressive portfolio of designs includes samplings from every style and type of architecture. Georgian to Spanish, Contemporary to Tudor, and one-, 1½-, two-story, and multi-level homes are all represented. Behind each beautiful facade is a complete blueprint package which includes virtually everything needed for construction. Special extras, such as materials lists and plumbing, electrical, and construction details, are also available — offering even more information and alternative ideas. The unique Plan-a-Home® kit helps with design considerations for a variety of building and remodeling projects.

With 135 books and magazines to its credit, Home Planners has sold over 2.0 million sets of blueprints since its inception in 1946. The company's plans are featured in such popular magazines as *House Beautiful, Better Homes and Gardens, Practical Homeowner, Homeowner, Decorating/Remodeling,* and others. Among the many books published by Home Planners are collections of exterior styles, design categories, and portfolios. *Vacation Homes* is a medley of designs for the perfect get-away. *The Signature Series Portfolio* is a gathering of luxurious homes in a variety of styles. *Home Plans for Solar Living* brings together designs that are attractive as well as being energy efficient.

In addition to the plans, many of the publications provide special sections offering advice, building and design tips, and helpful hints. Glossaries in some of the books define architectural terms. Guides for learning to read floor plans and choosing the right contractor are valuable for the first-time builder. A special section in *Home Plans for Outdoor Living* focuses on outdoor accents to enhance and improve any home's surroundings.

The Landscape Plans in this book have been designed to match or correspond to 40 popular Home Planners House Plans. The index on the opposite page lists each plan, its page number and price code. Pages 180 to 199 show the floor plan and another front view of the house. To order a complete Blueprint Package for any of these exciting House Plans, turn to page 200.

Home Plan Index

STYLE	DESIGN	PAGE	PRICE SCHEDULE
Ranch	F1343	193	B
Ranch	F1920	192	B
Traditional	F1981	195	B
French Provincial	F1993	186	D
Gambrel-Roof Colonial	F2131	180	B
Southern Colonial	F2140	183	C
17th-Century Medieval	F2191	192	C
New England Barn-Type	F2224	184	B
Spanish Adobe	F2231	198	C
Florida Rambler	F2268	197	B
Tudor	F2356	189	D
Courtyard Contemporary	F2386	198	B
California Stucco	F2517	196	C
Cape Cod	F2520	181	B
Ranch	F2534	193	D
Fieldstone Farmhouse	F2542	185	D
French Manor House	F2543	189	D
Tudor	F2606	191	A
New England Colonial	F2610	183	C
New England Cape	F2615	184	D
Gothic Victorian	F2645	190	C
Cape Cod	F2657	180	B
Cape Cod	F2661	181	A
Brick Federal	F2662	188	C
Spanish Contemporary	F2670	199	D
Georgian	F2683	187	D
"Raised-Porch" Farmhouse	F2694	182	C
Contemporary	F2711	194	B
Western Contemporary	F2729	196	B
Classic Colonial	F2731	182	B
Farmhouse	F2774	185	B
Country French	F2779	188	D
Contemporary	F2781	194	C
Tudor	F2802	190	B
Contemporary	F2857	199	D
Georgian	F2889	187	D
Traditional	F2921	186	D
Northwest Contemporary	F2952	197	E
Queen Anne Victorian	F2953	191	E
Contemporary	F4334	195	B

Plan F2657

SPECS

Type: Two-story
Style: Cape Cod
First floor: 1,217 square feet
Second floor: 868 square feet
Total: 2,085 square feet
Cubic footage: 33,260
Bedrooms: 3
Bathrooms: 2½
Price schedule: B

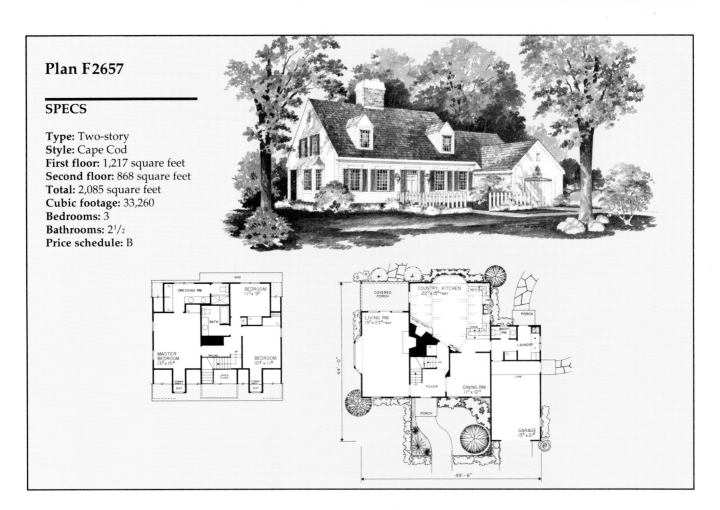

Plan F2131

SPECS

Type: Two-story
Style: Gambrel Roof Colonial
First floor: 1,214 square feet
Second floor: 1,097 square feet
Total: 2,311 square feet
Cubic footage: 28,070
Bedrooms: 3
Bathrooms: 2½
Price schedule: B

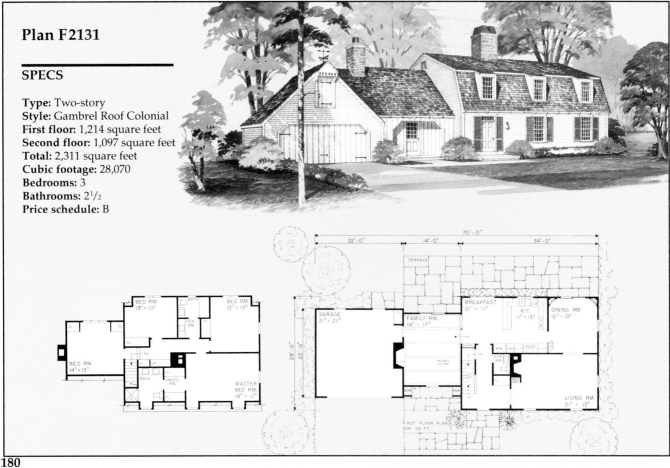

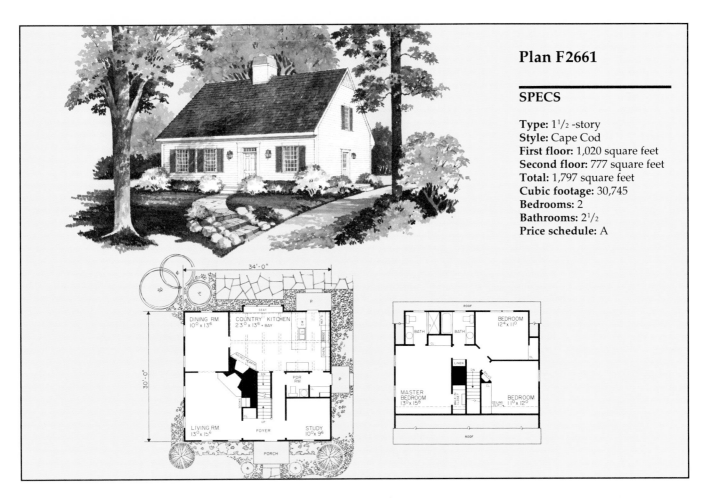

Plan F2661

SPECS

Type: 1$\frac{1}{2}$ -story
Style: Cape Cod
First floor: 1,020 square feet
Second floor: 777 square feet
Total: 1,797 square feet
Cubic footage: 30,745
Bedrooms: 2
Bathrooms: 2$\frac{1}{2}$
Price schedule: A

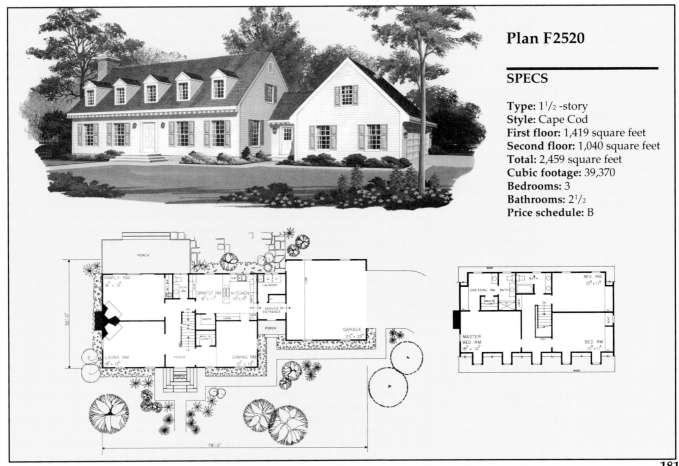

Plan F2520

SPECS

Type: 1$\frac{1}{2}$ -story
Style: Cape Cod
First floor: 1,419 square feet
Second floor: 1,040 square feet
Total: 2,459 square feet
Cubic footage: 39,370
Bedrooms: 3
Bathrooms: 2$\frac{1}{2}$
Price schedule: B

Plan F2731

SPECS

Type: Two-story
Style: Classic Colonial
First floor: 1,039 square feet
Second floor: 973 square feet
Total: 2,012 square feet
Cubic footage: 29,740
Bedrooms: 3
Bathrooms: 2¹/₂
Price schedule: B

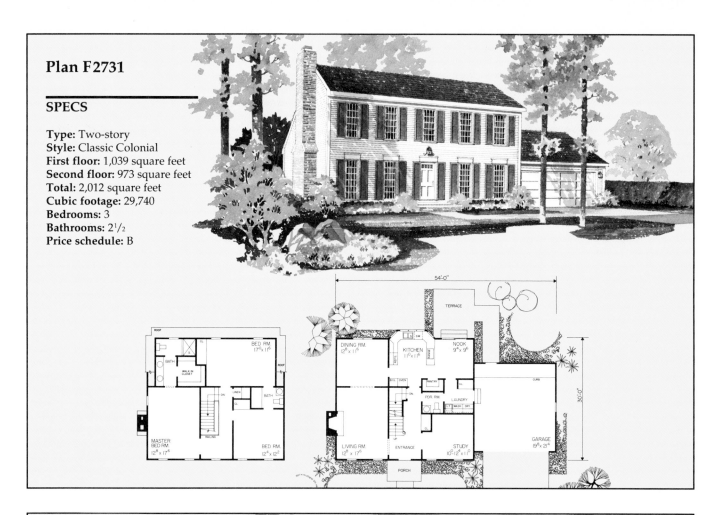

Plan F2694

SPECS

Type: Two-story
Style: "Raised Porch" Farmhouse
First floor: 2,026 square feet
Second floor: 1,386 square feet
Total: 3,412 square feet
Cubic footage: 69,445
Bedrooms: 3
Bathrooms: 2¹/₂ + powder room
Price schedule: C

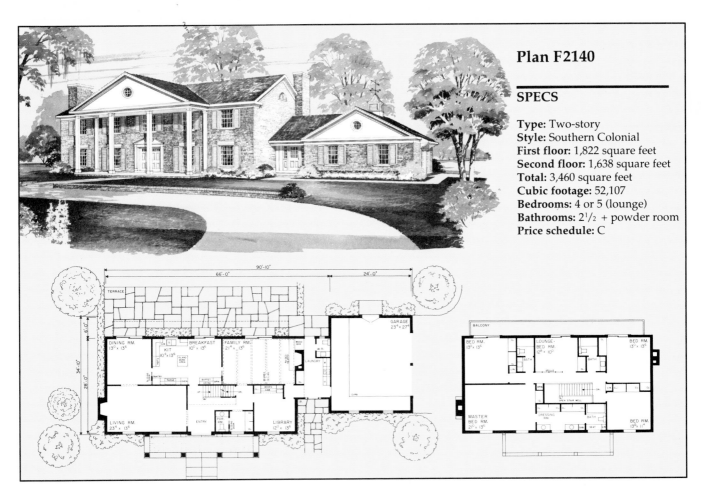

Plan F2140

SPECS

Type: Two-story
Style: Southern Colonial
First floor: 1,822 square feet
Second floor: 1,638 square feet
Total: 3,460 square feet
Cubic footage: 52,107
Bedrooms: 4 or 5 (lounge)
Bathrooms: 2$\frac{1}{2}$ + powder room
Price schedule: C

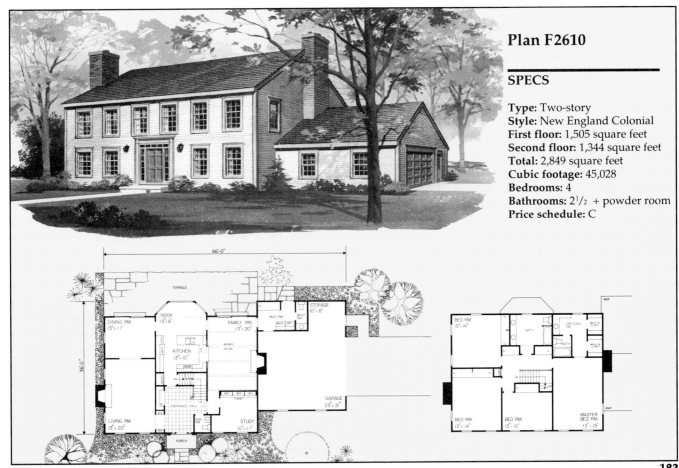

Plan F2610

SPECS

Type: Two-story
Style: New England Colonial
First floor: 1,505 square feet
Second floor: 1,344 square feet
Total: 2,849 square feet
Cubic footage: 45,028
Bedrooms: 4
Bathrooms: 2$\frac{1}{2}$ + powder room
Price schedule: C

Plan F2224

SPECS

Type: Two-story
Style: New England Barn-Type
First floor: 1,567 square feet
Second floor: 1,070 square feet
Total: 2,637 square feet
Cubic footage: 37,970
Bedrooms: 3
Bathrooms: 2½
Price schedule: B

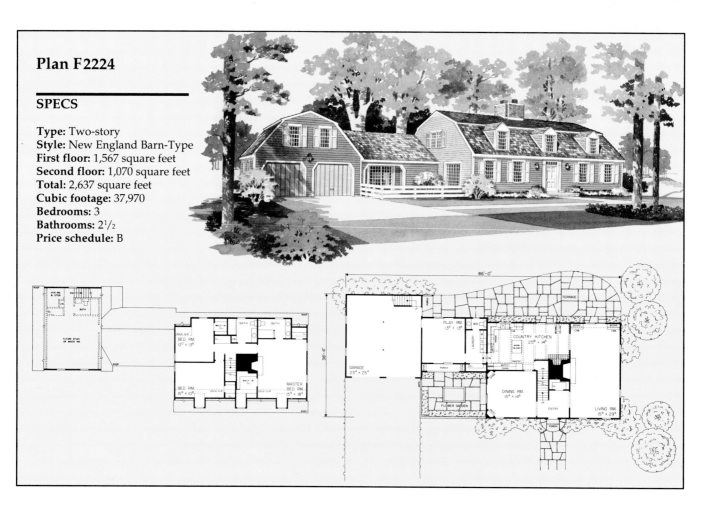

Plan F2615

SPECS

Type: 1½-story
Style: New England Cape
First floor: 2,563 square feet
Second floor: 552 square feet
Total: 3,115 square feet
Cubic footage: 59,513
Bedrooms: 3 or 4 (study)
Bathrooms: 2½ + powder room
Price schedule: D

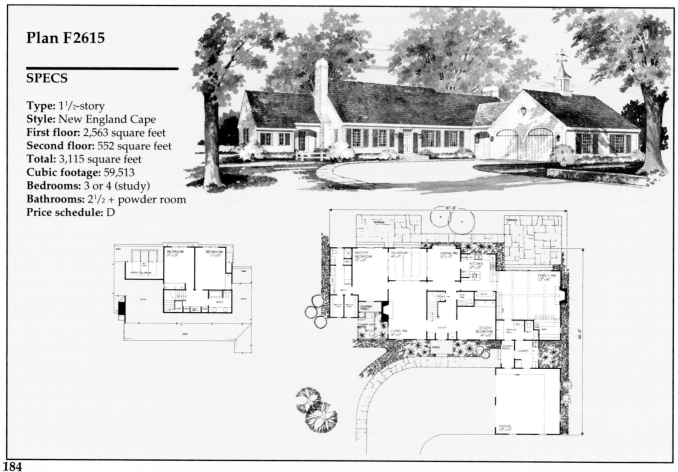

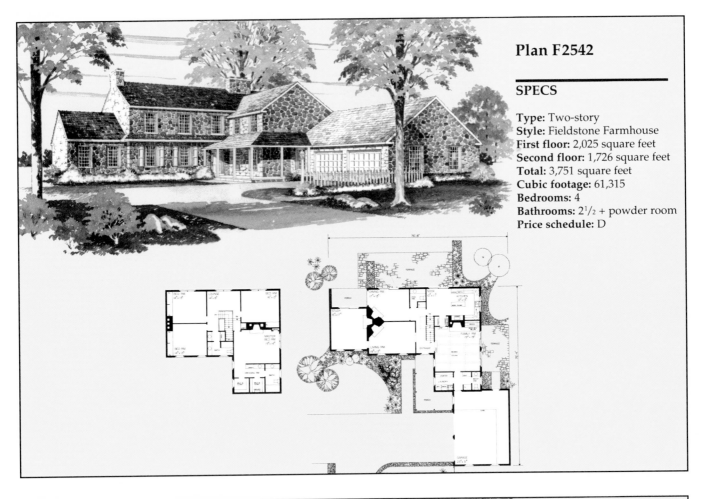

Plan F2542

SPECS

Type: Two-story
Style: Fieldstone Farmhouse
First floor: 2,025 square feet
Second floor: 1,726 square feet
Total: 3,751 square feet
Cubic footage: 61,315
Bedrooms: 4
Bathrooms: $2\frac{1}{2}$ + powder room
Price schedule: D

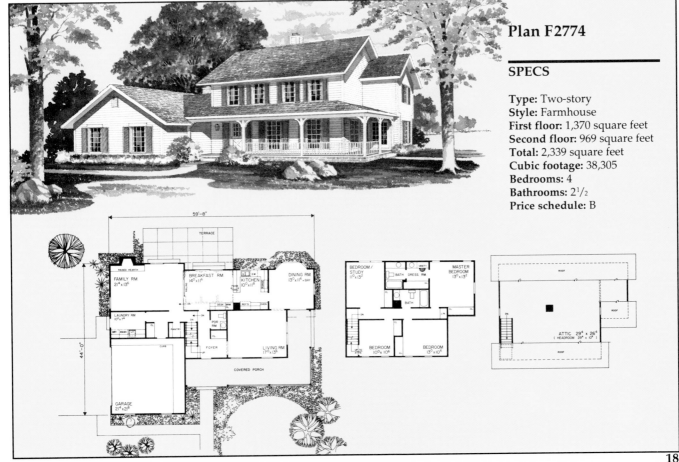

Plan F2774

SPECS

Type: Two-story
Style: Farmhouse
First floor: 1,370 square feet
Second floor: 969 square feet
Total: 2,339 square feet
Cubic footage: 38,305
Bedrooms: 4
Bathrooms: $2\frac{1}{2}$
Price schedule: B

Plan F2921

SPECS

Type: 1½-story
Style: Traditional
First floor: 3,511 square feet
Second floor: 711 square feet
Total: 4,222 square feet
Cubic footage: 69,991
Bedrooms: 3
Bathrooms: 2½ + powder room
Price schedule: D

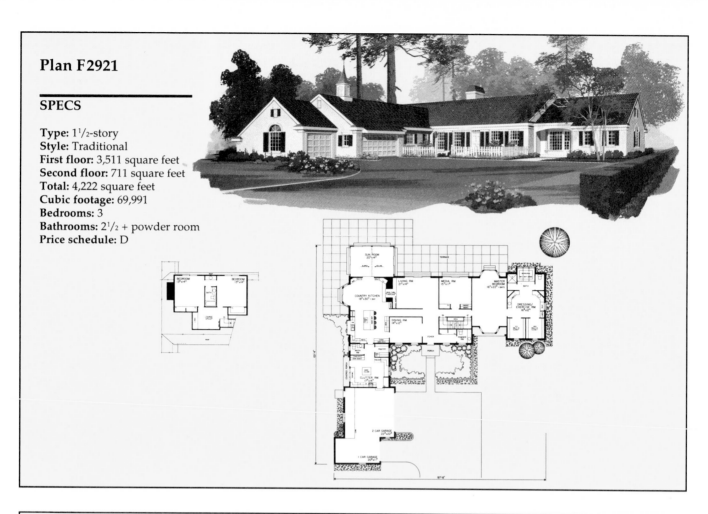

Plan F1993

SPECS

Type: Two-story
Style: French Provincial
First floor: 2,658 square feet
Second floor: 1,216 square feet
Total: 3,874 square feet
Cubic footage: 57,057
Bedrooms: 4
Bathrooms: 3½ + powder room
Price schedule: D

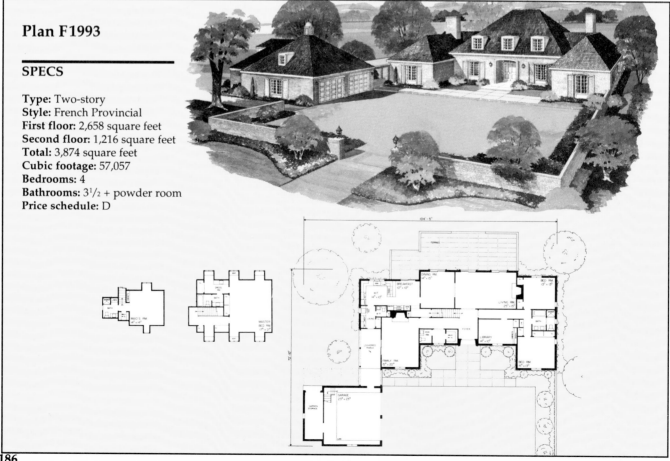

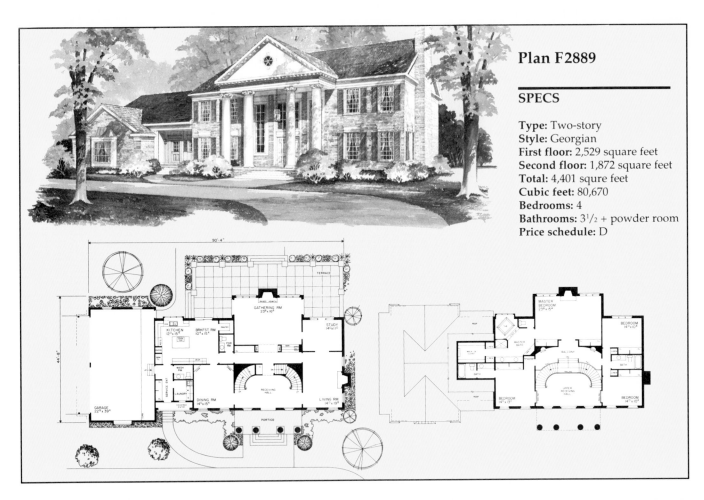

Plan F2889

SPECS

Type: Two-story
Style: Georgian
First floor: 2,529 square feet
Second floor: 1,872 square feet
Total: 4,401 squre feet
Cubic feet: 80,670
Bedrooms: 4
Bathrooms: 3½ + powder room
Price schedule: D

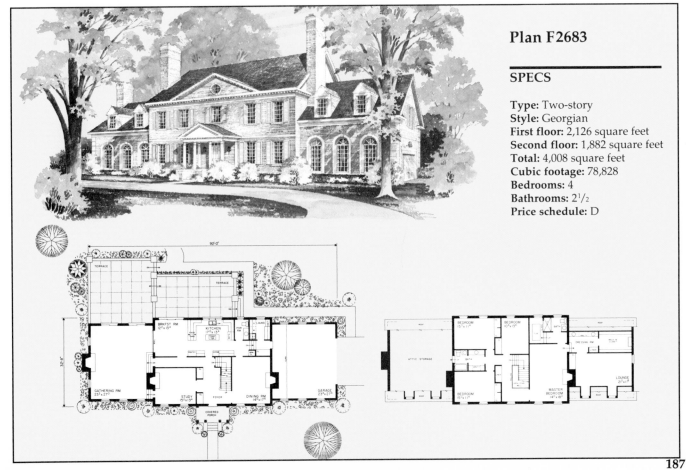

Plan F2683

SPECS

Type: Two-story
Style: Georgian
First floor: 2,126 square feet
Second floor: 1,882 square feet
Total: 4,008 square feet
Cubic footage: 78,828
Bedrooms: 4
Bathrooms: 2½
Price schedule: D

Plan F2779

SPECS

Type: One-story
Style: Country French
Square footage: 3,225
Cubic footage: 70,715
Bedrooms: 3 or 4 (study)
Bathrooms: $2^{1}/_{2}$
Price schedule: D

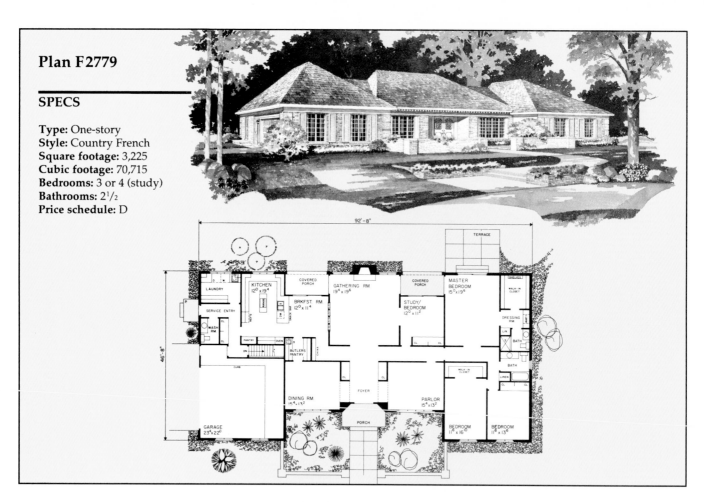

Plan F2662

SPECS

Type: Three-story
Style: Brick Federal
First floor: 1,735 square feet
Second floor: 1,075 square feet
Third floor: 746 square feet
Total: 3,556 square feet
Cubic footage: 49,165
Bedrooms: 5
Bathrooms: $3^{1}/_{2}$
Price schedule: C

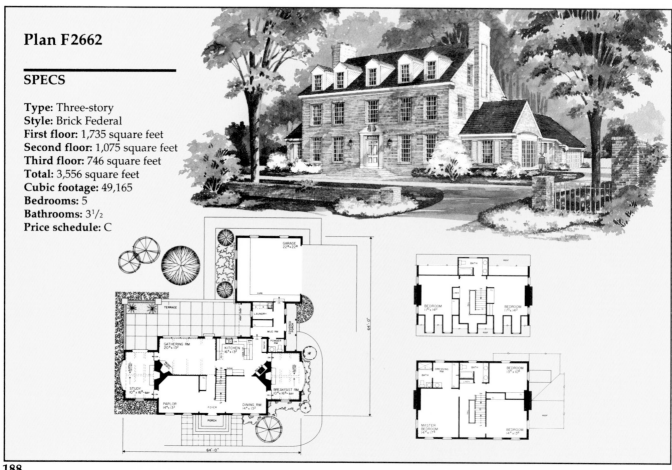

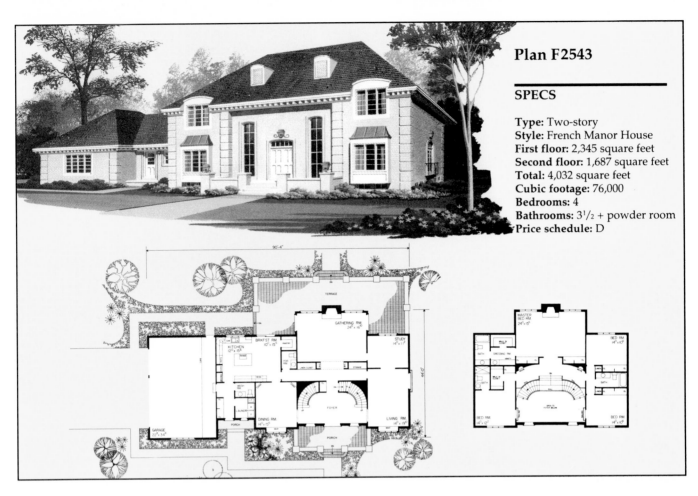

Plan F2543

SPECS

Type: Two-story
Style: French Manor House
First floor: 2,345 square feet
Second floor: 1,687 square feet
Total: 4,032 square feet
Cubic footage: 76,000
Bedrooms: 4
Bathrooms: $3^1/_2$ + powder room
Price schedule: D

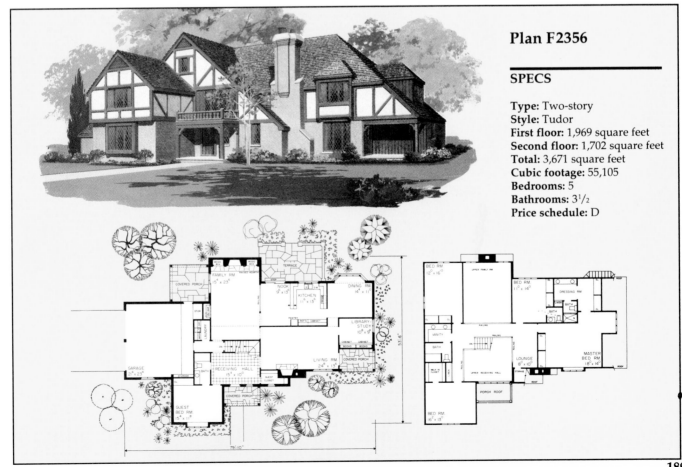

Plan F2356

SPECS

Type: Two-story
Style: Tudor
First floor: 1,969 square feet
Second floor: 1,702 square feet
Total: 3,671 square feet
Cubic footage: 55,105
Bedrooms: 5
Bathrooms: $3^1/_2$
Price schedule: D

Plan F2802

SPECS

Type: One-story
Style: Tudor
Square footage: 1,729
Cubic footage: 42,640
Bedrooms: 2 or 3 (study)
Bathrooms: 2
Price schedule: B

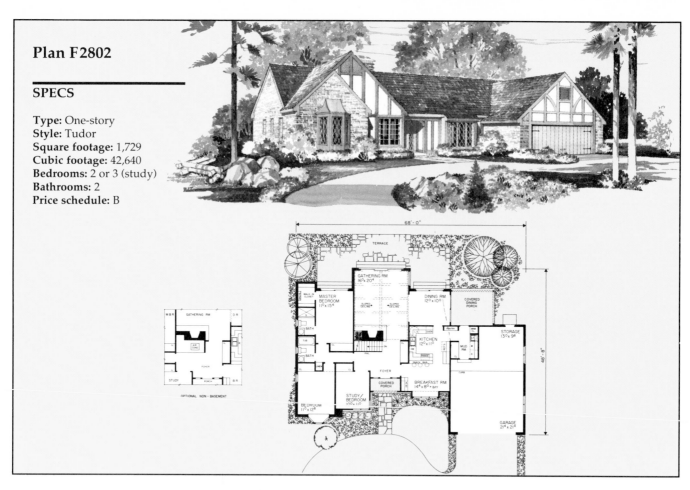

Plan F2645

SPECS

Type: Three-story
Style: Gothic Victorian
First floor: 1,600 square feet
Second floor: 1,305 square feet
Third floor: 925 square feet
Total: 3,830
Cubic footage: 58,355
Bedrooms: 5 or 6 (study)
Bathrooms: 3½
Price schedule: C

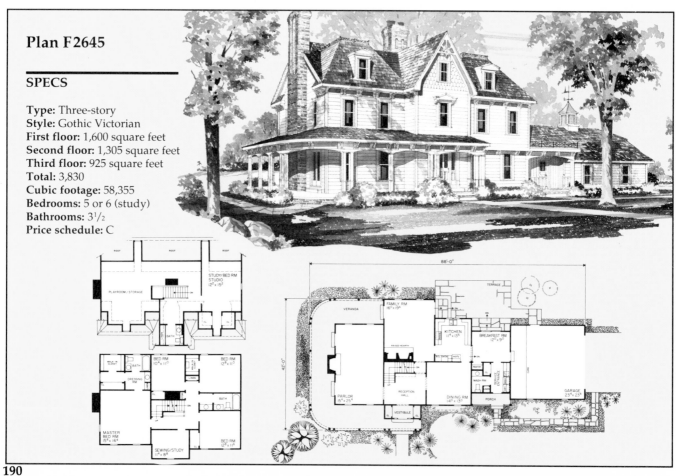

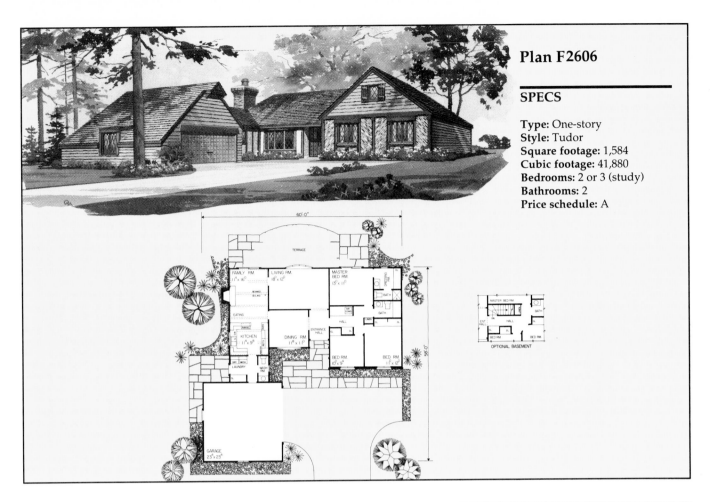

Plan F2606

SPECS

Type: One-story
Style: Tudor
Square footage: 1,584
Cubic footage: 41,880
Bedrooms: 2 or 3 (study)
Bathrooms: 2
Price schedule: A

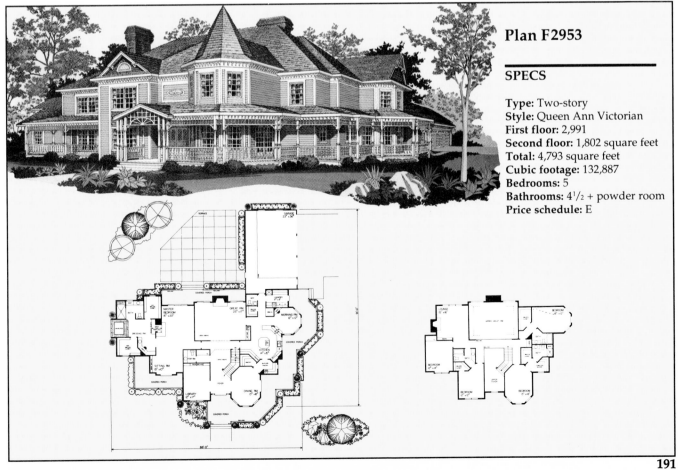

Plan F2953

SPECS

Type: Two-story
Style: Queen Ann Victorian
First floor: 2,991
Second floor: 1,802 square feet
Total: 4,793 square feet
Cubic footage: 132,887
Bedrooms: 5
Bathrooms: $4^1/_2$ + powder room
Price schedule: E

Plan F2191

SPECS

Type: Two-story
Style: 17th Century Medieval
First floor: 1,553 square feet
Second floor: 1,197 square feet
Total: 2,750 square feet
Cubic footage: 47,906
Bedrooms: 3
Bathrooms: 2½
Price schedule: C

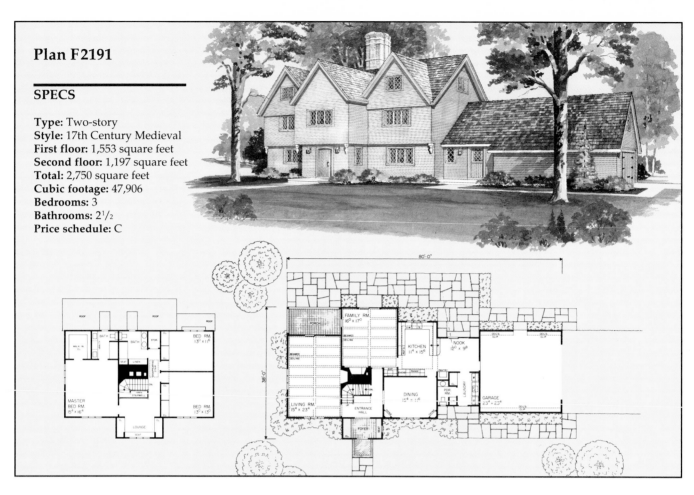

Plan F1920

SPECS

Type: One-story
Style: Ranch
Square footage: 1,600
Cubic footage: 18,966
Bedrooms: 3
Bathrooms: 2½
Price schedule: B

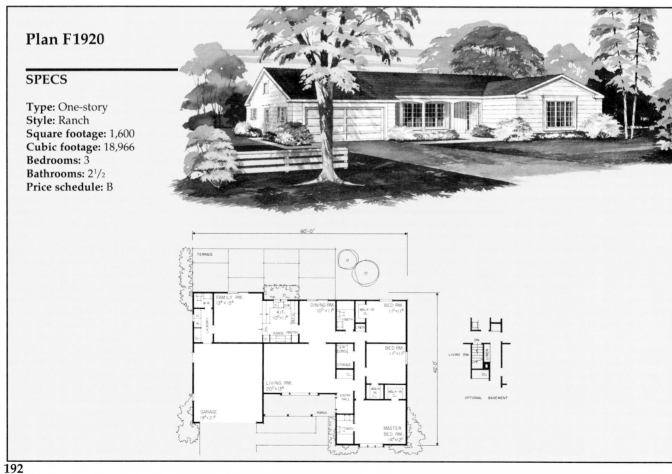

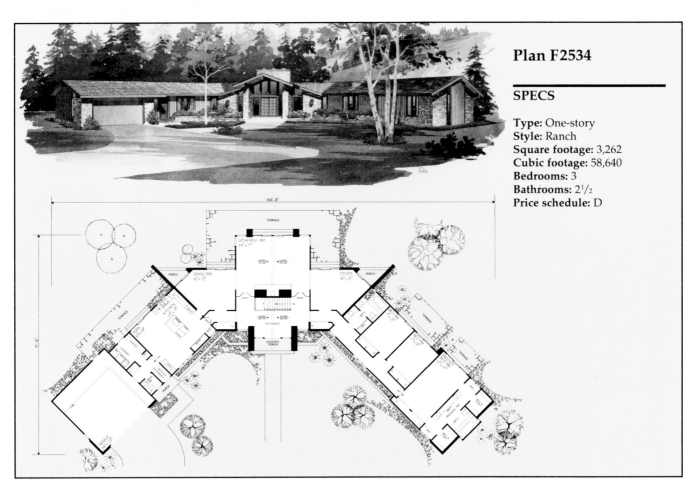

Plan F2534

SPECS

Type: One-story
Style: Ranch
Square footage: 3,262
Cubic footage: 58,640
Bedrooms: 3
Bathrooms: 2½
Price schedule: D

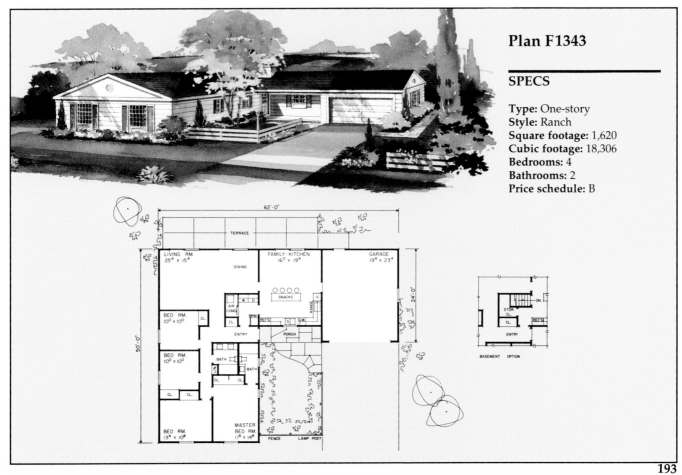

Plan F1343

SPECS

Type: One-story
Style: Ranch
Square footage: 1,620
Cubic footage: 18,306
Bedrooms: 4
Bathrooms: 2
Price schedule: B

Plan F2781

SPECS

Type: Two-story
Style: Contemporary
First floor: 2,132 square feet
Second floor: 1,156 square feet
Total: 3,288 square feet
Cubic footage: 47,365
Bedrooms: 3 or 4 (study)
Bathrooms: 2½
Price schedule: C

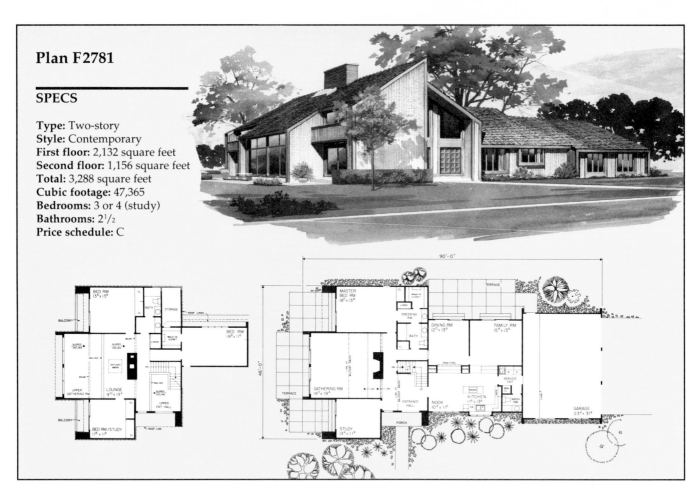

Plan F2711

SPECS

Type: Two-story
Style: Contemporary
First floor: 975 square feet
Second floor: 1,024 square feet
Total: 1,999 square feet
Cubic footage: 31,380
Bedrooms: 3
Bathrooms: 2½
Price schedule: B

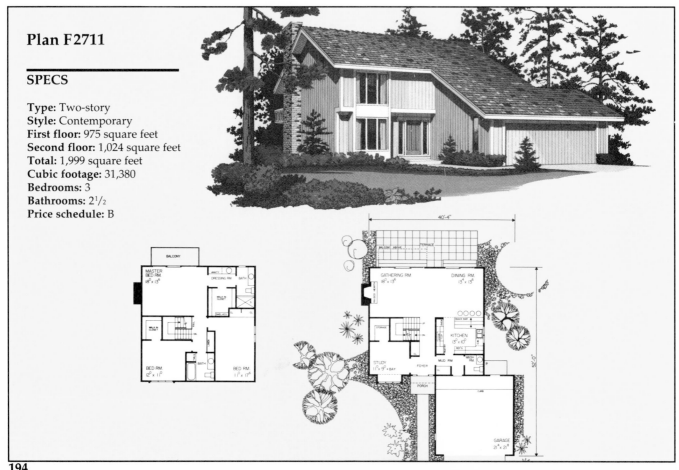

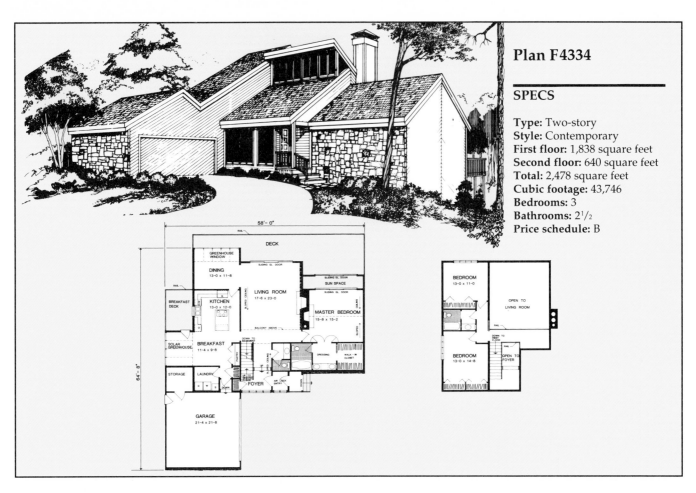

Plan F4334

SPECS

Type: Two-story
Style: Contemporary
First floor: 1,838 square feet
Second floor: 640 square feet
Total: 2,478 square feet
Cubic footage: 43,746
Bedrooms: 3
Bathrooms: 2½
Price schedule: B

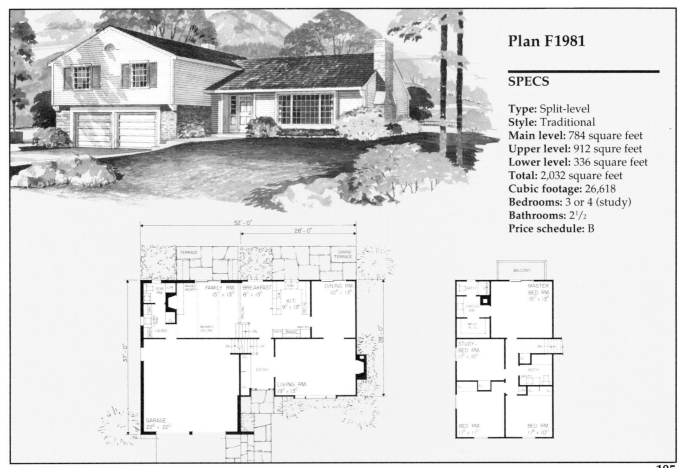

Plan F1981

SPECS

Type: Split-level
Style: Traditional
Main level: 784 square feet
Upper level: 912 squre feet
Lower level: 336 square feet
Total: 2,032 square feet
Cubic footage: 26,618
Bedrooms: 3 or 4 (study)
Bathrooms: 2½
Price schedule: B

Plan F2517

SPECS

Type: Two-story
Style: California Stucco
First floor: 1,767 square feet
Second floor: 1,094 square feet
Total: 2,861 square feet
Cubic footage: 50,256
Bedrooms: 3
Bathrooms: 2½
Price schedule: C

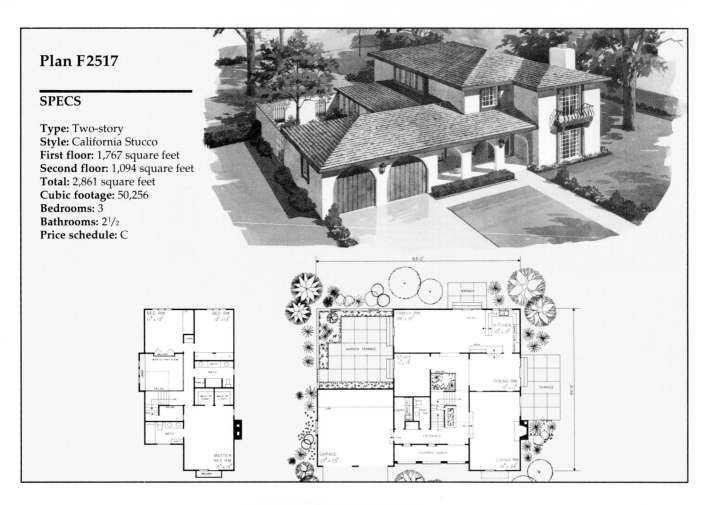

Plan F2729

SPECS

Type: Two-story
Style: Western Contemporary
First floor: 1,590 square feet
Second floor: 756 square feet
Total: 2,346 square feet
Cubic footage: 39,310
Bedrooms: 3
Bathrooms: 3½
Price schedule: B

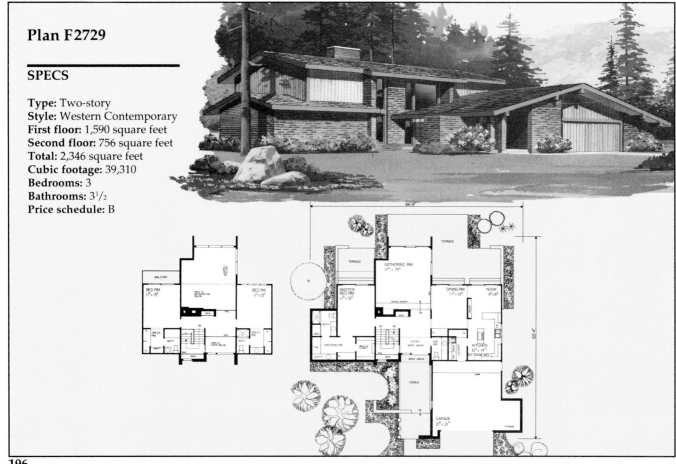

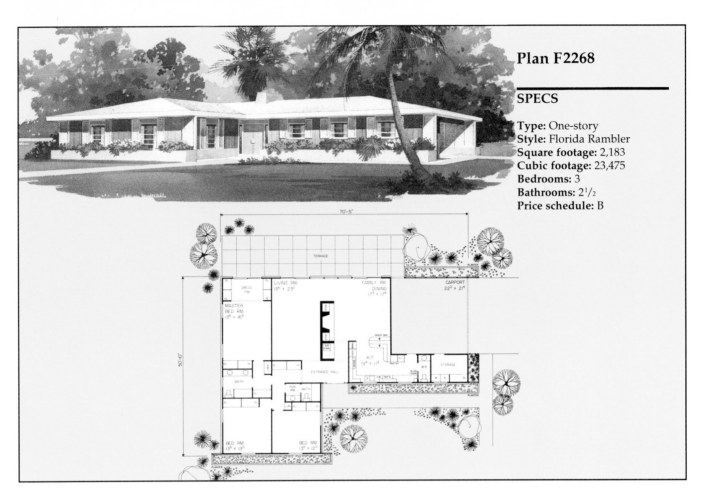

Plan F2268

SPECS

Type: One-story
Style: Florida Rambler
Square footage: 2,183
Cubic footage: 23,475
Bedrooms: 3
Bathrooms: 2$\frac{1}{2}$
Price schedule: B

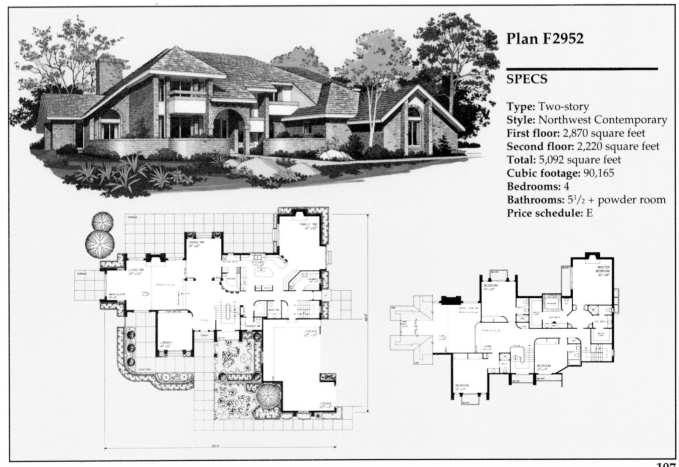

Plan F2952

SPECS

Type: Two-story
Style: Northwest Contemporary
First floor: 2,870 square feet
Second floor: 2,220 square feet
Total: 5,092 square feet
Cubic footage: 90,165
Bedrooms: 4
Bathrooms: 5$\frac{1}{2}$ + powder room
Price schedule: E

Plan F2231

SPECS

Type: One-story
Style: Spanish Adobe
Square footage: 2,740
Cubic footage: 31,670
Bedrooms: 3
Bathrooms: 4
Price schedule: C

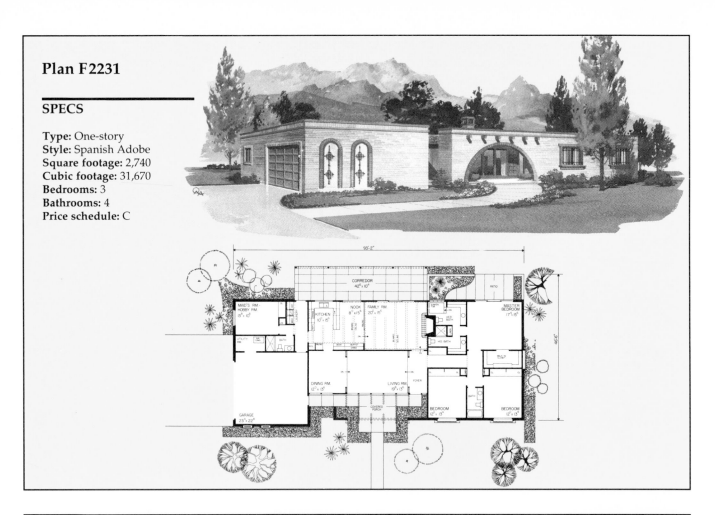

Plan F2386

SPECS

Type: One-story
Style: Courtyard Contemporary
Square footage: 1,994
Cubic footage: 22,160
Bedrooms: 4
Bathrooms: 2
Price schedule: B

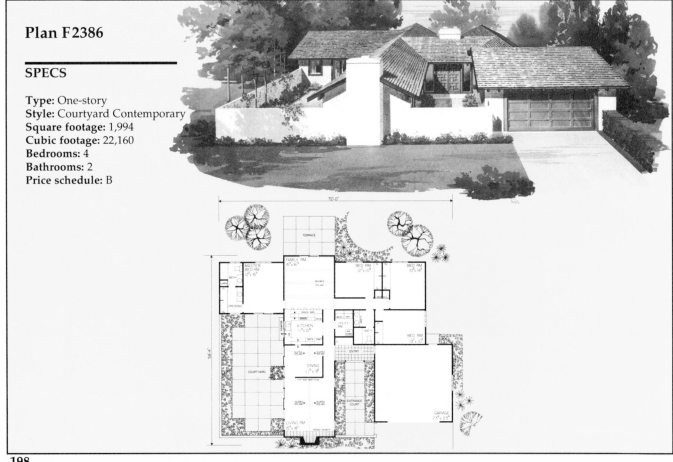

Plan F2670

SPECS

Type: 1¹/₂-story
Style: Spanish Contemporary
First floor: 3,058 square feet
Second floor: 279 square feet
Total: 3,337 square feet
Cubic footage: 44,210
Bedrooms: 4
Bathrooms: 2¹/₂ + powder room
Price schedule: D

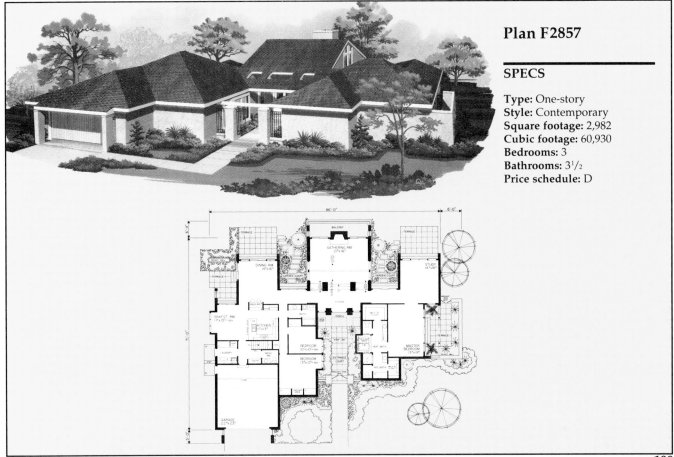

Plan F2857

SPECS

Type: One-story
Style: Contemporary
Square footage: 2,982
Cubic footage: 60,930
Bedrooms: 3
Bathrooms: 3¹/₂
Price schedule: D

The Home Plans Blueprint Package . . .

Take a look at our complete set of high quality plans.

Building a home? Planning a home? The Blueprint Package from Home Planners, Inc. contains nearly everything you need to get the job done right, whether you're working on your own or with help from an architect, designer, builder or subcontractors. Each Blueprint Package is the result of many hours of work by licensed architects or professional designers.

QUALITY
Hundreds of hours of painstaking effort have gone into the development of your blueprint set. Each home has been quality-checked by professionals to insure accuracy and buildability.

VALUE
Because we sell in volume, you can buy professional-quality blueprints at a fraction of their development cost. With Home Planners, your dream home design costs only a few hundred dollars, not the thousands of dollars that custom architects charge.

SERVICE
Once you've chosen your favorite home plan, we stand ready to serve you with knowledgeable sales people and prompt, efficient service. We ship most orders within 48 hours of receipt and stand behind every set of blueprints we well.

SATISFACTION
We have been in business since 1946 and have shipped over 1 million blueprints to home builders just like you. Nearly 50 years of service and hundreds of thousands of satisfied customers are your guarantee that Home Planners can do the job for you.

ORDER TOLL FREE 1-800-521-6797
After you've studied our Blueprint Package and Important Extras on the following pages, simply mail the accompanying order form on page 205 or call toll free on our Blueprint Hotline: 1-800-521-6797. We're ready and eager to serve you.

Each set of blueprints is an interrelated collection of floor plans, interior and exterior elevations, dimensions, cross-sections, diagrams and notations showing precisely how your house is to be constructed.

Here's what you get:

Frontal Sheet
This artist's sketch of the exterior of the house, done in two-point perspective, gives you an idea of how the house will look when built and landscaped. Large ink-line floor plans show all levels of the house and provide a quick overview of your new home's livability, as well as a handy reference for studying furniture placement.

Foundation Plan
Drawn to 1/4-inch scale, this sheet shows the complete foundation layout, including support

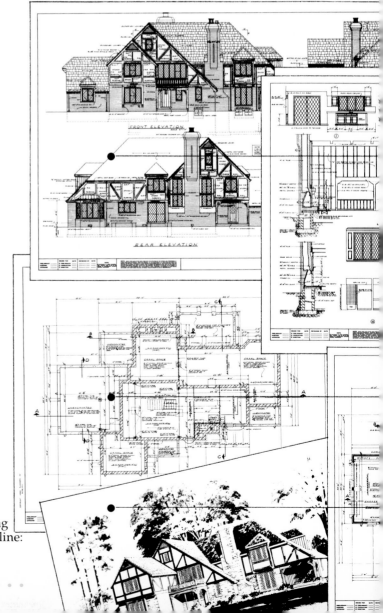

walls, excavated and unexcavated areas, if any and foundation notes. If slab construction rather than basement, the plan shows footings and details for a monolithic slab. This page, or another in the set, also includes a sample plot plan for locating your house on a building site.

Detailed Floor Plans

Complete in 1/4-inch scale, these plans show the layout of each floor of the house. All rooms and interior spaces are carefully dimensioned and keys are provided for cross-section details given later in the plans. The position of all electrical outlets and switches are clearly shown.

House Cross-Sections

Large-scale views, normally drawn at 3/8-inch equals 1 foot, show sections or cut-aways of the foundation, interior walls, exterior walls,

floors, stairways and roof details. Additional cross-sections are given to show important changes in floor, ceiling or roof heights or the relationship of one level to another. Extremely valuable for construction, these sections show exactly how the various parts of the house fit together.

Interior Elevations

These large-scale drawings show the design and placement of kitchen and bathroom cabinets, laundry areas, fireplaces, bookcases and other built-ins. Little "extras," such as mantelpiece and wainscoting drawings, plus moulding sections, provide details that give your home that custom touch.

Exterior Elevations

Drawings in 1/4-inch scale show the front, rear and sides of your house and give necessary notes on exterior materials and finishes. Particular attention is given to cornice detail, brick and stone accents or other finish items that make your home distinctive.

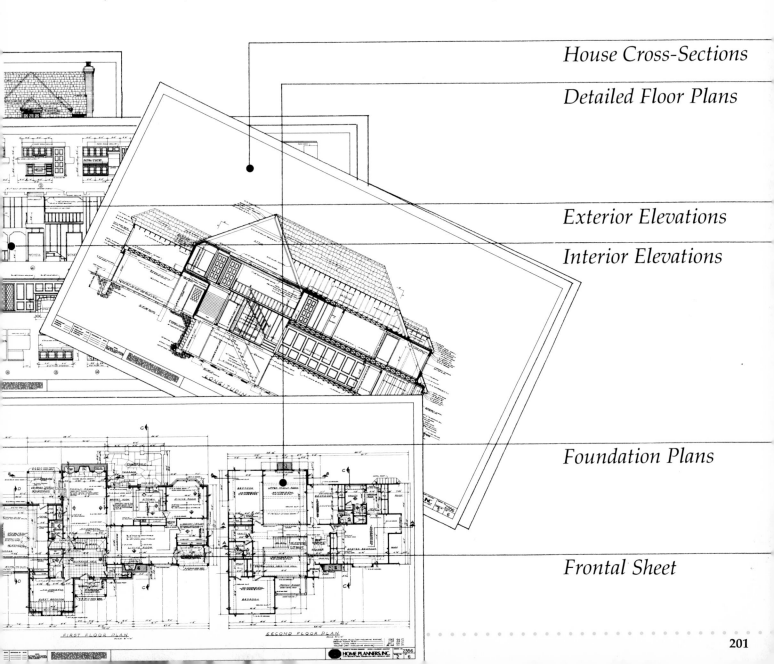

House Cross-Sections

Detailed Floor Plans

Exterior Elevations

Interior Elevations

Foundation Plans

Frontal Sheet

Important Extras To Do The Job Right!

Introducing seven important planning and construction aids developed by our professionals to help you succeed in your home-building project.

To Order, Call Toll Free 1-800-521-6797

To add these important extras to your Blueprint Package, simply indicate your choices on the order form on page 205 or call us Toll Free 1-800-521-6797 and we'll tell you more about these exciting products.

MATERIALS LIST

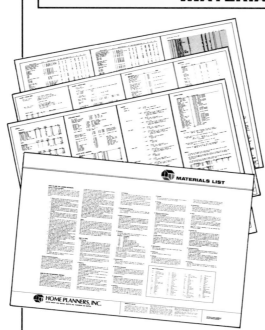

For each design in our portfolio, we offer a customized materials take-off that is invaluable in planning and estimating the cost of your new home. This comprehensive list outlines the quantity, type and size of material needed to build your house (with the exception of mechanical system items). Included are:

- framing lumber
- roofing and sheet metal
- windows and doors
- exterior sheathing material and trim
- masonry, veneer and fireplace materials
- tile and flooring materials
- kitchen and bath cabinetry
- interior drywall and trim
- rough and finish hardware
- many more items

(Note: Because of differing local codes, building methods, and availability of materials, our Materials Lists do not include mechanical materials. To obtain necessary take-offs and recommendations, consult heating, plumbing and electrical contractors. Materials Lists are not sold separately from the Blueprint Package.)

This handy list helps you or your builder cost out materials and serves as a ready reference sheet when you're compiling bids. It also provides a cross-check against the materials specified by your builder and helps coordinate the substitution of items you may need to meet local codes.

SPECIFICATION OUTLINE

This valuable 16-page document is critical to building your house correctly. Designed to be filled in by you or your builder, this booklet lists 166 stages or items crucial to the building process.

For the layman, it provides a comprehensive review of the construction process and helps in making the specific choices of materials, models and processes. For the builder, it serves as a guide to preparing a building quotation and forms the basis for the construction program.

Designed primarily as a reference for the homeowner, this Specification Outline can become a legally binding document. Once it is filled out and agreed upon by owner and builder, it becomes a complete Project Specification.

When combined with the blueprints, a signed contract and schedule, the Specification Outline becomes a legal document and record for the building of your home. Many home builders find it useful to order two of these outlines—one as a worksheet in formulating the specifications and another to be carefully completed as a legal document.

DETAIL SHEETS

If you want to know more about techniques—and deal more confidently with subcontractors—we offer these remarkably useful detail sheets. Each is an excellent tool that will enhance your understanding of these technical subjects.

Plan-A-Home®

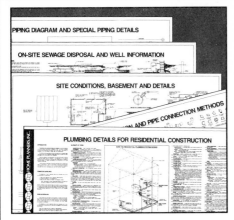

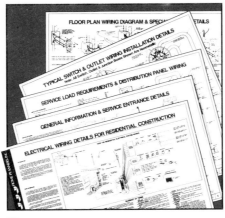

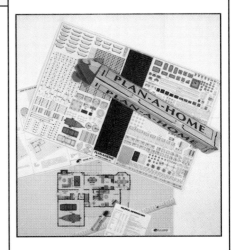

PLUMBING

The Blueprint Package includes locations for all the plumbing fixtures in your new house, including sinks, lavatories, tubs, showers, toilets, laundry trays and water heaters. However, if you want to know more about the complete plumbing system, these 24x36-inch detail sheets will prove very useful. Prepared to meet requirements of the National Plumbing Code, these six fact-filled sheets give general information on pipe schedules, fittings, sump-pump details, water-softener hookups, septic system details and much more. Color-coded sheets include a glossary of terms.

ELECTRICAL

The locations for every electrical switch, plug and outlet are shown in your Blueprint Package. However, these Electrical Details go further to take the mystery out of household electrical systems. Prepared to meet requirements of the National Electrical Code, these comprehensive 24x36-inch drawings come packed with helpful information, including wire sizing, switch-installation schematics, cable-routing details, appliance wattage, door-bell hookups, typical service panel circuitry and much more. Six sheets are bound together and color-coded for easy reference. A glossary of terms is also included.

Plan-A-Home® is an easy-to-use tool that helps you design a new home, arrange furniture in a new or existing home, or plan a remodeling project. Each package contains:

- More than *700 peel-off planning symbols* on a self-stick vinyl sheet, including walls, windows, doors, all types of furniture, kitchen components, bath fixtures and many more. All are made of durable, peel-and-stick vinyl you can use over and over.

- A reusable, transparent, *1/4-inch scale planning grid* made of tough mylar that matches the scale of actual working drawings (1/4 -inch equals 1 foot). This grid provides the basis for house layouts of up to 140x92 feet.

- *Tracing paper* and a protective sheet for copying or transferring your completed plan.

- A *felt-tip pen*, with water-soluble ink that wipes away quickly.

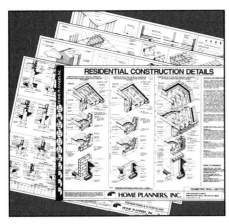

CONSTRUCTION

The Blueprint Package contains everything an experienced builder needs to construct a particular house. However, it doesn't show all the ways that houses can be built, nor does it explain alternate construction methods. To help you understand how your house will be built—and offer additional techniques—this set of drawings depicts the materials and methods used to build foundations, fireplaces, walls, floors and roofs. Where appropriate, the drawings show acceptable alternatives. These six sheets will answer questions for the advanced do-it-yourselfer or home planner.

MECHANICAL

This package contains fundamental principles and useful data that will help you make informed decisions and communicate with subcontractors about heating and cooling systems. The 24 x 36-inch drawings contain instructions and samples that allow you to make simple load calculations and preliminary sizing and costing analysis. Covered are today's most commonly used systems from heat pumps to solar fuel systems. The package is packed full of illustrations and diagrams to help you visualize components and how they relate to one another.

With Plan-A-Home®, you can make basic planning decisions for a new house or make modifications to an existing house. Use with your Blueprint Package to test modifications to rooms or to plan furniture arrangements before you build. Plan-A-Home® lets you lay out areas as large as a 7,500 square foot, six-bedroom, seven-bath house.

House Plans Price Schedule & Index

These pages contain all the information you need to price your blueprints. In general, the larger and more complicated the house, the more it costs to design and thus the higher the price we must charge for the blueprints. Remember, however, that these prices are far less than you would normally pay for the services of a licensed architect or professional designer. Custom home designs and related architectural services often cost thousands of dollars, ranging from 5% to 15% of the cost of construction. By ordering our blueprints you are potentially saving enough money to afford a larger house, or to add those "extra" amenities such as a patio, deck, swimming pool or even an upgraded kitchen or luxurious master suite.

To use the index below, refer to the design number listed in chronological order (a helpful page reference is also given). Note the price index letter and refer to the House Blueprint Price Schedule at right for the cost of one, four or eight sets of blueprints or the cost of a reproducible sepia. Additional prices are shown for identical and reverse blueprint sets, as well as a very useful Materials List to accompany your plans.

House Blueprint Price Schedule
(Prices effective through December 31, 1994)

	1-set Study Package	4-set Building Package	8-set Building Package	1-set Reproducible Sepias
Schedule A	$210	$270	$330	$420
Schedule B	$240	$300	$360	$480
Schedule C	$270	$330	$390	$540
Schedule D	$300	$360	$420	$600
Schedule E	$390	$450	$510	$660

Additional Identical Blueprints in same order .....$50 per set
Reverse Blueprints (mirror image) ....$50 per set
Specification Outlines..$7 each
Materials Lists
       Schedule A-D $40
       Schedule E $50

To Order: Fill in and send the Order Form on page 205 — or call us **Toll Free 1-800-521-6797.**

 Toll Free 1-800-521-6797

Normal Office Hours:
   8:00 a.m. to 8:00 p.m.
   Eastern Time
   Monday through Friday

If we receive your order by 5:00 p.m. Eastern Time, we'll process it the same day and ship it the following day. When ordering by phone, please have

your charge card ready. We'll also ask you for the Order Form Key Number on the opposite page. Please use our Toll-Free number for blueprint and book orders only.

By FAX: Copy the Order Form on the next page and send it on our International FAX line: 1-800-224-6699.

**Canadian Customers
Order Toll Free 1-800-561-4169**
For faster service and plans that are modified for building in Canada, customers may now call in orders directly to our Canadian supplier of plans and charge the purchase to a charge card. Or, you may complete the order form at right, adding 30% to all prices and mail in Canadian funds to:

 The Plan Centre
20 Cedar Street North
Kitchener, Ontario N2H 2W8

By FAX: Copy the Order Form on the next page and send it via our Canadian FAX line: 1-519-743-1282.

Before You Order . . .

Before completing the coupon at right or calling us on our Toll-Free Blueprint Hotline, you may be interested to learn more about our service and products. Here's some information you will find helpful.

Quick Turnaround

We process and ship every blueprint order from our office within 48 hours. On most orders, we do even better. Normally, if we receive your order by 5 p.m. Eastern Time, we'll process it the same day and ship it the following day. Because of this quick turnaround, we won't send a formal notice acknowledging receipt of your order.

Our Exchange Policy

Since blueprints are printed in response to your order, we cannot honor requests for refunds. However, we will exchange your entire first order for an equal number of blueprints plus the following exchange fees: $40 for the first set; $10 for each additional set; $60 total exchange fee for 4 sets; $90 total exchange fee for 8 sets.... *plus* the difference in cost if exchanging for a design in a higher price bracket, or *less* the difference in cost if exchanging for a design in a lower price bracket. (Sepias are not exchangeable.) All sets from the first order must be returned before the exchange can take place. Please add $8 for postage and handling via ground service; $20 via 2nd Day Air.

About Reverse Blueprints

If you want to build in reverse of the plan as shown, we will include an extra set of reversed blueprints (mirror image) for an additional fee of $50. Although lettering and dimensions appear backward, reverses will be a useful visual aid if you decide to flop the plan.

Modifying or Customizing Our Plans

With over 2,500 different plans from which to choose, you are bound to find a Home Planners' design that suits your lifestyle, budget and building site. In addition, our plans can be customized to your taste by your choice of siding, decorative detail, trim, color and other non-structural alterations.

If you do need to make minor modifications to the plans, these can normally be accomplished by your builder without the need for expensive blueprint modifications. However, if you decide to revise the plans significantly, we strongly suggest that you order our reproducible sepias and consult a licensed architect or professional designer to help you redraw the plans to your particular needs.

Architectural and Engineering Seals

Some cities and states are now requiring that a licensed architect or engineer review and "seal" your blueprints prior to construction. This is often due to local or regional concerns over energy consumption, safety codes, seismic ratings, etc. For this reason, you may find it necessary to consult with a local professional to have your plans reviewed. This can normally be accomplished with minimum delays, for a nominal fee.

Compliance with Local Codes and Regulations

At the time of creation, our plans are drawn to specifications published by Building Officials Code Administrators (BOCA), the Southern Standard Building Code, or the Uniform Building Code and are designed to meet or exceed national building standards. Some states, counties and municipalities have their own codes, zoning requirements and building regulations. Before starting construction, consult with local building authorities and make sure you comply with local ordinances and codes, including obtaining any necessary permits or inspections as building progresses. In some cases, minor modifications to your plans by your builder, local architect or designer may be required to meet local conditions and requirements.

Foundation and Exterior Wall Changes

Most of our plans are drawn with either a full or partial basement foundation. Depending upon your specific climate or regional building practices, you may wish to convert this basement to a slab or crawlspace. Most professional contractors and builders can easily adapt your plans to alternate foundation types. Likewise, most can easily convert 2x4 wall construction to 2x6, or vice versa. If you need more guidance on these conversions, our handy Construction Detail Sheets, shown on page 203, describe how such conversions can be made.

How Many Blueprints Do You Need?

A single set of blueprints is sufficient to study a home in greater detail. However, if you are planning to obtain cost estimates from a contractor or subcontractors—or if you are planning to build immediately—you will need more sets. Because additional sets are cheaper when ordered in quantity with the original order, make sure you order enough blueprints to satisfy all requirements. The following checklist will help you determine how many you need:

_____Owner

_____Builder (generally requires at least three sets; one as a legal document, one to use during inspections, and at least one to give to subcontractors)

_____Local Building Department (often requires two sets)

_____Mortgage Lender (usually one set for a conventional loan; three sets for FHA or VA loans)

_____TOTAL NUMBER OF SETS

Additional Plans Books

THE DESIGN CATEGORY SERIES

1.

ONE-STORY HOMES
A collection of 470 homes to suit a range of budgets in one-story living. All popular styles, including Cape Cod, Southwestern, Tudor and French. **384 pages. $8.95 ($11.95 Canada)**

2.

TWO-STORY HOMES
478 plans for all budgets in a wealth of styles: Tudors, Saltboxes, Farmhouses, Victorians, Georgians, Contemporaries and more. **416 pages. $8.95 ($11.95 Canada)**

3.

MULTI-LEVEL AND HILL-SIDE HOMES 312 distinctive styles for both flat and sloping sites. Includes exposed lower levels, open staircases, balconies, decks and terraces. **320 pages. $6.95 ($9.95 Canada)**

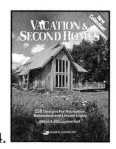

4.

VACATION AND SECOND HOMES 258 ideal plans for a favorite vacation spot or perfect retirement or starter home. Includes cottages, chalets, and 1-, 1½-, 2-, and multi-levels. **256 pages. $5.95 ($7.95 Canada)**

THE EXTERIOR STYLE SERIES

9.

THE ESSENTIAL GUIDE TO TRADITIONAL HOMES
Over 400 traditional homes in one special volume. American and European styles from Farmhouses to Norman French. "Readers' Choice" highlights best sellers in four-color photographs and renderings. **304 pages. $9.95 ($12.95 Canada)**

10.

THE ESSENTIAL GUIDE TO CONTEMPORARY HOMES More than 340 contemporary designs from Northwest Contemporary to Post-Modern Victorian. Four-color section of best sellers; two-color illustrations and line drawings throughout the remainder. **304 pages. $9.95 ($12.95 Canada)**

11.

VICTORIAN DREAM HOMES 160 Victorian and Farmhouse designs by three master designers. Victorian style from Second Empire homes through the Queen Anne and Folk Victorian era. Beautifully drawn renderings accompany the modern floor plans. **192 pages. $12.95 ($16.95 Canada)**

12.

WESTERN HOME PLANS
Over 215 home plans from Spanish Mission and Monterey to Northwest Chateau and San Francisco Victorian. Historical notes trace the background and geographical incidence of each style. **208 pages. $8.95 ($11.95 Canada)**

OUR BEST PLAN PORTFOLIOS

NEW ENCYCLOPEDIA OF HOME DESIGNS
Our best collection of plans is now bigger and better than ever! Over 500 plans organized by architectural category including all types and styles and 269 brand-new plans. The most comprehensive plan book ever.

15. **352 pages. $9.95 ($12.95 Canada)**

AFFORDABLE HOME PLANS For the prospective home builder with a modest or medium budget. Features 430 one-, 1½-, two-story and multi-level homes in a wealth of styles. Included are cost saving ideas for the budget-conscious.

16. **320 pages. $8.95 ($11.95 Canada)**

LUXURY DREAM HOMES At last, the home you've waited for! A collection of 150 of the best luxury home plans from seven of the most highly regarded designers and architects in the United States. A dream come true for anyone interested in designing, building or remodeling a luxury home.

17. **192 pages. $14.95 ($17.95 Canada)**

HOME IMPROVEMENT AND LANDSCAPE BOOKS

5.

6.

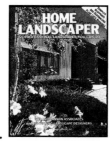

7.

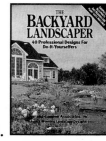

8.

THE HOME REMODELER
A revolutionary book of 31 remodeling plans backed by complete construction-ready blueprints and materials lists. Sections on kitchens, baths, master bedrooms and much more. Ideas galore; helpful advice and valuable suggestions. **112 pages. $7.95 ($10.95 Canada)**

DECK PLANNER 25 practical plans and details for decks the do-it-yourselfer can actually build. How-to data and project starters for a variety of decks. Construction details available separately. **112 pages. $7.95 ($10.95 Canada)**

THE HOME LANDSCAPER 55 fabulous front and back-yard plans that even the do-it-youseifer can master. Complete construction blueprints and regionalized plant lists available for each design. **208 pages. $12.95 ($16.95 Canada)**

BACKYARD LANDSCAPER Sequel to the popular *Home Landscaper*, contains 40 professionally designed plans for backyards to do yourself or contract out. Complete construction blueprints and regionalized plant lists available. **160 pages. $12.95 ($16.95 Canada)**

INTRODUCING THE NEW BLUE RIBBON DESIGNER SERIES

13.

200 FARMHOUSES & COUNTRY HOME PLANS Styles and sizes to match every taste and budget. Grouped by type, the homes represent a variety from Classic Farmhouses to Country Capes & Cottages. Introductions and expertly drawn floor plans and renderings enhance the sections. **224 pages. $6.95 ($9.95 Canada)**

14.

200 BUDGET-SMART HOME PLANS The definitive source for the home builder with a limited budget, this volume shows that you can have your home and enjoy it, too! Amenity-laden homes, in many sizes and styles, can all be built from our plans. **224 pages. $6.95 ($9.95 Canada)**

Please fill out the coupon below. We will process your order and ship it from our office within 48 hours. Send coupon and check for the total to:

HOME PLANNERS, INC.
3275 West Ina Road, Suite 110, Dept. BK
Tucson, Arizona 85741

THE DESIGN CATEGORY SERIES—A great series of books edited by design type. Complete collection features 1376 pages and 1273 home plans.

1. _____One-Story Homes @ $8.95 ($11.95 Canada)	$ _____
2. _____Two-Story Homes @ $8.95 ($11.95 Canada)	$ _____
3. _____Multi-Level & Hillside Homes @ $6.95 ($9.95 Canada)	$ _____
4. _____Vacation & Second Homes @ $5.95 ($7.95 Canada)	$ _____

HOME IMPROVEMENT AND LANDSCAPE BOOKS

5. _____The Home Remodeler @ $7.95 ($10.95 Canada)	$ _____
6. _____Deck Planner @ $7.95 ($10.95 Canada)	$ _____
7. _____The Home Landscaper @ $12.95 ($16.95 Canada)	$ _____
8. _____The Backyard Landscaper @ $12.95 ($16.95 Canada)	$ _____

THE EXTERIOR STYLE SERIES

9. _____Traditional Homes Plans @ $9.95 ($12.95 Canada)	$ _____
10. _____Contemporary Homes Plans @ $9.95 ($12.95 Canada)	$ _____
11. _____Victorian Dream Homes @ $12.95 ($16.95 Canada)	$ _____
12. _____Western Home Plans @ $8.95 ($11.95 Canada)	$ _____

THE BLUE RIBBON DESIGNER SERIES

13. _____200 Farmhouse & Country Home Plans @ $6.95 ($9.95 Canada)	$ _____
14. _____200 Budget-Smart Home Plans @ $6.95 ($9.95 Canada)	$ _____

OUR BEST PLAN PORTFOLIOS

15. _____New Encyclopedia of Home Designs @ $9.95 ($12.95 Canada)	$ _____
16. _____Affordable Home Plans @ $8.95 ($11.95 Canada)	$ _____
17. _____Luxury Dream Homes @ $14.95 ($17.95 Canada)	$ _____
Sub-Total	$ _____
Arizona residents add 5% sales tax; Michigan residents add 4% sales tax	$ _____
ADD Postage and Handling	$ 3.00
TOTAL (Please enclose check)	$ _____

Name (please print) _____

Address _____

City _____ State _____ Zip _____

CANADIAN CUSTOMERS: Order books Toll Free 1-800-561-4169. Or, complete the order form above, using Canadian prices and adding postage, and mail with your check in Canadian funds to: The Plan Centre, 20 Cedar Street North, Kitchner, Ontario N2H 2W8. FAX: 1-519-743-1282.

 TO ORDER BOOKS BY PHONE CALL TOLL FREE 1-800-322-6797

TB20BK

INDEX